*Civil Passions*

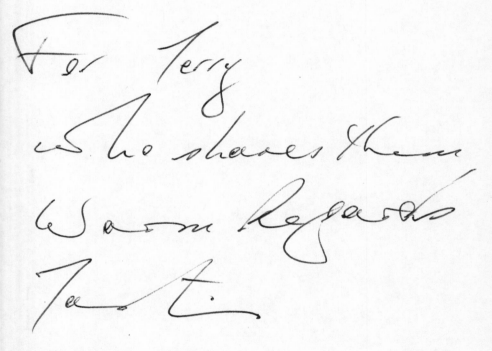

For Terry

who shares them

Warm Regards

[signature]

22. iii. 2012

# CIVIL PASSIONS

*Selected Writings • **Martin Krygier***

Published by Black Inc.,
an imprint of Schwartz Publishing Pty Ltd
Level 5, 289 Flinders Lane
Melbourne Victoria 3000 Australia
email: enquiries@blackincbooks.com
http://www.blackincbooks.com

The National Library of Australia Cataloguing-in-Publication entry:

Krygier, Martin, 1949- .
Civil passions : selected essays.

ISBN 0 9750769 8 1.

1. Politics and culture - Australia.  2. Social change - Australia.
3. Australia - Politics and government.  I.
Title.

320.994


Book design: Thomas Deverall
Typeset by J&M Typesetting Pty Ltd

The cover features a detail of *Allegory of Good Government: Effects of Good
Government in the City* by Ambrogio Lorenzetti.

Printed in Australia by Griffin Press

# Contents

*for Julie*

# *Preface*

The essays in this volume are a selection from my writings over the last twenty years. The principles of selection were straightforward. The essays should all raise or relate to issues of political morality broadly understood, and their imagined audience should not be confined to specialists in any of the subjects touched upon.

One occasionally finds a disdain among academics for writing intended for a non-specialist, even if sophisticated, audience. I have never shared that disdain. On the contrary, much of what I most like to read, indeed much of what I would most like to have written, is of just that sort: public writing about things that matter, for people who care. That sort of writing should never be writing *down* but *out* (if I can abuse a title from George Orwell, one of the greatest writers in the genre), not condescending to an audience thought incapable of understanding tricky stuff but engaging with people presumed to be as intelligent as the author, but who do other things. I admire that genre greatly, and have tried in these essays not to disgrace it.

In a variety of ways, the essays evince a taste for what I call civil passions. Examples are strewn through the book, but in 'Of Maggots and Angels' I seek to characterise such passions in general terms. I also commend them. Since there are circumstances in which one might need to be mad or brave or foolish to act on them, however, much of the book is concerned with the sorts of values and institutions that make indulgence of such passions a reasonable way to approach the world.

Part One, *Australian Identities*, begins with brief recollections of two such identities who most mattered to me: my parents, Richard and Roma Krygier. It has occurred to me that I'm not alone in having parents, but for better or worse mine had a great deal to do with why I write, what I write and what I write about. One thing I got from them, with my mother's milk so to speak, was a taste for hybrids of all sorts. Hybrids have contributed much to the variety of Australian identities, in a second sense of that word. This variety has enriched the country in many ways. I see little evidence that it has eroded the common attachments that every nation depends upon. Another thing my parents, their characters, their origins and experiences gave me is a taste for comparison. I say why and what might be gained from hybrids and comparisons, in the chapter so named.

I also gained from my parents a taste for civil societies. Theirs was born out of a horror of totalitarianism, two versions of which – Nazi and communist – they experienced directly. By the time I was born only one of these was left. My father spent an active life opposing it. Part of that activity was founding *Quadrant* magazine and publishing it till his death in 1986. In recent years there has been a decline in that magazine, but it had a distinguished and controversial past. Most of that controversy related to its anti-communist political commitments. To evaluate those commitments it helps to know something about communism. Yet it is remarkable how little communism was understood by so many in Australia who had views about it. In 'Worse than Provincial – Parochial', I speculate as to why.

'The Curate's Egg' arose from controversies in the late 1990s about issues to do with our treatment of immigrants and Aborigines. This essay deals with immigration. Subsequent ones focus on Aborigines. All of this writing tries in one way or another to work through the familiar but often denied truism that one can be proud and ashamed at the same time of things to which (and to whom) one is attached; indeed ashamed because proud, and both because attached. Had the chapter been written more recently there would have been consideration of our disgraceful treatment of refugees in mandatory detention. I would still resist the analogy of the curate's egg, but more sadly than once.

The other essays in Part One primarily concern aspects of settler–Aboriginal relations, where this truism is most painfully engaged. Several of them are also concerned with the way we discuss, and should discuss, these matters. The futility of single-shot characterisations of our past is starkly evident in 'Subjects, Objects and the Colonial Rule of Law.' So too, the complex virtues and limitations of the rule of law, one of my major academic, indeed life, concerns. The rule of law is a cluster of values, instantiated in this country better than in most. But, as I argue at some length, it requires a lot for law to count in a society and even more for it to do good. For many fairly obvious reasons, much of what is required was not available, particularly to Aborigines, in the early years of the colony. Nor is it easy to see how it could have been. The tragedy of settlement was, perhaps, predetermined. It was certainly overdetermined.

Were this book an attempt to survey Australian issues in systematic or comprehensive fashion, this stress on settler–Aboriginal relations would seem skewed. After all, other things happened. This is, however, not such a survey. I am interested in political morality, and I believe this is perhaps the central public moral issue Australians as a nation face and need to face up to. Since Australia is a young nation (though not country), physically separated from the rest of the world, we have not had the time nor been the place of the many complicated and tragic histories, such as the one I allude to in 'Neighbours', that have so scarred much of the rest of the world. We benefit from what one European friend has called our 'privileged provincialism'. As a result, there have been only a few overarching national tragedies since Europeans first came here, perhaps only one. And that one is not secreted somewhere in the margins of our national development, but is inextricably entwined with the birth of the nation itself.

'Of Maggots and Angels' hints briefly at values and institutions that civil passions support and that, in turn, support them. The essays in Part Two, *Public Values*, examine those values and institutions more closely. They also explore their implications in various contexts: attitudes to government; to prejudice; to political allegiances and ideologies. They are as much concerned with what we should avoid as what we should seek, with evils as with goods. The values I preach are of a rather ecumenical cast. I fantasise that there is something here for everyone, but perhaps there is simply something here to offend everyone. These essays were all written with Australia in mind, but they draw on experience from many places and they are intended to apply more generally. Were I ever to emigrate, this is what I would still believe and, I imagine, hope for wherever I landed.

Part Three, *Communism and Post-*, shifts to a different geographic terrain, east central Europe, where many of my concerns – political, intellectual, moral, emotional – have been focused for a very long time.

The first two essays are about communist Poland, whose terminal illness and then death I accidentally happened to witness. Perhaps these are best treated as period pieces, yet I am pleased to see them again. I certainly felt, and I hope they evoke, how unpleasant life was under communism, even in one of the least repressive communist states, and at a time when communist governments could no longer afford to be particularly horrifying, but were still pretty horrible. Weakened, demoralised, opposed, incompetent, they were only slightly caricatured by Adam Michnik, the hero of 'Of Maggots and Angels', as 'not communism with a human face but totalitarianism with its teeth kicked out'. It is hard for people who have not been there to imagine it, and it is easy for those who have been there to forget it. It should not be forgotten, both for its own sake and for a realistic appraisal of the achievements and non-achievements of its successors. No one begins with a clean slate, but not everyone has to deal with quite the pile of junk – institutional, psychological, moral, social and economic - that communism bequeathed.

The pathologies of late communism were easily observed, but it never occurred to me at the time that they were terminal, and my postmortem four years later, with its uneasy mixture of delight and anxiety, was also not a marvel of prophecy. Since I was not then an academic specialist on that part of the world, I could try to put some of my predictive inadequacies down to that, were I not in such good company. *No one* predicted the collapse of communism, and later predictions have also tended to have a short shelf-life. I have found that intriguing, and the last two essays have something to say about it.

Though I never imagined there would be a post-communist Europe, I am delighted, and not only because it gave me a new and congenial focus for some of my academic work. It was a great, as well as a world-historic, achievement. Since there are many misconceptions, amnesias, fantasies, prejudices, about that transformation, as much among 'experts' as others, my two last pieces are attempts to question a few of them.

'Gypsies' was a peculiar experience which shed a different, perhaps harsher light, on what later became my *leitmotif,* civility. Like all good things, civility has limitations, weaknesses, pathologies even. I discovered some.

*Sydney, February 2005*

*Acknowledgments*

I am more pleased than I can say that these essays, many no longer in print and others published in various, sometimes obscure, places have been saved from what Marx called 'the gnawing criticism of mice'. I am grateful for the generosity of their rescuers. First among them is Robert Manne, who proposed that a book of my essays be published. I have other reasons to be grateful to Robert, so this now can be added to a long list. He proposed it to Morry Schwartz, of Black Inc. Morry agreed to publish the book and showed a keen and helpful interest in its progress. I thank him. Robert and Black Inc.'s editor, Chris Feik, participated in a secondary cull of the essays I chose, and were politely resolute in discarding some of my darlings. Chris is an exemplary editor. Apart from what he tossed out he improved what stayed, by cutting some chapters with a keen eye for what was dead and what might still be saved or resurrected, repositioning others, and removing overlaps. Humble but not humiliated, I have been pleased to learn from him. Robert van Krieken generously allowed me to include 'The Character of the Nation', which we wrote together for *Whitewash*, even though he knew that some of his best lines might now be attributed to me. But then his worst ones will too. The book is dedicated to my wife, Julie Hamblin, for reasons too many, too obvious and too intimate to bear listing. Anyway she knows them all.

# Of Maggots and Angels

In 1979, before Solidarity was even a slogan, still less a world-transforming phenomenon, and when no one imagined communism would ten years hence wear a past tense, an exchange between two dissident writers appeared in an underground Polish quarterly. The subject of the debate was maggots.

One author, Piotr Wierzbicki, found Polish public life infested with them. In his 'treatise on maggots', he mercilessly attacked with this term intellectuals who, in his view, had compromised with communism. In reply, Adam Michnik, to whom I will return often in this book, published 'Maggots and Angels'.

Michnik was no less anti-communist than Wierzbicki, and he confessed that his first reactions on reading this treatise were 'both enchantment and envy ... How many times have I sharpened my pen, issued threats, and launched fiery tirades, driven by the "maggotty" behavior of my fellow men. But each time I ended up writing nothing. Not only because I did not have enough talent for it but also because as soon as my ardour left me, I would feel a certain falseness behind these emotions.'

The enchantments Michnik felt are easily understood. Righteous anger is peculiarly satisfying; it has a kind of purity and intensity that more complex emotions lack. And the more maggot-like one finds one's opponents the more angelic, by contrast, one is likely to feel oneself. If putative maggots repay in similar coin, one's virtues are further confirmed by their hatred. If they were to respond civilly you might be caught short, humbled even; instead their attacks are your vindication. There is then a kind of fateful feedback between the ease with which opponents judge each other to be maggots, and the assumption that they themselves are on the side of the angels. A circle of paraded virtue that can actually become quite vicious.

I have felt such enchantments and not always resisted them. But if the enchantments are evident, so too are their many dangers. As Michnik observed, they commonly involve 'abandoning a world view that encompasses the complexity of human obligations and achievements and replacing it with a crystal-clear picture of simplistic judgments and harmful verdicts'.

If he was reluctant to categorise as maggots those he opposed, he was conversely uneasy with angels, even if he and they had the same enemies. Indeed he confessed himself frightened of angels. Michnik was a heroic figure in the dissident movement, spent seven years in gaol and was harassed whenever he was free. He remains a towering if controversial figure in post-communist Poland, leader of its most influential newspaper. He is not easily frightened. But speaking of some vengeful angels of Polish history who had killed for causes he supported, he comments: 'the people who committed these murders were undoubtedly irreproachably honest and had heroic backgrounds. But the point is that they had no brakes; their Manichaean view of human obligations would not allow them to abandon these actions. They were consistent. Frighteningly consistent. Their goal justified everything.'

After years admiring his eloquent and elegant writings, full of a courageous mix of implacable opposition and principled restraint, I came to know Michnik. I expected a patient, quiet, measured man, calmly and thoughtfully taking the rough with the smooth. Given his record, I expected steel, but I also expected it to be finely tempered. Instead, I was overwhelmed by a force of nature, huge in passions and appetites, withering in his opinions, acerbic, brilliant, always and instantly the largest character in any gathering, always the funniest, not always – actually never – the most restrained. I once diffidently expressed my surprise at the distance between the sensibility that seemed to underlie his public moral commitments and the one he seemed to express in life. I had imagined such a relentlessly moderating impulse to stem from a pervasively moderate character. 'Oh no,' he roared. 'If I had allowed my character to take over, I would simply be a monster.' I concluded that he was wedded to civility, not because he had been born to it, nor, like some tepid English gentleman, brought up to deny passion of every sort, but rather because among his many passions he had developed a passion for it. And he indulged that passion, not because it flowed naturally from his temperament, but because he believed it was vitally important.

And so my title. Civil passions are not an oxymoron, like snowballs in Hell. Nor are they a silly joke, lampooning in some Monty Python fashion the ecstasies of a bureaucratic life. It may not always be obvious why they matter, particularly when civility is all round us and free as air. Yet with only apparent paradox, they are often readily appreciated and more deeply felt, as they were by Michnik, Václav Havel, Mahatma Gandhi, Martin Luther King and some other passionate civilians, when civility comes dear and the temptations to avoid it are cheap. And they are precious.

The essays in this book were written in response to particular provocations of one sort or another. Sometimes simply because I was asked, sometimes because I was annoyed, on occasion because I was moved. More than once all three motives have coalesced. So, depending on what occasioned the invitation, anger, emotion, their subjects are various. But as well as a number of common themes, there is a common sensibility at work, I believe, and not only because the same person happened to write them. Several elements of that sensibility are suggested by the story I have just told.

I have an aversion, partly innate partly acquired, to gleeful identification of maggots; even more to the urge to parcel the world between maggots and angels. That aversion has two components. One is directly related to Michnik's cautions, and is primarily a matter of public morality. The other is a rather more abstract question of intellectual hygiene. Let me take them briefly in turn.

What is a passion for civility a passion for? Is it a kind of self-denying ordinance, a passion for less passion? Hardly. Political argument is frequently about important values and the stakes can be high. So it naturally engages passions. I couldn't imagine it otherwise, nor would I wish it. My own public passions fuel most of the essays in this book.

And civility does not require some anaemic politeness, where everyone avoids saying what they mean. Civil debate can be, and often needs to be, heated, impassioned, angry. It can be bruising. But short of war, a serious business not lightly to be embarked upon, a society is blessed when passions are contained within civil limits. And it makes sense to be passionate about that very containment.

Sometimes that containment flows from personal decision and choice, as it did for Michnik, a choice one can exercise even when the political and social context gives you no support at all. That choice is as noble as it is rare. But it can also get you killed. And it pays to be brave.

We are not all brave, and a society in which one must be brave to be civil is a hard one to survive. I prefer a society of the sort Ernest Gellner praised in his *Conditions of Liberty: Civil Society and Its Rivals*:

> The price of liberty may once have been eternal vigilance: the splendid thing about Civil Society is that even the absent-minded, or those pre-occupied with their private concerns or for any other reason ill-suited to the exercise of eternal and intimidating vigilance, can look forward to enjoying their liberty. Civil Society bestows liberty even on the non-vigilant.
>
> Only the brave deserve the fair, says the poet. But may we not aspire to a social order in which even those of us who are timid can enjoy feminine beauty? Such has always been my pious hope. Civil Society is an order in which liberty, not to mention female pulchritude, is available even to the timorous, non-vigilant and absent-minded.

Such an unromantic vision deserves our passionate embrace. Our heroes are commonly less heroic and our villains less villainous, but we are better off when our social and political institutions and our public culture give us a foundation and frame for secure and civil relations, when they reward civil passions and punish uncivil ones, or at least their exercise, and transform the latter into the former; when incentives in public life point to restraint rather than excess. Such a framework involves many things, some having to do with institutions, some with cultures, some perhaps – as Montesquieu thought – with climate.

Constraint of unruly passions is part of the story, channelling them in ruly and productive directions another part. The upshot, briefly put here and less briefly in several of the chapters that follow, is a society where, even if you are not my friend you need not be my enemy. That is a very nice upshot and, as Donald Horne might have observed, a lucky one in our case. For it's not always clear what any of us did to deserve our luck.

Several of the essays here explore the conditions of civil societies, and look to their consequences, and also to their virtues. Angels in Australia are less frightening than those Michnik was writing about and dealing with; devils too. This is because, compared to most societies and polities that I know, ours is blessed with civilised and civilising institutions and a culture of civility of a generally high standard. Much of the time even a maggot might find it hard to do anything more horrible than merely sound off, and our angels are usually just talk as well.

Though most of us are indeed very lucky in this, it has not protected us all. Those whose consciences are disturbed by aspects of our history, and by our recent treatment of refugees, are rightly aware of that. It is appropriate that the failures of our institutions, and some of the dark sides of our achievements, be emphasised, and I have tried to address some of these failures and dark sides.

Some terrible things have happened 'on our watch' (and not always when we weren't looking but precisely when we were). It is appropriate, I would say necessary, to acknowledge those things truthfully, soberly and at the same time with passion and even pain. Sometimes, however, that recognition itself is touched with a sort of eager glee, as reason for condemning our society or civilisation as evil top to toe, because 'racist', 'xenophobic', 'sexist' or some other all-and-nothing explaining epithet. This is as satisfying as those glorifying mirror images about which I write in some of these pages, those unable even to allow the possibility that there might be some reason for a 'whispering in our hearts'.

Keith Windschuttle is right to say these debates have to do with 'the character of the nation', but like most characters that is a matter more complex than he will ever be able, or it appears wish, to understand. Most early settlers were neither maggots nor angels, just ordinary people in an extraordinary situation, where it was often hard to behave well, easy to behave badly, incentives to the former were often relaxed and to the latter strong, and where the consequences were often tragic, though not for them. Just as that does not set to nought the many fine features of our history and society, so too the many blessings for most of us of life here do not cancel the pains exacted from others, already here or trying to come. At a moral level, we have to deal with them all, and together.

And if the substance over which we debate is more complex than commonly admitted in our public debates, so too might be the reasons people have for their views. At least one does well to start with that presumption, rather than join one or other of the packs in which Australian polemicists like to hunt. So often those identified with another pack are readily dismissed by category, preparatory to being savaged, rather than engaged in civilised debate. Yet apart from the fact that a label is not an argument, maggot-hunts in the Antipodes are no more inviting than elsewhere. Less lethal, fortunately, but not more attractive.

Apart from the moral dubiousness of habitually dividing up the world in Manichaean terms, there is a simple intellectual fallacy commonly at work in such divisions. It is extraordinarily common in our public life, and in the ways we talk more generally. That, simply put, is the tendency to cast our problems as matters of inexorable choice between exclusive and exhaustive alternatives. I have absorbed from an American sociologist/philosopher, Philip Selznick (who learnt it from *the* American philosopher, John Dewey), a general suspicion of overdramatised, starkly dichotomous presentations of aspects and alternatives in social life. I have often written against that tendency in my academic work, and my allergy to it is evident pretty well everywhere in this book.

Such dualisms remain remarkably popular. Again and again we are confronted with false, all-or-nothing alternatives, false *because* all-or-nothing; stark and apparently incompatible understandings of complex pasts, presents and available futures. Allegedly necessary choices proliferate: right versus left, individual (or civil society or the market) versus the state, liberty versus equality, liberalism versus communitarianism or conservatism or socialism, universal versus particular,

Australian versus ethnic, maggots versus angels; the list could without difficulty be extended. It is left to a few old fogies to mumble that they might just be aspects of complex phenomena which can manage, sometimes more happily sometimes less, to include them both.

Few find such reminders convincing, still less interesting. Nuance, complexities, tensions, blurred boundaries, shades of grey, complex and fraught predicaments, are all so much less dramatic than dilemmas, contradictions, clarity, bright lines, black and white, the choice between maggots and angels. Nevertheless, I'm with the fogies. At least most of the time.

There are many things wrong with the taste for dichotomies. I will mention just two. One is the implication that the choice on offer is exhaustive, that one is faced with *nothing but* the alternatives presented. This rules out, *a priori,* such wisdom as Michnik displayed, in the answer to the question whether he would prefer General Jaruzelski who had gaoled him and others, or General Pinochet, who had gaoled (and killed) others. Michnik replied that offered such alternatives, he would choose Marlene Dietrich. I applaud the choice and the taste which guides it.*

Second, familiar dichotomies often present as incompatible – as unable to share the same space – elements that might well, and might need to, be combined. Out of differences that might be complementary, or tensions that might be resolved or need to be lived with (as we live with many tensions), irreconcilable contradictions are postulated, between which one *must* choose. This argumentative practice used to be common among Marxists and other revolutionaries, but it has outlived them and it doesn't encourage civility. It does not merely present what might be a false choice, but by the way it frames a problem it

---

* In recent years, Michnik has come, to the surprise and anger of many, to appear to prefer Jaruzelski to Pinochet, if not Dietrich. One of the complexities of Michnik's character and development, and in part a tribute to his extreme passion for civility, is that since the collapse of communism he has been one of the most outspoken protectors of several of the generals who gaoled him. Whether that passion for civility and conditional amnesty, transmuted into hostility to public reckonings with the past, is a condition of civil society (as he believes) or a threat to it (as a significant number of Poles believe) are issues that I cannot explore here. But they are important questions in the transformation of post-dictatorships.

makes *choice*, between exclusive and binary alternatives, the first task of thought and action. By implication, that excludes other, and perhaps more appropriate, ways of thinking and doing. Like refusing to choose.

Presented with stark options, apparently inescapable choices, one does well at least to begin with a Deweyite presumption and try to finesse them. The presumption might be quickly rebutted and finessing may not be possible, for sometimes stark choices are inescapable. The Second World War presented such choices, and I believe the Cold War did too. Some of my reasons for believing that are to be found in this book.

But we should not be impatient to multiply such situations. Rather, since the questions we ask delimit the answers we give, we often do better to ask how the two sides of an alleged dichotomy might and do combine and connect, and how best they might be made to combine and connect.

There is a moral aspect to this too. For a penchant for dichotomies is a penchant for exclusion: this *or* that, not *and*. For moral reasons among others, civility hopes to include. Of course, not everyone can be included, since civil societies have real enemies. Members of such societies must be clear-headed enough to recognise enemies and strong enough to resist them. But not everyone with whom one disagrees is an enemy.

Some are, though. This again was a lesson of the Second and the Cold Wars. It is also true of the current war against fundamentalists who practise terror. In each case, though it is the least that can be said, our enemies have been enemies of civility. Civil passions are neither logically nor practically linked to pacifism: if uncivil forces threaten civil societies with degradation or extinction, the latter need to be able to defend themselves, lest uncivility and a great deal worse overtake them.

How such defence should be undertaken raises many questions of judgment: strategic, tactical, prudential and moral. This book does not deal with such questions, but particularly relevant to its concerns are: what are the limits of civility, when are they reached, and what is appropriate when they are reached? What should one do in a civil society if internal opponents are determined to subvert the rules of civility?

What about defending such a society against attack, rarely civil, from without? And if conflict occurs, are all bets off, or does civility – and even more, our common humanity with our enemies, as Raimond Gaita has powerfully insisted – rule certain behaviours simply and always off limits? What are such behaviours?

These are real and difficult questions, aspects of that broad problem, alive today, about how a civil society might defend itself even *in extremis,* without losing the character that justifies the defence. If the questions are difficult, adequate answers are even more so, dependent as they are on complex judgments of principle and particular assessments of the state of the world in which one lives, the character of existing threats, their power, one's resources, and many other things. In discussing such issues, it helps to acknowledge that often we face complex *predicaments* rather than simple choices. And these issues are only worth discussing if you are committed to civility and common humanity in the first place.

Finally, though I write a lot about civil society, in fact I don't regard it as the pinnacle of human or social achievement. Far from it. Not every relationship is best when civil. Love surpasses civility. But it doesn't happen all the time and it can't happen with everyone, so civility is important when love is absent or dies. It certainly beats hatred, though there is even a place, one hopes a rare place, for that. Moreover, love is not the only passion that surpasses civility. Even among strangers, one can build more than civil societies. A civil society is not a ceiling but a floor, better a foundation. And what an important thing a foundation is. On it, we can stand and interact with some security, ease and confidence. Without it, one spends a lot of time just trying to keep one's balance. In a civil society, there will be many people we don't love, but we don't therefore need automatically to hate or fear them. One can strive for more, even much more, and I think there are many reasons to do so. But one should never settle for less.

That realism might be combined with idealism, to the support of both, is another message from Selznick that took me time to learn. While communism was alive, I was so convinced of the evil nature of communist regimes, so often unacknowledged or denied, that whenever better societies were heavily criticised, I was quick to ask,

'Compared to what?' That is not a trivial question, and we should always have it in mind. But it should not paralyse thought or imagination. For if we're not as bad as something else, even nowhere near as bad, we might still be better than we are.

*2005*

# AUSTRALIAN IDENTITIES

# Richard Krygier*

My father died in 1986. I loved him, and continue to love him, beyond measure. That is no great achievement, since he was easy to love. He was also simply the finest man I have known.

This combination of love and praise must seem unpersuasive; the latter rendered suspect by the former. But it shouldn't be so. Love does not have to be blind. After all, I don't say that he was the slimmest man I have known, or the tallest, or even – though he was very clever – the cleverest. Simply the finest.

That fineness had many features, and many were discussed by contributors to the special issue of *Quadrant* devoted to him (November 1986). They wrote of his talent for friendship, his courage, optimism, vitality, honesty, gaiety, and many other things. All of this is true and there is more. But I have been asked to speak in honour of him, not about him. So I will not go on much. But I will go on a bit. For apart from the pleasure in recalling him, it connects with my theme.

His fineness was easy to observe. He had, for example, a calm dignity which one might call serene, except that he was never still. And it was not merely a public face. His dignity was seamless. As anyone who knew him – anyone who *saw* him – could tell, he was no ascetic. He was too fat and joyful for that. (I used to call him the magic pudding, with the emphasis shared equally between adjective and noun.) But while he enjoyed himself he was also selfless, and that too was easy to spot. He

---

* While Robert Manne was editor of *Quadrant,* he inaugurated an annual lecture in honour of my father, who founded the magazine and published it until his death. I was asked to deliver the third of these lectures. In the course of it, I reflected briefly upon his character and stature.

had *no* small motives. Though his commitments were often unpopular and he had opponents, some bitter, he never did a petty thing. And, notwithstanding the depth and passion of those commitments, he was never a fanatic, not even a fanatic of virtue, though he was a profoundly virtuous man. He was – as deeply as can be – civilised.

He encountered much opposition, not all of it civil and some of it hurtful, but he never complained. Indeed, he considered it bad form to do so. As he reminded some of his more tender intimates, he had chosen to do what he was doing, and anyway he loved doing it. He was, to the core of his being, an *inteligent* in the old Polish understanding of that term, a man defined by his commitments and sense of public mission – in his case lightly worn – not by his job or prospects for advancement. So even when times were hard, he simply went on doing the best he could do. And that was formidable.

I described him as *simply* fine, both for emphasis and because many of the finest features of this complex man were extraordinarily simple. His courage, for example, was simple indeed. It flowed directly – without agonies, trimming, second thoughts, and without fuss – from his commitments. These commitments were simple too. They are nicely captured in the remark Peter Coleman quoted, in his eulogy at my father's funeral: 'I was anti-Nazi before the war; I'm anti-communist today. I haven't changed.' More could be said on these matters, and of course a great deal has been said. But there is a deep sense in which nothing more needs to be said. And it remains a matter of astonishment to me how much *has* been said that failed to understand, when it did not seek to deny, the deep and simple moral truth of this position.

He was not a theorist and he did not go in for disquisitions on political morality. But he understood profoundly the gulf between decent and evil political orders. Among the societies he knew to be decent, one was Australia. It had accepted him and my mother as refugees and then – also simply and without fuss – it afforded them the opportunity to live active, peaceful and happy lives. He saw no reason to waste that opportunity, and he valued it because he understood its worth.

Nazism and Communism were pre-eminent among the evil regimes he knew. They gave him an understanding, and some experience, of the very worst that people can do. His own life was directly and dramatically affected by both. But he well knew that millions of others had suffered immeasurably more, and that millions continued to do so. Nazis had murdered my mother's family and many of my parents' friends, and destroyed their earlier ways of life. Communism made it impossible for them to return to Poland, which despite all they loved and missed very much. But they themselves had escaped Europe relatively early in the war, and had emerged from it alive, together and relatively unscathed, ending up in one of the gentlest and fairest countries that have been. They knew tragedy, they knew sadness, and they knew their luck. My father somehow emerged from this mix a remarkably resilient and happy man, but he was not complacently happy.

His good fortune was something he continually savoured, and was grateful for. In a sense, his subsequent life was an expression of that gratitude. It took the form of cheerful and unstoppable – if often thankless – support for decent polities and opposition to evil ones.

In one of his last conversations with me before his death in September 1986, he expressed regret that he would not outlive the communist system which was born in the same year as he, 1917. He sniffed something in the air, and since he was always an optimist he hoped. But no more than anyone else did he know what would happen. As it turned out, communism collapsed, ignominiously and in a heap, and it is a matter of specific distress to those who loved him that he was not able to witness that. It would have delighted him. And rightly so.

The collapse of communism was a marvellous thing, no less so because life after communism is not a picnic. Whereas communists and other fanatics were inclined to think that there was only one source of evil in the world, pragmatic liberals like Richard Krygier were used to seeing the struggle for decency as a perennial one. So while he might be disappointed, he would not be dismayed that post-communism – like the proverbial German joke – is no laughing matter. It would simply have suggested that there was more work to be done.

There appears to be no genetic code for his virtues, but even those who do not have them can admire them, and I do. And while it would be foolish to try to emulate him, it would be equally foolish not to be influenced. And I have been.

*1996*

# Roma Krygier

My parents' passage to Australia is one of those extraordinary stories of which their generation of Europeans, and particularly European Jews, is full. Roma, my mother, often reflected that she had had a very rich and full life, and a very fortunate one too. And though that transitional period of her life, which took her from Warsaw to Sydney, was full of tragedy it was also blessed with good luck. She understood and respected both elements.

In 1938, Roma finished her university studies in Warsaw and went to the University of Nottingham where after a few months, as she later recalled with amusement, she obtained the Cambridge Certificate of Proficiency in English. The reason for that success may well have been her genius in improving English idioms, for it was there that she declined seconds offered her at an elegant dinner, by explaining that she was 'fed up'. That inaugurated a fertile and successful vocation: admonishing her children not to make 'mountains out of molecules', speaking condescendingly of 'country pumpkins', or warning me on my first trip to then-communist Poland that I must 'mince [my] words', something by the way that she never did in her life.

She returned to Poland in December 1938, married Richard in January '39, and then, after the Nazi invasion eight months later, saw him ordered east with the aim of joining a regrouped Polish army. In the meantime the Russians invaded eastern Poland and there was no army to join there. Two months later, learning that he was in Vilnius, she managed to join him, not without danger or difficulties, travelling with her aunt and seven-year-old cousin through Nazi-occupied Warsaw into Soviet-occupied Poland.

After my mother's death, I received a letter from my father's cousin, Henryk Schoenman. Among other moving recollections, he included the following, which I translate: 'I have a precise recollection of the last time I saw Roma before her exodus [from Warsaw]. She and my mother were very fond of each other, and Roma came to farewell her before she left to go to Richard. I remember a young, pretty, very determined girl, whom everyone warned against making this dangerous trip, but who had decided to go out into the world to find her husband whatever it cost. When we received a postcard from Vilnius saying that they were together and intended to go "further", I remember my father opening a bottle of Rothschild and toasting their success.'

Her parents remained in Warsaw and were later murdered by the Nazis as they tried to escape from the ghetto. Her seventeen-year-old brother joined the Polish army and was executed by the Germans, probably the following year (or so my mother was told. She was never absolutely sure, and every time she travelled to Europe, she would look for his rather unusual name – Ewald Halpern – in the phone book of every city she visited. Once, in Switzerland, she found the name, but it was another Ewald).

In Lithuania, they lived off money sent by an uncle of Richard's in Egypt and, as she told her grandson Jonny in an interview for a school project, 'You will laugh, but I was also giving English lessons to two ladies … who paid me for that and always took me for afternoon tea to a very nice coffee shop.' The Russians took over Lithuania in 1940 and liberated my mother from her former political sympathies. As a student, she had been a member of a secret communist student organisation in Warsaw, and apparently had been quite passionate in that attachment, but the Russians, with a little help from her husband, managed to re-educate her in the year the couple spent under Soviet occupation. The Soviets took their Polish passports and so they could not leave Lithuania. Were it not for the now-famous intervention of the Dutch and Japanese consuls there, who saved several thousand people by quasi-fraudulently combining to give them papers which would get them to Japan, they would presumably have remained where they were, to be killed in mid-1941 when the Nazis invaded that country and exterminated all the Jews there.

Instead they spent New Year's Eve, 1940 on the Trans-Siberian railway, getting dangerously drunk on *Sovietskoie Shampanskoie*, and after ten days arriving in Vladivostok, from where they went to Japan. They spent almost a year there, working for the Polish Relief Committee, attached to the Polish Embassy. They obtained visas to Canada 'for the duration of the war' but by that time there were no ships sailing direct to Canada, and instead they got one via Australia, where they arrived in late November 1941 on papers allowing them a transit stop of two weeks. Then the Japanese bombed Pearl Harbor and my parents decided to stay here 'for the duration' and then return to Poland. The rest is history. My father never saw Poland again. My mother did in 1991, after fifty-odd years away. She was profoundly moved by the experience, but was happy to come 'home', as she put it.

My mother loved Australia. She loved its civility, its gentleness, its tolerance, its democracy. She delighted in those panels of opponents who politely discuss results on election night. She thought it wonderful that they were so pleasant to each other; even laughed at each other's jokes, rather than merely at each other's expense. She couldn't, how-ever, abide our fascination with sport, and stopped reading newspapers in hospital earlier this year, ostensibly because she couldn't stand reading about the Olympics. But she was a grateful citizen. For she knew she had enjoyed rare good fortune.

*1999*

# Hybrids and Comparisons

I am an Australian. I was born, brought up and educated here. I have spent the bulk of my life here. I watch cricket for days without being bored. I expect Christmas to be hot. These facts are central to my make-up. Were they otherwise, so would I be. And yet they are not the only pieces that make me up. For, like so many Australians, I am the lucky beneficiary of other people's tragedies, most immediately those of my parents. That, too, is relevant to who I am and what I think about.

My parents arrived here during the Second World War, Polish-Jewish refugees from Nazism. Their lives, families, friendships and country were ripped apart by the war. Both my mother's parents and her brother were murdered by the Nazis; other relatives spent years fighting or being imprisoned by them, and what was left of the family was dispersed around the world. My parents left Poland from necessity, arrived in Australia by accident, and stayed because, after the Communist take-over of Poland, they couldn't go home. They came to love this country and to participate actively in its affairs, but that was later.

I mention these far from exceptional facts not to claim some exotic authority for my views, nor – in accordance with a budding Australian tradition – to launch a prize-winning novel, but because they inform the way I think about things, what I think about and – above all – what I think matters. Combined with my birthplace, they have made me what I am: a congenital cultural hybrid, a hybrid from birth. If you prefer, a mongrel.

My parents were already hybrids in Poland, since they were cultur-ally both Polish and Jewish. Each *ish* had significance for them, and so their lives were already complicated. They became Australian hybrids differently, however, over time. What they came to learn and expect, and grew to be, in Australia interacted with their already formed personalities and cultural identities. Their hybrid condition was acquired, as is that of most, if not all adult migrants: they become culturally something different from what they once were while remaining something different from those among whom they now are. If over 20 per cent of Australians were born overseas, and 40 per cent were either so born or their parents were, there are a lot of us about.

There is also a third sort of hybrid, and I am one of them too. I study and write about the societies of post-communist Europe, and their fate matters a lot to me. So I am also a vocational hybrid: coming from one world, and preoccupied with another. There are, of course, fewer vocational hybrids than congenital and acquired ones, and many of them are hybrids of the other kinds as well, a connection which is psychologically not difficult to explain. Perhaps it is just a way of mixing business with pleasure, but it has consequences. When I am there I think of here; when here, of there. That makes comparisons ever-present and unavoidable.

All hybrids are affected, some afflicted, by overlapping cultural residues within them. Pure vocational hybrids might slough such residues off as simply parts of their jobs, but congenital and acquired hybrids often find that difficult to do. They often discover to their surprise, rather than as a matter of deliberate choice, aspects of their personality – their sense of identity, belonging, sometimes longing – which define them and have moulded them, whether they like it or not.

There is no reason to romanticise hybrids. Sometimes their cultural condition is just a source of confusion, sometimes of defensive fundamentalism, sometimes of unattractive social climbing, sometimes of raw pain. Some hybrids find the combinations within unbearable, and some try to suppress some of their cultural elements, usually the foreign ones, for their own sakes or those of their children. That is often an excruciating experience, particularly for those who find that cultural integration comes more slowly than the wish for it. Worse still must be the discovery that it can all be for nothing: the host and dominant culture, which you imagined you were joining or had long joined, spits you out and then tramples on you. At its most tragic, that was the discovery made by German Jews in the 1930s.

Even when the threat is incomparably less, it must always be a source of immediate shock and continuing distress when people who have adopted a country, and with it aspects of a culture, discover that they are nevertheless still, or again, treated as aliens. Were the Pauline Hanson phenomenon to be generalised and sustained, I imagine that many Asian-Australians, even those who have lived here for generations, must feel something of that shock and distress. To say nothing of Aborigines, who have lived here forever and whose cultural adaptation was, to put it gently, not of their choosing.

Other times, or for other people, there is nothing problematic about being a hybrid. Some rejoice in the variety of their inheritance and find it, or make out of it, a rich and coherent whole. Some just do, and others just don't, feel that particular aspects of their cultural inheritance matter to them, are significant parts of what they are. Many children of migrants naturally or deliberately leave their parental culture behind and think little of it, in both senses of that phrase.

All these responses can change over a person's life, and over generations. Resolutely Aussie kids of hybrid parents – I was one – can gradually find themselves resonating to cultural melodies which had earlier left them cold. And whatever *they* do, they might, to their surprise, find their own children re-establishing links with the culture of their grandparents, links which the generation in-between rejected, ignored or simply forgot.

Even contented congenital hybrids, like myself, at times find themselves envying people whose sense of who they are and where they belong seems uncomplicated: grounded in local geography, family and tradition; supported and interwoven with others by generations of overlapping public and private narratives; apparently settled, and settled here, for longer than life. For many hybrids, however happy in the condition or unconscious of it, there are moments of awkwardness when we don't quite know where we belong, or when it occurs to us that there is no group which we feel completely inside, though there are several where we don't feel completely outside, either. Of course not only hybrids have this experience and it's by no means all bad. Indeed

I've come to think that such complication has compensations. Hybrids share a particular condition which might yield some insights.

Hybrids have a specific resource available to them: a range of values, experiences, traditions which is different from the range one might find in the heads of those with whom they mix. That can be enriching both to them and those who meet them. Moreover, where these components are psychologically salient – where they have meaning and significance for the hybrids themselves – they are not merely options from which to choose, like goods in a shop, or a background of exotic food, strong coffee or stronger spirits. They enter into people's lives and souls. They shape values, ambitions, horizons, expectations, ways of talking, of drinking, of laughing and of loving. And they shape the values (and all the rest) which people from these traditions pass on to their children. Whether these are good values, and whether they mesh easily or well with local ones, are particular and variable matters. Some are good and do mesh, some are good and don't, some aren't and do, some aren't and don't. All that has to be worked through and worked out.

There is something else hybridity can generate, however, which I think is a totally good thing. Comparisons. Part of a hybrid's make-up grows out of experience, cultural traditions, a sense of other histories and possibilities, models of thought, speech and behaviour, which are different from local ones. On the one hand, this can open windows for them into other, often very different and complex, cultures which complete outsiders find harder to penetrate. On the other hand, it offers to hybrids a vantage point, a perspective and a quite peculiar place to stand. That metaphorical space is simultaneously inside and outside the cultures in which they were raised, in which they live, of which they are parts and which are parts of them. That can make them critical of some things. It can also allow them, however, to appreciate distinctive accomplishments that non-hybrids, who have not known their absence, might regard as natural and unremarkable. More generally, it can offer a powerful antidote to parochialism, which has, perhaps, cosy charms *as* a way of life, but is not much help in understanding or evaluating a way of life.

Parochialism is common enough everywhere, though its sources and character differ widely. There is a lot of it in America, for example,

because it's often hard for Americans to imagine that anything important happens anywhere else. In Australia, by contrast, so much that is
important happens somewhere else, and everywhere else is a long way
away. A common response is to overrate the importance of that far-
away stuff and then court the risk of cultural cringe, which is a wonderful Australian phrase but a far from exclusively Australian disease. It
is found in all provincial settings. Since there are many ways of being
provincial, one can find it among Eastern Europeans when they listen
to Westerners, particularly rich ones, and among Americans, and some
Australians, when they listen to Alistair Cooke. The opposite extreme is
to puff up whatever is near at hand and insist that Australians have
nothing to learn from the experience of anyone else. That also is not
a specially Australian condition, and everywhere it is a silly one. It
allows one to be not only provincial but a little ridiculous, and narcissistic as well.

For narcissism is not just an individual phenomenon. The morbid
self-obsession characteristic of narcissistic individuals can be observed
among groups too. National narcissism thrives in many countries, in
both positive and negative varieties. Positive narcissism is more
familiar. The positive narcissist is confident that his country is the
centre of the world. What matters happens there, and it can't be bet-
tered. This is a viewpoint well captured in Saul Steinberg's marvellous
*New Yorker* cover, 'View of the world from 9th Avenue'. The foreground, which occupies half the canvas, is occupied by one New York
block, between 9th and 10th Avenues. Beyond the Hudson River, there
are a few major American states and cities and then, across the ocean in
the far distance, China, Japan and Siberia. Australia doesn't appear.

Positive narcissism is easy to mock, and it is rightly mocked. We
have seen quite a bit of it in Australia in the last couple of years, and it
is not a pretty sight. It contrives to combine boastfulness, ignorance,
insecurity and hostility in ample and self-reinforcing measures.

Not that its melacholy twin, negative narcissism, is more attractive
or less parochial. It differs from the celebratory kind, but only by inver-
sion of value, not of subject. The subject is again one's own country
and it's also superlative, in a way. However, what occurs there is not the
best but the worst.

America has always had plenty of positive narcissists. From the 1960s, for a decade or two, it gained many negative narcissists as well. (Australia had some too, though ours have often been happier to damn the Americans, and us only secondarily as their satraps or cultural colonies. This is another provincial privilege.) In a century which boasts Stalin's Russia and Mao's China, Hitler's Germany and Pol Pot's Kampuchea, this position was always absurd, though it was popular enough, particularly among intellectuals. More generally, unless one has really thought about the many goods and evils the world has to offer, narcissism – both positive and negative – is a frivolous way to think about anything that matters.

One antidote to such narcissistic tendencies, whether positively or negatively charged, is to look around. Anyone can do it. Hybrids merely have a strong temptation and good access. They have the option close at hand, indeed under the skin. That option, more specifically, consists in reflecting upon a deceptively simple question which I consider one of the most important of all for social understanding and evaluation. That question, in all its glory and complexity, is: 'Compared to what?'

I have not seen this point made better than by the late Robert Haupt, who went from being a good Australian journalist to a great one, when he moved from Australia to become the Moscow correspondent for my local, and often parochial, newspaper, the *Sydney Morning Herald*. I found the passage I will quote so arresting, that I have appropriated it in several places. It bears repetition.

In October 1993, shocked by the way in which Boris Yeltsin had managed, bloodily and for the time being, to re-establish control in Moscow by storming the Russian house of parliament – the so-called 'White House' – Haupt was moved to reflections of a sort rarely evident among Australian political journalists, or among Australians generally, but which are nevertheless distinctively Australian in character. In an article entitled 'It's no way to run a country', he wrote:

Acres of scholarship have been devoted to the question of how Russia – rich, cultured, the bridge between East and West – got to this constitutionless point. Square-inches are given in the Australian syllabus to how we arrived at Federation. Is it time, one wonders, for a comparative study between [*sic*] the thought of Sir Henry Parkes and of Bakunin, the relative achievements of Lenin and Deakin? When one sees Russians killing Russians in a country 88 per cent Russian while Serbs and Croats apparently live in peace in Australia, an explanation must be sought beyond the effects of SBS and surf.

Here [in Moscow], all the boring things of life are missing. There are no Premiers' Conferences, no shire councils, no chambers of commerce, no solicitors, accountants, real estate agents, no double-entry bookkeeping. There are soldiers everywhere, but very few police, and none you could rely on for help in a sticky situation. There is no head of State, no Scout movement, no civic progress associations and few charitable groups.

All of this, the texture of civic order, strikes an Australian as so natural and ordinary that to investigate its origins seems superfluous, while to speculate on how evanescent it might become is an exercise in sheer wonder, or perverseness. Yet the worth of something can generally be better seen from its absence than its presence.

Like Haupt, I believe that one can better appreciate what seems 'natural and ordinary' by comparing it with circumstances where it is neither. One can always ask, and it is commonly worth asking: why here and not there, or there and not here? This naive question can help us to see more distinctly – rather than merely see through – much that frequently goes unobserved, because it so often goes without saying.

Compared to what, then? Anyone is in a position to compare – for better or worse – what they have with what they had, the present with the past. This is often useful and it is often done, whether it is useful or not. It is common both for reactionaries within a dominant culture, and for unhappy immigrants, to compare the present unfavourably with the past, but the pasts they have in mind often have little to do with each other, and often not much to do with what actually happened either. We can also compare what we have and do with what others like us have and do. This can be an important stimulus to reform or, if we're lucky, satisfaction. Third, we can compare what we have with what we would like to have, or believe we should have. Hopes and ideals drive us to these comparisons.

All of these are legitimate comparisons to make and to draw upon, so long as we are conscious of what in particular we are comparing and why. Critics often fail to make clear whether they think things are worse than before, worse than elsewhere, worse than they should be, or all of the above. Those happy with the way things are, are often equally undiscriminating. They are all important sorts of judgments to make, but they are not the same judgment. There is not even much reason to assume that they will point in the same direction.

The first and the third of these comparisons – with the past and with an idealised future – can largely be accomplished without leaving home, actually or even imaginatively. The second – with societies similar to one's own – requires some physical or mental travel, but if you choose your comparisons well it can be quite comfortable. It is useful to know what happens in societies with which one shares many features but not all, and it is not too hard – particularly if everyone speaks English there.

But there are some comparisons which are culturally more taxing, and which take up most of my time. One is with societies and cultures which seem utterly or drastically to lack what seems normal at home. Another, really the converse of the first, is with societies which seem to regard as normal what is inconceivable here. Each of these comparisons raises questions about the naturalness of what otherwise goes without saying (here or there), and each encourages thought about the causes and worth of whatever matters to us, when we find it is not universally shared.

Sometimes these sorts of comparisons can be made through deliberately fanciful but finely constructed thought experiments, as in the novel *Lord of the Flies,* where William Golding transports his young characters to an uninhabited island, and has us observe their behaviour – *our* behaviour – in these culturally and institutionally unconstrained circumstances. The great eighteenth-century French analyst of political institutions, Montesquieu, populated his fictional *Persian Letters* with stories of Persian despotism and its consequences, about which he knew nothing much, but which were intended to warn of dangers of French despotism and despotism in general, about which he knew a great deal. Or we can reflect on the *Utopia* of Sir Thomas More and its many successors, or the unsettling *dystopias* – Zamyatin's *We*, Huxley's *Brave New World*, Orwell's *1984* – in which our century is so unusually rich.

More deeply and powerfully, Thomas Hobbes, the greatest of English political philosophers, asked us to consider the uses of political authority by inviting us to consider what life would be like without an established state, law and the related institutions of which many people complained in the war-torn century and country – seventeenth-century England – in which he lived. His argument is relentless and his conclusion quite fearfully grim: life in what he called a 'state of nature' would be a predicament so terrible that people would lay down everything save their lives to escape it. So the existence of a state is a powerful good, as long as it can protect our lives. If it does that indispensable job, Hobbes notoriously insisted, little else can be demanded of it. For without institutions powerful enough to keep the lid on, life would necessarily be plagued by constant, unremitting insecurity, the consequences of which he portrayed in his *Leviathan*, in one of the most famous and most eloquent passages in political philosophy:

> Whatsoever therefore is consequent to a time of war, where every man is enemy to every man; the same is consequent to the time, wherein men live without other security, than what their own strength, and their own invention shall furnish them withal. In such condition, there is no place for industry; because the fruit thereof is uncertain: and consequently no culture of the earth; no navigation, nor use of the commodities that may be imported by sea; no commodious building; no instruments of moving, and removing, such things as require much force; no knowledge of the face of the earth; no account of time; no arts; no letters; no society; and which is worst of all, continual fear, and danger of violent death; And the life of man, solitary, poor, nasty, brutish, and short.

Though such hypothetical comparisons might not be provable, they need not be empty. Many thinkers have disagreed with Hobbes about what a society of people something like us might be like without a political order something like ours. But only frivolous or privileged people can ignore the depth and fearfulness of the comparisons he made and the dangers of which he wrote.

This sort of comparison does not have to rely merely on intuition and speculation. International relations have often amounted to a state of nature. Countries riven by civil war too. Think of Bosnia or Somalia or Zaire or Cambodia or whatever other country is being ripped apart by the time this essay is read. And really to think about such possibilities is especially important in a society like ours, just because they are so alien from everyday experience (though not every one's experience) here. It is one thing to know that the world is full of strange and tragic places and events. Another harder and more important thing, to try to learn about and from them.

Of course, few lessons can simply be transferred from one society to another, still less from fantasy to reality, and it is not for recipes that one makes comparisons. It is to help consideration of one's own circumstances from a vantage point not limited by one's own horizons.

We belong to a privileged group of countries – relatively rich, peaceful, democratic and law-governed – whose apparent successes some people are trying to emulate. This is especially true of the post-communist world which interests me, where many would like to witness similar successes without having to travel. It is worth examining what our luck might rest upon, both for their sakes and our own. That must involve self-examination, but not self-absorption. We should be in a position to say why here and not there or there and not here. That we are not yet in that position is clear from the fate of some of our prescriptions, for other societies' ills and for our own. Thinking about our values, in the light of apt comparisons, might enable us better to help others; but it also might allow us to help ourselves, and to discover how much or little we know about ourselves. It might reveal how well or ill our rights are secured, and it might reveal, too, how well or ill we have discharged our responsibilities. It might also reveal to us costs, failures and inadequacies in the social accomplishment we represent. For we will not do well out of every comparison, and we should pay equal heed to those where we don't as to those where we do.

And if we are encouraged to try some new initiative – ignorant, belligerent and racist populism, to take a random example – we should certainly think about the fate and consequences of similar initiatives wherever else they have been tried. Conceivably we might find the comparisons encouraging. More likely, we will not. Either way we will be less ignorant for having made them. In any event, that is what I believe.

*1997*

# Worse Than Provincial – Parochial

James McAuley was a multi-talented poet, writer and public figure. He was also a complex man, a compelling presence, not a bad pianist and a remarkable drinker. Through his life, and at any one time, he played many public roles: member, with a team of unusually but disparately talented and later prominent Sydney University mates, of Alf Conlon's bizarre wartime Directorate of Research and Civil Affairs (in connection with which he went to New Guinea, source of several encounters which changed his life); co-progenitor of Ern Malley; influential member of the Australian School of Pacific Administration which sought to develop policy and train officials for post-war Papua New Guinea; Roman Catholic convert and political activist; founding editor of *Quadrant*; Professor of English, poet and writer; political organiser; uneasy participant in modernity. He was notable and controversial in many of these roles.

Cassandra Pybus didn't know McAuley, and acknowledges that there were many aspects to his protean personality, attested to by those who did, which she 'cannot find … on the printed page'. Nevertheless her book, *The Devil and James McAuley*, is the most detailed chronicle of the life so far. It is also an attempt to explain the course it took. As chronicle, it has several virtues. It contains a lot of information, usually delivered lightly, brightly and at times engagingly and wittily. Even cheekily. The book is rarely dull. The man is more than commonly interesting and so his story is interesting to tell. Pybus is a gifted story-teller and chronicles it well.

Since she seems tantalised by the young McAuley, he emerges from

her telling as a person one would very much want to meet. As her distaste grows, which it does pretty soon – towards the end of the war and
increasingly afterwards – she can't resist a derisive, condescending tone
when he offends her sensibilities, which he often does. Here one feels
(more precisely, I feel, for reasons that will emerge below) that one is
learning more about the author than her subject. The story comes to be
driven more and more obviously by her prejudices (in the classical and
not necessarily pejorative sense of unthought prejudgments) and less
and less by what drives him. And the prose flags, too. It leans increasingly
and repetitively on stock epithets: 'intemperate', 'strident', 'dogmatic',
'crude', 'rabid', 'virulent'; so much so that they become superfluous. We
*know* that the next anti-communist we meet must be one or the other, or
one and the other, without being told. But we are always told. Still even
here her difficulties with McAuley and his ilk (among them my father, I
should here declare) do not always, though they do commonly, swamp
her capacity to record some things that speak well of him, particularly
the calm and courageous way he faced death.

Pybus is not infrequently careless with facts and her interpretations
are often tendentious. But if you are curious about details of McAuley's
life and interested in a sometimes shrewd dissection of a complex and
not easily penetrated personality, you will find the book informative.
Particularly if you aren't interested in poetry. But if you are after a perceptive and nuanced report of the causes which animated him, the reasons he might have had for adopting them or the character of the
period in which he lived, Cassandra Pybus's book will disappoint. It
might even annoy, as it has me.

Pybus clearly is intrigued by McAuley, and, as far as I can tell, she
tries within her lights to be fair. She doesn't always find it easy, though,
as her taste for him dwindles noticeably and fast. For he confronts her
with a problem that her whole book is a struggle to resolve. How did
the awesomely gifted, irreverent pre-war poet and piano player, of aes-
theticising and anarchist leanings, whom she describes with some
affection, change so? How did he come to emerge from New Guinea
and the war so *plus catholique que* ..., so combatively (a.k.a. 'stridently',
'rabidly' etc.) anti-communist and at the end so passionately, if
ambivalently, anti-counter-cutural? Prince to frog.

Her answer, hinted at throughout the text, but only fully revealed in the book's last chapter, has the following three steps. They appear consecutively in the work, each less weighed down by evidence, more buoyed up by what might gently be called imagination, than the preceding one. And as the evidence dims, a somewhat desperate assertiveness glows.

The first step, for which Pybus adduces ample evidence, is that McAuley was, or often was, deeply tormented by what we might metaphorically call inner demons, and he might have non-metaphorically called the same. In particular he suffered, she surmises, from deep inner conflicts, self-disgust and guilt.

The second step owes more to the *Zeitgeist* of the analyst than to the evidence at her disposal: the source of the torment, in case you need it spelt out, is sex. What else could screw you up so, so to speak?

The third emerges from a welter of speculation, several strategically placed 'could' and 'may' have beens, acknowledgment of the central importance of women – particularly his wife – in his life and the candid confession that 'I simply don't know, nor will I ever know.' Undaunted by these rather heavy-duty qualifiers, Pybus builds to her climax: 'my supposition that McAuley's terrors are related to guilt about homosexual desire is not wildly speculative'. Given the flimsiness of her evidence on this point, that is a matter on which judgment and perhaps taste might differ.

But Pybus's reluctance to give up on her speculations is understandable, since so much of the explanatory offering of the book depends upon them. For they are, we learn, the key to McAuley's Catholicism, anti-communism, editorship of *Quadrant*, support for the Vietnam War, opposition to student sit-ins, ability to drink anyone else under the table, and much else. Everything really.

Let me mention three examples: religion, drink and anti-communism, without which, it is pretty clear, the mature McAuley would have been someone else. First is religion, a central element in his post-war life and in Pybus's account: 'In my reading McAuley's way of dealing with what he hated and feared in himself – the suppurating wound that would never heal – was to externalise his guilt on to the malevolent, preternatural force [the Devil].' And so his Catholicism and its stringently – astringently – orthodox character: 'this faith enabled him to externalise his fear and give it a name.'

Second, though there is no suggestion that he was an alcoholic, McAuley was a serious drinker. According to Pybus, his 'frenetic alcohol consumption would seem to me to be an indication of the chaos and terror that lingered at the edges of his rigid self-control'. But only at the edges, because he almost never appears to get drunk, though all around him drop about. That too is grist for Pybus's accommodating mill: McAuley always needed to be so in control of his rampaging netherworld that 'The mask rarely slipped'. It's this terror-concealing *mask* and not his apparently heroic liver that is the key. Oh for such a mask. Oh for such a liver.

Pivotal to the story, however, is McAuley's anti-communism, and it is in relation to this that Pybus delivers her psychobiographical *pièce de resistance*:

> Having said that McAuley was a contradictory and complex man, it is not my intention to try to render him simple and transparent. My thesis is only that McAuley was troubled by – terrified by – his sexual urges, especially the homoerotic, which he displaced onto the Devil and his communist agents. He was not alone in this. The Cold War provides some outstanding examples of the mechanism: J. Edgar Hoover, long-time Bureau chief of the FBI, was one; Roy Cohn, the over-zealous counsel for the House of Un-American Activities, was another.

Had Hoover and Cohn also written poetry and fathered six children, the case would have been clinched. As things stand it is not completely clear from Pybus's account whether suppressed homoerotic urges are sufficient or merely necessary conditions for anti-communism. Perhaps that will be sorted out in a second edition.

I have praised the book as an interesting chronicle of an interesting life. But as a source of understanding and explanation, the work is merit-free. This is not because Pybus entertains the hypotheses she does about McAuley's psyche. For all I know, all three of them might be true, though on the evidence provided I would only consider betting on the first. Nor is it simply because I – who didn't know McAuley well (though my father, who founded *Quadrant*, knew him very well) – find the analysis unpersuasive. That is of no importance to anyone but me. Anyway Pybus, expert in psychological cliché, would expect it. The problem is, rather, that she seems to have no idea how to establish the significance of the psychological factors upon which she lights, in what she wants so desperately to explain: the public life, in a particular epoch, of a complex and strenuously thoughtful man.

Among his many parts and roles, Pybus explicitly chooses to focus on McAuley as 'political intellectual'. He certainly was one, and the phrase deserves to be taken seriously. Let us treat it so, starting with the noun. McAuley was a man of ideas, an erudite and driven *thinker*; not only but also. Pybus recognises that he has *conclusions,* for it is those that she wants to explain and debunk. But she shows no acknowledgment that this deeply intellectual man might also have had *reasons,* that is thoughts, arguments, considerations, that on reflection he took to point one way and not another. Her McAuley comes to conclusions simply as a result of drives, just like Bill Clinton I guess, or rather as an attempt to stop up drives, unlike Bill. It is a bit like those familiar and crude understandings of judicial decisions, that they are just 'the result of' the judges' personalities, socio-economic status, religions, etc. All of these things are potentially relevant, as is McAuley's psychic playground, but judges also deliver reasons, and many of them, the best of them, take seriously the reasons they give. McAuley also published many of his reasonings. Automatically to see through them is not always the best way of seeing what these are, where they might lead and where they might have led him. These reasons might be good or bad, we might accept them or not, but it is arrogant to assume they count for nothing and philistine to imagine that it is enough simply to tune in to the 'bottom line'.

Apart from this political intellectual's ideas, what of his politics? If a thinker is anti-communist, for example, how much should his biographer understand communism? Or, more precisely, how much should she enter into how communism, and what he knew and understood of it, affected his thinking about it?

You can't write about everything, of course. In one of several increasingly shrill sallies – strident even – against reviewers who displeased her,

Pybus reminds us that it matters what the book was intended to do. Robert Manne had suggested that her work was 'both a political-spiritual biography of [McAuley's] movement towards anti-communism and a cultural interpretation of the Australian Cold War'. He goes on, 'Because Pybus is such an intelligent and attractive writer her portrait of McAuley is likely to prove persuasive. Because she appears to know so little about the nature of communism her portrait of the Australian Cold War is likely to perpetuate our current misunderstanding as to what was most seriously at stake.' In her angry response, Pybus claims that her book was no more than a 'study of the preoccupations of a very singular man and more than half of the book is in no way concerned with the Cold War'. She 'resent[s] being called to account for deficiencies in a book I did not write'.

Yet it is pretty obvious that she has both less and more than this singular individual in mind. I have already mentioned her lack of discussion of his ideas. Moreover, though he was above all else a poet, she is not concerned with his poetry. It appears only as a psycho-diagnostic aid. Rather, as she explains in her introduction, on the one time she saw McAuley, when he came to speak at a political function at Sydney University, 'It was not the poet I went to hear all those years ago. Then, as now, it was the political ideologist and cold war warrior who compelled my attention.' Her book is an attempt to 'make sense of [McAuley's] ideology and its political impulse , rather than a conventional biography'. But if she is interested in less than the whole McAuley, she is at the same time confident that he stands for something larger. Her aim is 'to foreground the political intellectual whose spirited engagement with public affairs in the three decades between the Second World War and the Vietnam War provides some insight into that unique time of turmoil and change'. So Manne might be forgiven for thinking that it was not just McAuley's singularity which so concerned Pybus.

And in any event, the point surely is not whether she should have written a history of the period as well as a biography of the man. Rather it is that one can't understand a man so immersed in the period unless you understand some aspects of it, important in themselves and important to him. One such aspect is communism.

In the beginning of the nineteenth century, Joseph de Maistre made a profound observation about the French Revolution: 'we must have the courage to acknowledge ... that for a long time we completely misunderstood the revolution, of which we were witnesses; we took it to be an *event*. We were mistaken: it is an *epoch*.' The communist revolution inaugurated an even more far-reaching epoch and much of the world is only beginning – with great difficulty and no assurance of success – to recover from it.

Whether one dates the end of what Hobsbawm calls 'the short twentieth century' at the collapse of European communism in 1989, or as he does at the collapse of the Soviet Union in 1991, communism was – in Hegel's phrase – a world-historical phenomenon pivotal to the development of that century. Its significance spanned the world, as Marx knew it would. It bore on hopes and on dreams, since it claimed to incarnate and fulfil the most influential secular prophecy of modern times. It bore on our understandings and evaluations of the societies in which we lived and on what we imagined alternatives to them might be, since globally communism represented just such alternatives: alternative ideals and alternative forms and models of social, economic and political organisation, all available, as it were, in 'real time'. And it bore on foreign policy everywhere, since communism was an export industry of vast scale.

For almost the whole of the epoch, communism was never what it has become now, in those few places where aged communist parties still maintain their dictatorships, such as China, North Korea, Vietnam and Cuba: local and absurd anachronisms, no longer demoniacal (with the possible exception of North Korea), just malign; and abandoned by those whose enthusiasm was at its peak precisely when they *were* demoniacal. James McAuley (and my father) were born in the year the epoch began; they both died before it ended, McAuley thirteen years before.

In the month I write (October 1999), the English translation of a monumental and very important book has just been published by Harvard. It appeared originally in French two years ago, as *Le livre noir du communisme*, and was quickly translated into many central and east European languages. I first saw it in Polish. It is over 800 pages, and based in part on new archival findings and hitherto unrevealed documents from former communist archives. The state crimes of every country that has endured communism are documented by some of the leading scholars of these matters in the world. Their editor estimates that between 85 and 100 million people died as the result of deliberate official action in these countries in this period. About 20 million in the Soviet Union, 65 million in Communist China, several millions more in Cambodia, North Korea, Vietnam and Eastern Europe. These estimates are controversial, of course, but whatever the figures, as Martin Malia puts it in his foreword, 'the Communist record offers the most colossal case of political carnage in history.'

And that is perhaps not the most important part of this tragic tale. Hundreds of millions of people were condemned to live stunted, thwarted lives, by regimes which sought to infiltrate every aspect of their subjects' beings and managed to crush, diminish and demean them, even as they slid from ruthless repression to slovenly despotism to collapse. A collapse, by the way, which unlike that of the Roman Empire or the Austro-Hungarian, or the British Raj, left *nothing* good in its wake. By the end, most of these regimes were shabbily horrible, rather than energetically and repressively horrifying as they were to begin with; but by then they had far fewer Western supporters.

The comprehensiveness, many of the details and the figures of the Black Book are new and some of them inevitably controversial. The contours are not new at all, however, to anyone who cared to look for them. But many people never did, and Pybus doesn't even now. Not because she would likely be interested to deny any of this, but because she seems to think it is irrelevant to her subject. But what if her subject thought differently?

The first issue of *Quadrant* appeared in December 1956. In his first editorial, McAuley wrote:

Suddenly this one huge glaring visage, this enormous mask made of blood and lies, starts up above the horizon and dominates the landscape, a figure of judgment speaking to each person in a different tone or tongue, but with the same question: And what do you think about *me*?

Pybus writes of the 'extraordinary performance' that this editorial represents. What is more extraordinary, as noted by Andrew Riemer (*Sydney Morning Herald*, 24 July 1999), is that she doesn't 'acknowledge the conjunction between McAuley's editorial and that defining moment in modern political history' which had begun the month before: the Soviet invasion of Hungary. This was not an event noticed only by anti-communists, of course. It had a profound resonance for millions, then and since. But like so much that happened in the world during the life of her subject, and notwithstanding her professed interest in the 'political impulse' of his views, Pybus passes it by in silence and, one suspects, ignorance.

There are many ways of accounting for the differences between Pybus and McAuley on these matters, but one is overarching. She has no understanding of something fundamental which weighed with him: the radical evil of communism. Without wishing to be cruel, I believe the reason is expressed in the subtle but important distinction Henry James makes, when he observes that Thoreau was 'worse than provincial – he was parochial'.

Provinciality is a geographical matter; no one to blame. Parochialism is a matter of will and imagination. One, of course, can foster the other; but it needn't and in McAuley it didn't; on the contrary, whatever else one thinks of his *Quadrant*, it was the least parochial of Australian magazines; indeed it was a self-consciously *de*-parochialising influence in this country. Of this significance, there is not a word from Pybus.

Parochialism comes in many variants. Peasants are often parochial, which is why Marx despaired of the 'idiocy of rural life'; they show no interest in things that do or have gone on, or might, in a wider world. Less obviously, and more commonly among parochial intellectuals, even clever ones, a real interest in larger things is combined with lack of awareness or ability to imagine that they might be qualitatively different from what one finds at home. Everything is measured on the local scale.

This is not merely Pybus's problem. It is a common feature in Australian responses to communism, and much else. A great deal of discussion of communism in this country never had anything to do with communism at all, but only with one's attitude to the social and political order here. And so it didn't depend, for many people it has never depended, on knowing anything about what was happening in communist countries, even when precisely that was the subject of bitter debate. What one thought about communism couldn't be refuted, even dented, by evidence of those things. This was true of many who had no wish (as many others, however, did) to believe anything particularly wonderful was happening under communism. They just had no imagination of catastrophe and were happy to misunderstand communism by accommodating their picture of it to the slack and easy standards of everyday Australian life. What mattered was where you lined up in the Australian debate, and who your friends would turn out to be, as a result of what you were prepared to say about this strange phenomenon of which you knew nothing.

Some people couldn't think of communism in this way, because they had experienced it 'on their skins', in the Polish phrase. As it happens, my father was one such, and so was Frank Knöpfelmacher. They didn't just pop up in this country, as they do in the book, without a past, ready to be walk-on extras – eccentric, devious, altogether excessive – in Pybus's petty psychodrama.

They were driven to make some things that seemed desperately important to them apparent to others, in this implausibly peaceable and complacent island on the other end of the world. They spoke of things beyond local experience. Some people believed them and were influenced by them, though it did not always come easily.

Even though I grew up in an anti-communist home, for example, it was in Bondi not Warsaw, and I had no privileged understanding of these things. I still recall a lecture on Czechoslovakia given by Knöpfelmacher in 1968, shortly before the Soviet invasion. Knöpfelmacher was a Czech Jew who, unlike most of his family, had escaped the other world-historical scourge of the century, Nazism. After fighting in the war, he returned to Prague and resumed philosophical studies (under Jan Patocka, later to influence Václav Havel). As he explained in the lecture, he resolved to escape again in 1948, when it became obvious the communists would take over. He tried to warn a friend, but his friend said he would stay because, as he was apolitical he'd be OK. Knöpfelmacher commented, without any emphasis, as though it went without saying, 'he didn't understand that this was a regime in which what you did or didn't do protected you from nothing.' I was stunned by this remark, realising at the ripe age of nineteen, and at a highly political time, that I had no understanding of such a regime either. That led to an obsessive attempt to gain such an understanding, which has yet to stop. I still am not confident I understand much, but there are some things that I have learnt.

And it was not so hard to learn. Certainly, no one was starved of information, neither then nor even much earlier. There were scarifying works by ex-communist writers such as Silone, Koestler, Miłosz, and later by former victims, such as Ginzburg, Nadezhda Mandelstam and Solzhenitsyn, which profoundly influenced people such as McAuley, and which, needless to say, Pybus never mentions. There was plenty of material available to convince anyone who cared that communism was a human calamity in every country on which it had been visited. People with an ability to imagine catastrophe, such as George Orwell who saw only a bit of what he so profoundly understood, or more recently Simon Leys of whom the same can be said, understood this material. They were not thanked for it at the time.

Certainly, for a very long time not everyone was convinced; indeed many reserved their hatred not for a system of rule responsible for so much unmitigated tragedy, but for those who sought to expose that system, and thought it important to do so. I have often wondered why.

I have no Pybusian explanation for why what was obvious to any ordinary Polish peasant was calumny to so many eminent Western thinkers. Instead I would venture a charitable explanation, which *is*, I confess, 'wildly speculative' and even if true could only be partial: in Australia, at least, radical and systematic evil, conducted on a mass scale, is hard to imagine. It might have been that McAuley, perhaps even for the reasons or some of them that Pybus gives, was more than usually receptive to understanding it, and to recognising its most powerful political site and source in the world at the time he lived. That would have been an interesting marriage of psychological predisposition and awareness of empirical reality. But it is not a hypothesis that Pybus ever entertains, since she appears to know nothing and care less about the realities that McAuley did know and did care about. Nor does she seem to think it important to know. And so, since nothing else, least of all communism, for example, is thought to have anything to do with McAuley's anti-communism, the answer must lie deep in his groin.

In the most remarkable passage in the book, Pybus explains in a crisp schoolmistressly way:

> McAuley's insistence that communism was an aggressive force of evil, rather than a political and social system created by human intelligence and practised by mortal men, made him uncompromising toward those who did not regard communism as an abomination.

Here we have it: either evil or human. Try substituting 'Nazism' or 'Pol Pot's regime' for communism in that sentence. How irresistible is the choice that poor Devil-obsessed McAuley is supposed to have overlooked? The plain truth is that communism *was* an aggressive force of evil *and* it was a political system (and the rest) … *and* it was an abomination. Nothing to choose. If it had been my fate to have to listen to much prating of this sort, I think I would have become pretty uncompromising too! I might have even been moved to religion; certainly to drink. Religion clearly informs McAuley's understanding of evil as it cannot mine, and perhaps he was better for it. It does appear to have helped him understand something Pybus can't.

None of this is to say that McAuley was necessarily right or admirable in all his particular views, hostilities, obsessions, that he wasn't tormented, that it was always the better course to be *contrarian* (to use a new and ugly coinage) in his manner. In the polarisation of the epoch, Manichaeanism came easily to people who found themselves continually derided for saying something important and true. It might well be that it came too easily at times, and hardened into a reflex rather than a considered response. But these are discriminations and criticisms which can only have purchase if, in making them, you understand the context in which they occurred. Pybus doesn't even see a need to.

It might also be that, if McAuley had lived past 1989, his view of the world and those of some others who had been in or around *Quadrant* would have diverged, on the grounds less of the state of their libido than of their beliefs. It is, for example, very plain in post-communist Poland, with which I am familiar and which has local resonance for me, that people who were once closely united against a common foe may come to discover they have less or nothing in common when that foe disappears. Polish Catholics of a traditionalist anti-modern bent, conservatives, nationalists, many for whom modernity is a problematic achievement at best, now respond in very different ways to the challenges of post-communist modernity, than do, say, Polish liberals, among them Catholics and others, for whom modernity and a tolerant civil society are ideals for Poland's future and grounds for conflict with friends of the past. Among those who agreed on the evil of communism, after all, are many who see it as but a development and heightening of modernity, and they dislike many features of the latter, even without the former. So did McAuley. Others, once equally opposed to communism, see it as a perversion of modernity. Much that was most objectionable about communism died with it, and grounds of political alliance and antagonism are no longer the same. Recent splits in what was once called the '*Quadrant* group' attest to some divisions and re-divisions of these sorts. What they had in common was fundamental, but new questions arise to which they now have conflicting answers.

But this is idle, if not completely wild, speculation. My point is merely that unless one penetrates the actors' own views of the world in which they lived and tries to see what in the world (both of action and of thought) might have led them to these views, psychological reductionism of Pybus's sort is not really a *conclusion* of one's research but its presupposition. When everything else of potential importance is filtered out, whatever is left wins by default.

To conclude, in anticipation of correspondence, I have not asked that Pybus answer a question she now repeatedly declares is 'of no concern to me … who was right or who was wrong about communism' (*The Australian*, 13 October 1999). That is not a bad question, by the way, and not one, as we have seen, on which she avoids expressing uninformed yet censorious opinions. But there is a different point, which has to do with the obligations of a biographer. One of these is to understand your subject. Ignoring the significance of ideas to an intellectual and communism to an anti-communist and poetry to a poet is not the best way to meet it.

*1999*

# The Curate's Egg

Over a century ago, a *Punch* cartoon gave an expression to the language: the curate's egg, good in parts. A young curate of meek appearance is dining in considerable formality with the family of his 'Right Reverend Host'. This severe-looking cleric observes that the curate has been served a bad egg. 'Oh no, my Lord, I assure you!' replies the miserably placed young man, 'parts of it are excellent.' Anyone who has tried to eat an egg which is good in parts will feel for the curate's predicament. For such an egg must be bad in parts too, and, since the parts are not easily separated, it is simply bad.

Societies are different, and altogether more complex. If good at all, they are typically good only in parts, though some have more good parts than others and some parts matter more to some people than others. But the parts don't easily add up or cancel each other out, nor do they all flow into each other. German culture, for example, gave the world Goethe and it gave us Hitler. Goethe doesn't make Hitler any better and Hitler doesn't make Goethe any worse. They are independent and incommensurable, and not only because Goethe wrote well and Hitler painted badly. Moreover, Goethe is an appropriate focus of pride for patriotic Germans; Hitler an appropriate focus of shame for decent ones. Even if you add Bach and Beethoven, you don't cancel Hitler. Nothing cancels Hitler. Germans simply have to live with the complex combination of genius, good and evil, which is their history. Sums don't add up. Goods and evils have to be accommodated on their own terms.

Australia is not Germany: no Goethe, no Hitler. But as Australians, we too have things of which to be proud and others of which to be ashamed. Some people seem to think that because we have examples of the one sort, the other kind don't count or don't count for much, or – as Geoffrey Blainey has suggested – they are 'balanced' out in our country's moral accounts. The truth is quite otherwise. There are aspects of our history of which we are right to be proud and others of which we should properly feel ashamed. Neither should be thought to wash away the other. Even more, we have something new to be ashamed of if we try to deny what else we have to be ashamed of.

In this essay, I tell one story, having to do with migrants to this country. In the four essays that follow, I discuss issues concerning relations between settlers and this country's indigenous inhabitants. In brief, I believe that Australians have good reason to be proud of the first story and good reason to be ashamed of the second. Indeed, pride in the way that migrants have been accepted into this society only makes moral sense if we admit that what has happened to Aborigines in the same society is shameful. Among other things, they have been treated indecently.

At an important time in my life, I studied under, and was much influenced by, Eugene Kamenka, professor of the history of ideas at the Australian National University. Kamenka's parents were Russian Jews who had fled Russia to Germany, and met and married there. He was born there, but the family was again forced to flee, this time from the Nazis. They arrived in Sydney in 1937 when Kamenka was nine. Through his life, Kamenka travelled a great deal and was intimately familiar with many societies, cultural traditions and ways of life. Intellectually and culturally, he was in the largest sense a citizen of the world, but he was in important ways an Australian citizen of the world.

In late 1993, a conference was held in his honour, as he was dying of cancer. Scholars came from several countries and from around Australia. In conjunction with the conference, Kamenka was invited to deliver the 1993 John Curtin Memorial Lecture. Though he was terminally and visibly ill, he did so with his customary eloquence, to a large and packed hall. The title of this lecture, his last and one of his best, was '*Australia Made Me ... But Which Australia Is Mine?*' It was moving to hear him wrestle with these issues of influence and identity at that moment in his life, and it is still powerful to read.

Kamenka began the lecture by outlining the complex and overlapping strains and cultural allegiances which formed him and which were parts of him: Jewishness, Russianness, European philosophical and intellectual traditions, the particular influence of Professor John Anderson of Sydney University, and aspects of the Australia which also, he insisted, 'made' him.

After pointing out that not everything about Australia appealed to him, and not everything that appealed to him was Australian, he then asked:

What, then, draws me back to Australia? What do I admire most about Australia? The Australia I came to in 1937 is now mostly portrayed as deeply racist, socially, religiously, and ethnically intolerant, full of cultural cringe, and ruled by undeserving elites. Coming from Nazi Germany, I was struck by the opposite: the basic kindness and ease of social relations (which did not extend to Aborigines, to our shame, but which did by the 1920s extend to some of the other races who had become long-term residents in Australia), the accessibility and lack of pomposity of people in positions of minor or major authority, the non-intrusive friendliness of neighbours, the diffidence about telling other people how to live. Jews and refugees were not, in all circles, considered the most desirable and admirable migrants. Yet Australians disliked making a fuss or being nasty to people more than they disliked Jews or foreigners and for each Australian who did dislike them there were literally dozens who went out of their way to be helpful, friendly, encouraging. I found that with neighbours, in school, with wolf-cubs and boy scouts, with council employees, with ordinary people all over the place. Europe, let me say it bluntly, was not like that; much of today's world is still not like that.

This is high and apt praise. My own parents' experience was much the same. When my parents arrived here, they were befriended by a distinguished Polish diplomat, Dr Sylwester Gruszka, uncle incidentally of an American hybrid of note, Zbigniew Brzezinski, National Security Adviser to President Carter. They worked for Gruszka in the pre-communist Polish Consulate. After the War he and my father started a

Polish book shop, *Vistula (Australia) Pty. Ltd.*, whose fortunes steadily eroded as its customers learnt English.

When he first met them, Gruszka told my young parents that they would experience real democracy here, for the first time in their lives. They knew nothing much about that, as they heard themselves called 'bloody reffos', worked in (and were fired from) assorted menial jobs, were abused in trams for speaking German (it was Polish) and were reported to the police for their raucous parties.

These were not dramatic experiences, but they were also not always pleasant. For of course the arrival of millions of people like my parents (and unlike them) was a real shock to this strange anglomorph outpost perched – as Mr Keating is supposed to have observed, with cartographic precision – on 'the arse-end of the world'. As my parents came to learn, however, and as they never stopped appreciating, Dr Gruszka was right.

The distance this country has come in the relatively brief span of time from then to now is extraordinary. We now have over one hundred ethnic groups and eighty languages here. The peaceful way in which all these 'aliens' have become citizens should be at the forefront of any account of immigration in Australia. This was a real social experiment which could have gone awfully wrong. It didn't, notwithstanding the frequently simmering and often outspoken, vulgar and ugly resentments between Anglos and ethnics, and ethnics and ethnics.

Over time, ethnic resentments, hatreds, prejudices, have not all disappeared but they have been moderated and kept pretty tame. On the whole, that has happened with remarkable success in this country, if not always in the countries from which many of our migrants have emigrated or fled. Indeed disputes over the very same issues that have torn at the heart of societies such as Croatia and Bosnia, northern Ireland and southern Lebanon, Vietnam and Cambodia, come to have an altogether cooler temperature, oddly enough, when reheated in the Antipodes.

That is not to say that the migrant experience here has always been smooth, uncomplicated, welcoming. It is hard to be a migrant, more still a refugee. You commonly start from scratch, not everyone wants or likes you, and you don't always want or like them. And there is so much to learn. It begins with simple words, and it never really ends. For it is not just new things to do, but new ways to be. Migration leaves nothing untouched. How could one expect it to be easy? Why should one expect that success will be quick? More particularly, where has it been easier or quicker than here? Certainly not in most of the countries that our migrants have left. As the historian John Hirst has rightly observed, 'The secret is now out. No nation in the modern period has accepted such a rapid change in its ethnic composition and with such a high degree of social peace.'

This is not merely a good thing but grounds for legitimate pride: pride in our institutions, in the texture of our social relations, in our political practices, and in their results. Not only are the results good, but the ways in which they have been achieved are also. As one of my closest, recently naturalised, friends puts it, in an accent it would be defamatory to mimic: 'It makes me proud to be an Aussie.' It does me too.

Of course, this is not the only way the story of immigration to Australia can be told. Some ethnic activists, on the one hand, and some anti-ethnics, on the other, tell it very differently. Here as always I am moved to ask, *compared to what?* And here, as often, I am struck by the contradictory but symmetrical exaggerations in which multicultural and monocultural antagonists indulge.

The multicultural excess consists in pushing a valid point too far. It reminds us all, as Al Grassby was wont to do, that, at least from the First Fleet, 'every Australian is really a migrant.' And of course we all are, at least genetico-geographically. But some people then go on to deny anything other than temporal priority to the culture of the 'Anglo-Celts' who were the first non-Aboriginal settlers here. Worse still, some suggest that they were some sort of drab and negative presence until redeemed by all us colourful multi-cultis. That is deeply foolish. Not every migrant influence is as formative, pervasive, built into institutions, traditions, values and language as every other. And on this score, the debt owed by the immigrant Australians who flooded into the country after the Second World War, to the particular complex of practices, traditions, institutions and people that awaited them is enormous. For the legal, political, cultural, linguistic and moral space was not empty and nor was it formless when they arrived. And very many of them, I would guess most, were fortunate that what filled it was so benign to them. The success story of post-war migration to Australia speaks to a deep civility in this society and culture, a civility that belongs to our best traditions and one for which we beneficiaries have reason to be grateful.

A priceless element in these 'Anglo' traditions, of which I will say more in the next essay, is the rule of law, expressed in a whole battery of legal and constitutional institutions and traditions and, even more important, in the apparently simple, but actually rare and complex, fact that law *counts* as a restraint on power in the life of this country. That was a strong British influence. Indeed it was a profoundly important part of our cultural inheritance which, as David Neal has shown in his exemplary book *The Rule of Law in a Penal Colony,* was transported with the convicts and their gaolers on the First Fleet. On this basis was built, in remarkably short order, a stable liberal democracy which works and which, if rarely edifying, is also rarely horrifying. Those of us whose families fetched up here recently have been lucky that this was so.

Australia is also a society which has elaborated – indeed mythologised – traditions of tolerance, equality and a 'fair go', a fondness for 'mates' who are less than lovers and more than others, and can even come to include newcomers with accents. There is also a distrust of 'bullshit' and 'bullshit artists', which is not always great for academics but is healthy in the main. The Australian language is full of local terms or terms full of local significance like these, and it is hard to find foreign equivalents of them. They don't describe everyone's beliefs or relationships, but they inscribe distinctive values into language and into life and these values have profound cultural resonance. I find all those values attractive. I am charmed when called 'mate' by a stranger with a foreign accent who never knew the word before coming here and whose original language has no equivalent to it. It beats *Herr Dr Professor* or the Polish equivalent which is even more complicated but also compulsory. These values and traditions appear to be local products, perhaps a benefit of not inheriting an aristocracy, and I find that charming too.

It didn't have to be this way. Not all cultures have traditions of this sort, and nor does every culture within which our immigrants were born. Many come from societies which outsiders can never join or which were and remain bitterly and often fatally divided by race, by religion, by genealogy, by madness. Still others are riven by what Freud called the 'narcissism of minor differences', differences which are invisible to outsiders but for which insiders routinely kill each other. These, after all, are among the reasons why so many travelled so far to get here, and why many of them consider their arrival a blessed event.

Of course, institutions and traditions of a society, which for most of its history was a British dominion, need to be altered, amplified, made more accessible and in different ways, when so many citizens of the country come in a brief period from so many different places. Of course these institutions and traditions will be found to be inflexible here, condescending there, to beg these cultural assumptions and ignore those. Of course, too, many inhabitants of this peaceful provincial outpost must have found it unsettling to be invaded by so many different people carrying such a Babel of different languages, cultures, experiences and ways of life. Not to mention good food and coffee. Nevertheless, it was precisely these inhabitants within these traditions who have overall coped so calmly and well with the vast transformation of their ways of life.

They were not saints and one should not overdo their virtue in all this. The migrant boom came when the need to populate the country was uncontroversial and employment was plentiful. Moreover 'Anglos' did well by the change, and so did Australia as a whole: economically, culturally, intellectually and in many other ways. But they also did well in enabling it. It would be a shame if the good that has been done were denied or undone by ethnic entrepreneurs or alienated Australians who say too little about the character of that achievement, or by 'old Australian' populists who pretend that it was a great sacrifice.

For the second sort of error – the opposite of the first – is made by those who wish to puff up this crucial and enduring significance of our 'old Australian' heritage into a ground for racial exclusiveness in favour of old Australians or those who can pass as such. The virtues that I have enumerated have been inclusive ones, not exclusive. They have been the virtues of a tolerant, law-abiding, democratic and above all open society, framed and supported by institutions and traditions which embody them. They have not been virtues of the blood. One reason is that there are no virtues of the blood. No vices either. The effects of good institutions and good public values are transferable to people of many origins who live under these institutions and learn to practise and trust these values, so long as the institutions are determined to enforce them and the environing culture nurtures and requires them. As the distinguished liberal philosopher Chen Liew Ten has observed:

> it is no part of a liberal political order that there should be comprehensive shared ends and values which identify our way of life. A crucial element of our social identity is a common political morality that tolerates different ways of life. Immigrants who want to pray to God in their own way, to build their mosques and temples, to perpetuate some of their cultural practices, do not thereby threaten our way of life. On the contrary, it is the intolerance of such cultural diversity that is the real enemy, and that can come from those with unpronounceable names, who speak in broken English with strange accents, as well as from those whose impeccable pedigrees do not exempt them from the crude bigotries of the worst forms of nationalism.

This is a crucial matter. Nations, Benedict Anderson has observed in a famous phrase and title, are 'imagined communities' which purport to find something in common among millions of people who never meet each other. There are few incontestable facts of the matter in these imaginings, and what facts there are, are variously imagined and re-imagined. What matters is, in another felicitous phrase of Anderson's, 'the style in which they are imagined'. Some styles are admirable, and give people a place to stand and a group within which to feel at home without treating the rest of the world as lesser beings. Others lay claim to an ethnic purity which is usually spurious but for which nothing else can substitute.

The first style is commonly known as civic nationalism. It had its origins in Britain, but became a model only after the American and French Revolutions. It maintains, as Michael Ignatieff has written in *Blood and Belonging*:

that the nation should be composed of all those – regardless of race, color, creed, gender, language, or ethnicity – who subscribe to the nation's political creed. This nationalism is called civic because it envisages the nation as a community of equal, rights-bearing citizens, united in patriotic attachment to a shared set of political practices and values.

Such nationalism is in principle inclusive, since people of any sort can be accepted as citizens. The United States is the most prominent example of this sort of nationalism. Ethnic nationalism, on the other hand, rests on ancestry, real or purported – more often than not, unreal yet purported. It is the source of many of the worst miseries that have afflicted the modern world. Militant ethnic nationalists, such as some Serbs and Croats in recent times, have no doubt that their *ethnos* is superior to any other, in particular to the particular others whom they are busy killing, and that conviction allows them to keep killing. Nazi nationalism was of course of this sort, and democratic German nationality, while no longer virulent, is still ethnically based. Thus Turks who have lived for several generations in Germany, and have never been to Turkey, are still Turks and can never be Germans.* 'Germans' from Poland and Russia who speak no German, on the other hand, can classify as Germans. Non-ethnics may live within, but they can never join ethnic nations.

In Australia, of course, things are different. Our law has no ethnic component today, and it is unfashionable publicly to suggest that others should be excluded because they are inferior. It is also implausible. Rather, concerns are presented as being about social tensions, or cultural incompatibility, or incomprehensibility, or the future of a way of life. These are all possibilities that deserve discussion, but they are rarely addressed in a persuasive way. For they commonly treat cultural differences as given and ineradicable features of the world, rather than features we make of the world, and they pretend that the more obvious the differences between cultures the greater the dangers. History is against both of these suggestions.

---

* In 2000, this was changed by the new German citizenship law.

Partly we are misled by the way we crudely and misleadingly lump people together into ethnic categories – Anglo-Celt, ethnic, Asian – which are useless for historical and sociological purposes, indeed for all purposes other than polemics, since they manage to homogenise peoples and histories which have often spent millennia apart or, in the Anglo-Celtic case, together and at each other's throats. They also suggest that culture, or ethnicity, or language have essential, unchangeable characters. This is manifestly a myth in Australia, full as it is of an extraordinary array of hybrids, different from their ancestors and likely to be different from their heirs. It is also a myth more generally, as has been well observed by Chandran Kukathas, a Malaysian-Sri Lankan-Australian teaching at the Australian Defence Force Academy:

> the fundamental point … is that ethnicity and culture are not static but constantly changing in response to economic, social and political conditions. In looking at culturally pluralistic societies – that is to say, most societies – what we find are neither melting pots nor mosaics but ever-shifting kaleidoscopic patterns. In absolute terms, there are few if any stable cultural formations, since nearly all are affected not only by immigration and intermarriage but also by trade in cultural products and information, and by the expansion of the world's largest industry: tourism.

Moreover, marked ethnic differences are neither necessary nor sufficient for ethnic tensions. Nationalism is a European invention and it has been the basis of the slaughter of innumerable Europeans by innumerable others who, to a non-participant, are indistinguishable from those they come to hate and kill. For virtually anything can be a basis for group antipathies at some time and place and not at other times and places.

We know that Catholics and Protestants have often been keen to kill each other, indeed considered it obligatory, in European history. After all, the idea of tolerance, the basic condition of civil society, first developed as a reaction to the terrible European religious wars of the seventeenth century. Today in northern Ireland, the ancestral home of many Australian Anglo-Celts, some Catholics and Protestants still consider it a virtue to kill their compatriots. We also know that Catholic/

Protestant hostility was formative in Australian history, indeed very recent history. But when was the last time an Australian Catholic gunned down, or was gunned down by, an Australian Protestant? The relationship has been transformed, with difficulty and over time but with undoubted success, under the benign ministrations of the secular Australian state and a society which does not just practise tolerance but in important ways breeds it.

Again, whatever their leaders say, Serbs and Croats speak a virtually identical language and lived together in civil peace for a great deal of their history. It is a large question why they don't now, but it has nothing much to do with cultural distance from each other and nothing to do with physical differences. And when Serbs and Croats come to Australia, they also stop shooting, by and large. And whatever parents do, children start to act differently, to intermarry and to raise hybrids. And I, of course, see nothing wrong with that.

Of course, generational changes take time, and some migrants to Australia – particularly many Asian migrants – have not had much time. Yet recent controversies appear to focus on Asian migration. A lot of nonsense is said about unbridgeable cultural differences, for example, when the only indicator we have is physical appearance. Though an immigrant fresh from Hong Kong or Singapore or Delhi is likely to know far more about how a society like ours operates, and have a much better grip on the language, than do many of my parents' compatriots, there is more outcry against 'Asian immigration' than Polish. That might suggest that, just as people use one social marker – say, skin colour – as a kind of proxy for others, so some forms of argument are just proxies for prejudice, or at least insufficient thought.

What is most wrong with current attacks on Asian immigration is not that they will offend our neighbours, though they might; nor that they will scare off tourists, though they might; nor that they might lower international student enrolments, from which we skim hefty fees, though they might do that too. What is most wrong with such attacks is that they are morally objectionable and, being so, they violate our best traditions (though, unfortunately, not all our traditions).

Of course, no country is obliged to admit everyone. There are complex issues about how many and who should be admitted. The appropriate numbers, mix of skills, proportions between skill-based immigrants, refugees and family reunions are all legitimate matters of argument and decision. And what is appropriate at one moment in a nation's history might not be appropriate at another. But the principles invoked as grounds of limitation must be morally defensible, otherwise no policy can be. Perhaps fluoridation has been so successful that we need fewer dentists. That might be an argument for admitting fewer dentists. No holes left to fill. But *Asians*? How would we defend that? Do we worry about social peace? Then we should export the Irish, or if we keep them, the English. And what about Serbs? Croats? Kurds? Turks? Greeks? Macedonians? Palestinians? Jews? Is the concern cultural difference? How's your Albanian? Or your Turkish? Or, for that matter, Afrikaans? Perhaps we worry about preservation of our, in any case constantly changing, way of life. With a total 4.7 per cent Asian-born residents recorded in the 1996 census and a few more to include their Australian children, many of whom will intermarry with other Australians from different backgrounds, we have some way to go for that to be even an arguable, let alone a serious consideration. Perhaps we can't stand all that good food. Now there is an argument for Anglo-Celtic exclusiveness, but it's not one I've heard. One hopes that the real consideration is not that staple of social madness throughout the world: our race, or colour, is superior to others.

It has been wisely observed that an ethnic nation is a collection of people who hate their neighbours and share a common illusion about their ethnic origin. The consequences of these illusions and hatreds are objectionable enough when aimed against residents of other countries, but when turned inward against one's own fellow citizens, such dispositions are vile. And as Avishai Margalit observes in *The Decent Society*, a book which has much influenced me, 'when the hated neighbors are residents of the country, and the national symbols are directed against them, the problem raised by these symbols becomes exceedingly important.' When we talk racist language about immigrants, we are saying what we think about our citizens, many of whom are former immigrants. It is not merely uncivil, but indecent to do that.

In later essays, I discuss Margalit's view that a decent society is one whose institutions do not humiliate people. Suggesting to some of one's citizens that they belong to a group that is unwelcome – though they pay their taxes, obey the law, do whatever citizens are obliged to do – is to humiliate them, to treat them indecently. That is a shameful thing to recommend, and since there are times in our history when – through the White Australia Policy – it has been national policy, it is a shameful thing that our society has done. It is shameful because it has no moral ground and it contradicts what is most admirable in our history. But it is not the most shameful thing we have done, and Asian immigrants are not the most humiliated or injured beneficiaries of our national indecency. That honour goes, of course, to the indigenous peoples of this country.

*1997*

# Subjects, Objects and the Colonial Rule of Law

Law first made its way here on the backs of convicts and Aborigines, with dramatically contrasting results. We have histories of both encounters, but specialists tend to focus on one group or the other and they are rarely closely juxtaposed. However, it is important to consider them in connection, for both analytical and historical reasons. Analytically, both have implications for our understanding and appreciation of the nature, conditions and consequences of the rule of law. Australia was a testing ground for many experiments in the late eighteenth and early nineteenth centuries. Transportation of the rule of law was one of them. Second they are both equally parts of our history and of each other's history. Moreover, there was a specific link between them from the start. For, as Alan Atkinson has observed, in the first volume of his *The Europeans in Australia*:

In Britain, with the end of the American Revolution, two great issues dominated the conversation of polite and ambitious men and women. These were, first, the status of Blacks throughout the empire and, secondly, penal discipline. Slaves and convicts both challenged the imagination of reformers. Both seemed to live within a restricted, oppressive and exotic culture of their own, beyond the sweetness and light of an improving civilisation. Both might be touched by the humanity of educated men and women and their lives enlarged.

A major institution through which both convicts and Aborigines were to be 'touched by the humanity of educated men and women' was law. I hope that from juxtaposing the markedly different ways in which law touched settlers and indigenes, we might gain a more complex appreciation of what the rule of law meant in Australia's early development and, more generally, of the character, virtues, limitations and presuppositions of the rule of law itself. Along the way we might also learn something about ourselves.

## Transplants and Transitions

In his Boyer lectures, *The Rule of Law and the Constitution*, the Chief Justice of the Australian High Court, Murray Gleeson, draws on a passage from Robert Bolt's *A Man for All Seasons*, in which Sir Thomas More defends his devotion and submission to the positive law of the land. More wouldn't transgress its limits, even at the risk of giving 'the Devil the benefit of the law'. Against his interlocutor's angry retort that he would 'cut down every law in England' to get the Devil, More hotly replies:

> Oh? And when the last law was down, and the Devil turned round on you – where would you hide, ... the laws all being flat? ... This country's planted thick with laws from coast to coast ... and if you cut them down ... d'you really think you could stand upright in the winds that would blow then? ... Yes, I'd give the Devil benefit of law, for my own safety's sake.

Gleeson endorses these sentiments, and though it is an old Australian habit to do so, he is not just thinking of England. For he takes from More the title of his first chapter, 'A Country Planted Thick with Laws', and the country of which he writes is Australia.

Yet, like so many things gained and lost in translation, More's metaphor has a somewhat different resonance in its new home. The laws with which England was 'planted thick' had to be transplanted here, and this is a more specific, deliberate, activity than is suggested by More's passive participle. Those laws were, after all, products of processes that had gone on, if not 'from time out of mind', then for a very long while indeed. It would be a real task to discern what parts were deliberately planted by anyone in particular, and what just grew. That can be done, but it is not More's task. For he is not interested in the process but in the product, in the result not its origins or sources. He believes the English are, and it is good that they are, protected by what he calls 'the thickets of the law'. But he is not concerned with, nor would it be easy or brief to say, how those thickets came to be planted, nourished and tended, how they came to grow or what they displaced as they came to flourish.

In Australia we can be more precise. The laws which govern this country do so because of a specific event, the landing of Governor Philip in Sydney in January 1788. With him came 9 officials, 212 marines, 759 convicts and, because the colony of New South Wales, where it all began, was regarded as 'settled' rather than 'conquered', all the laws of England that were, in Sir William Blackstone's phrase, 'applicable to their own situation and condition of an infant colony'. Once planted in local soil, law grew in a range of distinctive, even peculiar, ways, but its roots, and those who planted them, are easy to identify.

And this points to another difference between the way in which England was 'planted thick with laws' and what it means to say those laws were planted here. More speaks of dense 'thickets' that provide security, apparently for everyone, 'from coast to coast'. Get rid of them, he says, and no one could stand upright. But in Australia in 1788, none of *them* was here.

To be sure, there were the long-established laws of Aboriginal societies, but neither More nor Gleeson was speaking of them. In any event those laws were not developed to deal with conquest (the accurate, though not the legal, term in our context) by strange invaders from another country, who would not go away. These invaders, in turn, were ignorant of those laws, only sporadically interested in them, and never contemplated their applying to themselves.

So they brought their own. These were new to the place they came, as was everything else the British brought. And so, therefore, became everything touched by them from the time of their arrival. To be sure, Aborigines had lived here for thousands of years – *their* societies and laws were as old as could be. And the settlers weren't newly minted either, for all that convicts came to be called 'currency lads'. What was new was their existence and juxtaposition in this place, and *that* novelty affected everyone – Aborigines, convicts, free settlers, and all of us who live in the society formed out of their encounters.

In the last decade or so, we have come to be familiar with a new family of terms: 'transitional' societies, 'transitional justice', the 'transition to democracy and the rule of law', indeed transitions galore. Not to mention transitologists. Post-communist Europe is full of them, so too Latin America, South Africa, and only a little earlier Spain and Portugal. Many scholars consider the post-communist transformations in particular to be unprecedented, since they involve *simultaneous* political, economic and social transformation. But so did our own. One hundred years after Federation, and a little over two hundred after white settlement began, Australians might usefully recall their contribution to transitology.

Many scholars who consider the contemporary developments now demur at talk of transitions, notwithstanding the ubiquity of the term. They prefer less teleologically loaded terms such as 'transformations', since they are less confident than many were in 1989, where things are going. Australian transitologists around, say, 1800, might have felt something similar. Yet there are some things we can say about the results of Australia's transition. One of them is that it has issued in 'democracy and the rule of law'.

This was not inevitable, nor was the transition simple or seamless. Nor still did it bring equal good fortune for all. But it occurred, and more quickly than is common. In many ways, indeed, it is an exemplary transition, one of the best of its kind.

But a paradox lies at its heart: that is, that while benefiting the settler population almost immediately, it had no such salutary consequences for indigenous Australians. Indeed if the criterion for the end of transition is success, theirs is still continuing. That paradox might be explained in short order – 'imperialism', 'racism', 'hypocrisy', the 'culture cult' and so on – but these epithets, while often appropriate, do not take things very far and since they explain everything they do not take us into the specificity of anything. I want to focus on one specific thing: the paradoxical sway and effects of law, and the ambiguous bearing of the rule of law, in our early history.

I use 'early' loosely, and in fact will range over some distance in our short history, but I am discussing genealogy rather than current developments. Some of our formative moments have left direct marks on our present; some have led to reactions, occasionally salutary, which have moved us in different directions. Either way they are important for an understanding of what we were and what we have become.

## The Rule of Law

When Chief Justice Gleeson observes that 'The imagery of law as a windbreak carries an important idea. The law restrains and civilises power,' he speaks of what is certainly an important idea, but that idea needs to be unpacked. For clearly not every law or legal order 'restrains and civilises power'.

Many legal orders have no such ambition. In many states, law has been conceived of as an instrument for repression or at least top-down direction of subjects, and nothing more. Indeed the word 'subject' is ambiguous in regard to them. The ruled were subjected *to* the law, and in that sense more subjects than citizens. On the other hand, they did not relate to the law as active subjects, as a subject does to a verb, for example. They are better seen as the *objects* of power and the institutions through which it is exercised, including law. Its subjects were the rulers, who used laws, among other instruments, for their own purposes. Indeed law has often been a very useful vehicle (and at times equally useful camouflage) for the exercise of unrestrained and uncivilised power.

Consider this telling epitome of the long-lived Russian legal tradition: Count Benckendorff, the chief of police under Nicholas I, once said: 'Laws are written for subordinates, not for the authorities.' As a recent commentator has observed: 'as a logical consequence, laws did not need to be made public in order to go into effect. Those who broke the law would find out anyway.' Clearly when Benckendorff spoke of laws being written for subordinates, he did not mean 'for their sakes', or 'for their protection, guidance and use.' The Russian tradition is particularly striking in its starkly top-down, instrumental view of law, but it is far from unique. More rare, indeed, are regimes where laws, or a substantial proportion of them, *are* written for the protection, guidance and use of citizens, where this is widely assumed to be the case and thought properly to be so. In these regimes, the cluster of values known as the rule of law is strongly institutionalised.

Politically pliable, draconian, discriminatory laws; incompetent, venal, weak, suborned administrators of law; rulers who, to adapt the German philosopher Habermas's distinction, use law solely as a 'steering medium' for the effective exercise of power, leaving no room for it to serve as an 'institution' of the everyday life world itself, available to citizens as a resource and protection in their relations with the state and with each other; laws which, against other sources and forms of power, simply do not *count* either as restraints on power or as resources in everyday life. None of these sorts of law, and they are hardly rare, is likely either to restrain or to civilise power.

Alternatively a legal order might embody laws which do restrain some things, or in some spheres, or in relation to some people, yet in doing so contribute to a larger incivility. One example is what Ernst Fraenkel called, in his book of that title, a 'Dual State', dual for it includes both a 'normative' and a 'prerogative' component. In the former 'an administrative body endowed with elaborate powers for safeguarding the legal order' governs some classes, races or domains. The latter wields 'unlimited violence unchecked by any legal guarantees' over other classes, races or everyone in other domains (e.g. politics). In such orders, the 'prerogative state' has the final word, though it might often find it useful to allow the normative state to operate routinely in particular areas of life. Nazi Germany was Fraenkel's example; South Africa under *Apartheid* a more recent one. Law in such states is not well characterised as a 'windbreak'.

More's and Gleeson's encomiums, then, cannot serve as a blanket endorsement of everything that can be called, in some bland and undiscriminating sense, 'law', but rather a particular normative conception of what law can and should do, one which will only be realised by certain *kinds* of law that serve certain sorts of ends in certain sorts of ways. That normative conception is conventionally summed up as 'the rule of law'.

The rule of law is commonly understood by contrast with arbitrary exercise of power. That, above all, is the evil that it is supposed to curb.

The *reasons* one might want power to be so restrained are various, but they include most prominently what might be called a *protective* and a *facilitative* element. The protective aspect has to do with diminishing the chances that subjects will be assailed by unrestrained exercise of power; the facilitative with contribution to interpersonal knowability and predictability, from which might come mutual confidence, co-ordination and co-operation. These are both good reasons.

In societies with large and concentrated centres of power (traditionally political power, but the point can be generalised), we do better if we can rely on institutions that are able to lessen the chances of that power being exercised arbitrarily, capriciously, without authority or redress. We do better, too, in large societies, where we are constantly interacting with non-intimates, if we can know important things about people we may not know well in other respects. Such things include their and our rights, responsibilities, risks and constraints. In small societies, as in families, we can know many of these things from personal everyday experience. In larger agglomerations such knowledge is often not available. Where the rule of law *matters* in a society, however, we can know these things even about strangers. That makes their and our activities more predictable to each other and might make us less fearful of and more co-operative with them, and, of course, them of and with us. This can lead to a productive spiral of virtuous circles, where each gains by reasonable trust in others.

There is also, at the very least, a practical, if not a logical, connection between the rule of law and important values. It is a negative connection, important for what it seeks to block. A government which seeks to treat its citizens as mere means or in a substantially discriminatory way, even more in despotic or terroristic ways, is very likely to violate the rule of law. The rule of law conspires to bring exercises of power into the light, and it gets in the way. Since many rulers prefer the dark and do not like anything to get in the way, doing so is a central part of the point of the rule of law. Such rulers might well contrive to uphold a façade of the rule of law, but not the rule of law itself.

Moreover, the connection between the rule of law and the morality of law is not merely practical and negative but more immediate and positive as well. For, as a number of authors have remarked, the rule of law's assurance that citizens will be penalised only on the basis of laws knowable when they act, is a condition of the state's treating people with respect, as the subjects of laws rather than their objects, as responsible agents whose interests and projects the law should serve and facilitate, rather than things, beasts or children which the law can freely mould, direct and control.

These benefits are inherent in even the narrowest, most procedural, versions of the rule of law, but on another view, though formal regularity should be an important component, it should not be the limit of one's ambitions for the rule of law. Legal orders typically embody and generate certain values, both in their animating principles and in the complaints they provoke when their practices flout the values that give them legitimacy. These include values such as those of equality before the law, procedural fairness or due process, and in particular legal traditions much more. On this view, which I share, the rule of law is incomplete to the extent that those values are not honoured.

These, then, are reasons why the rule of law has been thought to matter deeply in certain sorts of societies: those with large populations and differentiated legal and political institutions. It seeks to protect citizens from arbitrary power, facilitate fruitful interaction among them and between them and the state, and secure that they are treated in accordance with important legal values.

Less easy to specify in the abstract is what in particular is necessary to achieve these ends. Different societies, with different traditions, have sought (and achieved) the rule of law in different ways, and arguably could not all have achieved them in the same ways. Achievement of the rule of law is, in any case, always a matter of degree, and similar degrees of achievement can be attained in various ways. Nevertheless, there are some general conditions which need substantially to be fulfilled. I will mention four, three of them having to do with the nature of legal institutions and official behaviour. These are staples of the jurisprudential literature. The fourth, which I consider more important, is rarely much explored.

First, *scope* of the law is crucial. To the extent that powerful players are above or beyond the law, the rule of law must suffer. Law must reach everyone, including those at what Lenin called the 'commanding heights' (though he made sure it never reached there), and it must do so in the polity, the economy and the society.

There have been many polities where the ideal of subjecting governments or notables or relatives to law was unknown and would seem outlandish. Even where the idea exists, the extent to which it is realised by a legal order will vary markedly between polities and over time. To the extent that the idea and the practice are lacking, however, so is a crucial element of the rule of law.

Second, people will not be able to use the law to guide their own acts or their expectations of others unless they can know and understand it (either directly or through agents such as lawyers, accountants, associates, etc.). So the law must be of a *character* such that it can be known.

The necessary thing is that the law be knowable. How that is to be done is harder to say than lawyers generally understand, for successful attainment of the rule of law is a *social* outcome, not merely a legal one. What matters, here as everywhere with the rule of law, is how the law affects subjects. The general truth is that no one can guide their actions by laws that they do not know. But since the distance between law in books and action is often long, and the space full of many other things, it is a matter of investigation and social theory, not merely legal elegance, what might best, in particular circumstances, in particular societies, further that goal.

A third condition of the rule of law takes us beyond the rules to the ways they are administered. The law must be administered and enforced by institutions and in ways that take its terms seriously, interpret it in non-arbitrary ways that can be known and understood publicly, and enforce it fairly.

Finally, to be of sociological and political, rather than purely legal, consequence the rule of law depends on law that does and is widely expected and assumed to *matter,* to *count,* as a constituent and as a frame in the exercise of social power, both by those who exercise it (which, where citizens make *use* of the law, should be far more than just officials) and by those who are affected by its exercise. What is involved when the law counts is a complex sociological question on which the law bears. It is not in itself a legal question, for it depends as much on characteristics of the society as of the law, and on their interactions. But the rule of law depends upon it.

What does it mean for law to count in a society, in such a way that we feel confident saying that the rule of law exists there? All the questions asked here have a sociological dimension, this one above all. It asks about the social *reach* and *weight* of law, and the answers, whatever they are, will have to attend to questions of sociology and politics, as much as of law. Indeed social and political questions are central ones to ask about the place of law in a society, and they will be answered differently in different societies, whatever the written laws say or have in common. This is not because the law has no significance, but because the nature and extent of that significance cannot be read off from the law itself. After all, if no one is listening it doesn't matter too much what the law is saying.

If the laws are there but governments by-pass them, it is not the law that rules. So exercises of governmental power must be predominantly channelled through laws that people can know. But governments, as we have seen, are not the only addressees of the rule of law. And for the rule of law to count in the life of its subjects, as important as mere *submission* to law, or even adequate *access* to and *supply* of laws and legal institutions, though far less remarked upon than either, is *demand* for, and (often unreflective) use of, legal services and resources. Such demand and use extend beyond, and frequently will not involve, direct enlistment of legal officials or institutions. They are manifest in the extent to which legal institutions, concepts, options and resources frame, inform and support the choices of citizens.

This can occur, and vary, in two ways. The most obvious is in direct invocation of legal institutions. Possibility of access to them varies greatly between societies and within them. Willingness and ability to take advantage of possibilities of access vary greatly as well. More socially significant than citizens' (generally rare) direct invocations of official channels, however, is the extent to which they are willing and able to use and to rely upon legal resources as cues, standards, models, 'bargaining chips', 'regulatory endowments', authorisations, immunities, in relations with each other and with the state, as realistic (even if necessarily imperfect) indicators of what they and others can and are likely to do. For it is a socio-legal truism, which still escapes many lawyers, that the importance of legal institutions is poorly indicated by the numbers who make direct use of them. The primary impact of such institutions is not as magnets for social disputes, a very small proportion of which ever come to them, but as beacons, sending signals about law, rights, costs, delays, advantages, disadvantages and other possibilities into the community. They mix with other signals from other sources, and different people receive and respond to them in different ways.

Preparedness to draw on legal resources and entitlements, then, is sign of the extent to which the rule of law is a living presence in a society, and that varies greatly. If people know nothing of the law, or knowing something think nothing of it, or think of it but don't take it seriously, or even, taking it seriously don't know what to do about it, then their lives will not be enriched by the rule of law (though if it applies to governments they might still be partly protected by it).

Another way of making this point is to say that, especially in its facilitative role, the rule of law presupposes a particular view of the people it affects. They are supposed to understand themselves to possess rights and duties defined by law, shared with others, and usable as reliable underpinnings for interpersonal relations, particularly among non-intimates, or even among intimates when things go awry. And such interaction is supported, that is, actually helped and also considered worthy of support, by the values inherent in the rule of law.

Treating such people in such a way, as legal 'right-and-duty bearing subjects', is, as we have seen, to treat them in just one of the ways among many in which power might treat them. It is a condition of the state treating them as subjects, not mere objects, of the law, or in another idiom, to treat them with respect. Refusing to treat such people in such a way is commonly to treat them as objects and without respect.

Understood to refer to the rule of law, then, there are in many circumstances serious grounds for the conviction shared by the Chief Justice and the Archbishop, that law 'restrains and civilises power'. Does the planting and growth of law in Australia bear that conviction out? The answer is clear: yes and no. I begin with 'yes' and move on to 'no'.

**Yes**

> The end of the law is, not to abolish or restrain, but to preserve and enlarge freedom. – John Locke

My primary text in this matter is David Neal's excellent book *The Rule of Law in a Penal Colony,* the thesis of which is simple and, though the word is unfortunate in this context, arresting.

Neal begins his book with an exemplary, extraordinary and now often told tale: that of Henry and Susannah Kable, separately sentenced to death for burglary in England, reprieved and transported to Australia, after having met and had a child in Norwich Castle Jail. The captain of the hulk onto which Henry and Susannah were loaded initially refused to take their child on board. A sympathetic prison turnkey took pity on the distraught parents, rode (with the child) the several hundred mile return journey to see, and successfully plead with, the Home Secretary, Lord Sydney, in London, and returned the child to his parents in time for them to travel together to the other side of the earth. His mission attracted great public interest, and led to a public subscription of a substantial amount (£20) with which the couple bought goods for their new life and which they loaded onto a transport ship, the *Alexander.*

A month after they arrived in New South Wales, Henry and Susannah were married, but the newlyweds were without their parcel of goods. So they began the first civil case ever held in Australia, against the captain of the ship which had charge of it. They won. Neal aptly sums up the significance of this victory:

> Thus, the first sitting of a civil court in Australia and the first civil case to be heard, occurred at the behest of two convicts under sentence. Moreover, it named an important figure in the colony, a ship's captain, as defendant, subjected him to the power of the court's jurisdiction and officers, and made an order against him. It vindicated the property rights of two convicts and publicly demonstrated the ability even of convicts to invoke the legal process in the new colony. Nor was it to be the last time that convicts used the legal system to assert their rights in the colony.

From that time on, Henry was unstoppable, becoming in 1789 a police constable, then chief constable of Sydney (from which position he was dismissed in 1802 for misbehaviour), a successful if somewhat shady businessman, father of eleven children, and ultimately a rich and fulfilled octogenarian. Still today his numerous descendants are scattered through the land. But the story is not really about him or them, but about what his treatment and his case symbolises. And this is Neal's topic.

Neal's book seeks to answer an intriguing question: how was it that an often harsh and brutal penal colony came, within the space of fifty years, to be a free society? After all, the first white settlers in Australia did not come here for a holiday, nor did they get one when they arrived. Early New South Wales was not a pleasant or easy place to be. Apart from the harshness of everyday life there was, as Neal comments, 'one fact that everyone in the colony knew, both convict and free: convicts were sent there as a punishment.' Against more sunny accounts of the early settlement, such as John Hirst's, Neal insists on the dark and stark significance of that for all those who first settled here. In accordance with that fundamental fact and purpose, the nascent penal colony had no representative political institutions, no jury trials, almost no lawyers (except for some convicts), a dominant military presence and governors whose formal powers were great and whose practical autonomy, in this wilderness at the end of the world, was even greater. Fifty years later, while the majority of its population was still convict or ex-convict, it was a free society, with considerable legal protection against arbitrary power, and a representative legislature. There is no evidence that the British government planned it that way. Nor was the result inevitable. Nevertheless the transformation occurred, and most Australians are its beneficiaries. Why that happened is a matter of more than local or antiquarian interest.

Neal is well aware that there are many reasons for the changes to which he draws attention. However the major argument of his book is that one of the central reasons that New South Wales became a free society has to do with law, in a very special sense. His argument is that it was not just convicts who were transported, but particular ideas and ideals – ideas and ideals about law. What transformed Australia from penal colony to free society was what the convicts carried from Britain in their heads, 'as part of their cultural baggage'. Central to that cultural baggage was belief in the rule of law, belief that the law should and could matter, that it should be respected by their rulers and that it should and could form the basis of challenge to these rulers. 'A cluster of ideas known as the rule of law provided the major institutions, arguments, vocabulary and symbols with which the convicts forged the transformation.' Convicts fought, and often won, political and other crucial battles in the courts. When they won, it was because their opponents' hands were tied. They too, after all, had the same baggage in their heads. And even where they didn't, the courts did, insisting on their independence under British law, and the subordination of the apparently autocratic governors to that same law.

There were many ways in which this could have been otherwise. What if the convicts had come from Russia? There would have been no tricky issues about the legal rights of free-born Russians. The penal colony would not have had – from the very beginning – courts in which convicts could sue their masters, and oftentimes win, and this for two reasons: courts would not have been provided, and had they been, few people would have thought to use them. There would have been no fuss about trial by jury. Nor would the governors of the colony have constantly had to battle against prickly judges, conscious of their independence and attached to their traditions, or free settlers against far-too-smart emancipist lawyers, such as Wentworth and Wardell, who were often able to best them in court.

What if – more plausibly – the convicts had been cynically dismissive of the legal system? What if they had been imbued with then current ideas of universal rights or had chosen strategies of armed revolt? It is clear that many convicts were aware of these options, but in the main they were not chosen. Instead, as Neal demonstrates:

> the terms of political debate in New South Wales proceeded on very traditional lines. The protagonists relied on their British birthrights and deployed the language of the rule of law to secure them and to forge new social and political order out of the penal colony at Botany Bay.

The reasons for this owed a great deal to British institutions. Institutional *structures* were pretty rudimentary at the start, but institutions in the sense of rules, norms, common understandings, were thick on the ground, or at least in people's heads. Institutions of this kind were not rudimentary, and not new, in any sense. For the Britain from which the convicts came was an unusually law-suffused country, and more than that, a highly rule-of-law suffused one. It had endured a century of struggle over the political centrality of law, a struggle full – as Neal observes – of 'powerful icons', among them Chief Justice Coke's rebukes to his sovereign James I: in particular his insistence that no one, including the king, was above the law. As E. P. Thompson has argued eloquently in his *Whigs and Hunters*, 'Turn where you will, the rhetoric of eighteenth-century England is saturated with the notion of law' and that law was not merely something which rulers used, but a language in which people of all classes spoke, argued, claimed, and a source of rights for which they demanded respect. Not always successfully, certainly not with equal power, but insistently. To an extent unmatched anywhere in the world then, except perhaps the other British offshoot, America, law mattered in England; and, as Neal shows, it mattered consequently – and in some ways uniquely – in the unpropitious circumstances of New South Wales too.

This cultural inheritance was exported with our first white settlers, implausible avatars of the rule of law. What political historians of Australia – H. V. Evatt apart – have tended to regard simply as political struggles over civil liberties, Neal locates as far deeper arguments over the proper role of law in political and social life; more traditional arguments too, understandable only in the light of far older struggles and arguments over Magna Carta, the liberties of British subjects, and a 'government of laws and not of men'.

Indeed in some ways the inheritance was augmented by transportation. It is already notable that, unlike most prisons of that time, this Antipodean one was provided with courts from the start. That was not intended, until as late as November 1786, when, according to Alan Atkinson, Lord Sydney 'seems to have decided that too much was being left to chance'. In the months before the departure of the First Fleet, it was decided both that convicts would be given the protection of a judicial system, and also be entitled to absolute rights in land. Both decisions were consequential. The first, in the absence of other available public institutions in which struggles over power and status could be transacted, made available institutions useful for political fights, in which talk of the rule of law was useful rhetoric. It was, however far more than that. Convicts fought battles for status and recognition in terms of their entitlements under the law, believed in the rule of law, insisted that the authorities should respect it, demanded rights that they believed flowed from it. A great deal flowed from these beliefs. In the term used in this essay, the *scope* of the law reached both high and low, to the Governor and to the convicts; convicts knew and insisted upon that; they were rather liberally granted legal rights; and they made use of them, often to good effect.

Indeed, convicts had several legal rights that they would not have had in England. As John Hirst emphasises in *Convict Society and Its Enemies*, masters were not allowed to beat their servants themselves. That could only happen at the hands of authorised floggers under court order. John Braithwaite nicely captures the significance of this in an important piece on 'Crime in a Convict Republic':

> Consider in historical context the procedural innovation involved here. Masters of convicts were being required to have their corporal punishment authorized by a court when British naval and military commanders were not so constrained, when masters under English common law could flog apprentices and indentured workers on the spot, schoolmasters could do so to students, and it was not long since husbands had a right/duty to do so to recalcitrant wives.

Convicts retained other important rights as well. They could petition the governor, could be witnesses in court against their masters, could bring actions against abusive masters, could not be punished except by due process of law, and, as Braithwaite observes, 'while the adversity of floggings was terrible, mostly it could be avoided by sticking to the rules.' They could, as we have seen, own property and sue to protect it. Australia's British subjects believed they had rights under the law and insisted that the authorities should respect them. Apart from all that, convicts ate and dressed better than at home as well, and the sun shone.

Sunshine apart, none of this had to happen. As felons, convicts forfeited their civil rights in English law and the various rights allowed them here could quite legally have been withheld. Even the Kables' suit could have been prevented from the start. How such a policy might have been sustained in a society where convicts constituted the majority is not obvious, and this was clearly a major reason that they were treated better than the law might have allowed. Their labour and their co-operation in building the colony were necessary, and seen to be so, from the start. So interest conspired with ideals to fashion a strange bitter-sweet concoction – rather quickly more sweet than bitter – for the convicts of New South Wales.

A striking feature underpinning this story, for all its brutality, corruption and harshness, is that convicts were conceived not only as 'British subjects', as they were in law, but 'subjects' in a much more robust sense of the word. There were things that could not be done to them, facilities that must be afforded to them, demands that they could make, and which were listened to. They could *use* the law, not merely suffer it. They would undoubtedly have preferred not to be convicts, and they were often treated harshly, but they could not complain that they were systematically treated in ways that denied their humanity or personhood.

A subject is the author of his acts. Not necessarily the author of the law that applies to him; that is the promise of democracy not the rule of law. Moreover convicts were subject to particular restrictions, for they were criminals sentenced to be punished; subjects under sentence, as it were. But like other British subjects, the law assumed convicts to be, in considerable measure, the real and proper authors *of their lives,* and many of them took advantage of this by proving that that is just what they were.

Unfortunately, I do not know of evidence that tells us how much convicts' sense of the law entered into their everyday affairs, as distinct from their demands on public institutions. What I have read about convicts and law has tended to focus on direct encounters or uses of such institutions. My guess is that a society whose inhabitants are self-conscious enough of their rights to use official institutions will be effectively aware of their rights in their interpersonal dealings, even though the reverse is not necessarily the case. But that is amateur speculation, and one could offer alternative speculations. Perhaps, for example, law was reserved for dealings with officials, and convicts were after all experienced in such dealings, but irrelevant to their everyday lives together. Evidence of how law entered everyday interaction would be important evidence to have, as an indicator of how much the rule of law entered into interpersonal, and subject–state relations in a way that might have facilitated the civil society that ultimately grew here. Were I a historian of this period it would be where I would next seek to look. Perhaps historians have done so, and I would welcome word of that.

There is, however, one indirect indication which may bear on what went on 'in the shadow of the law'. It suggests that the treatment of convicts as subjects was not merely a morally attractive fact, but turned out to be salutary in its larger implications. In the article mentioned earlier, John Braithwaite compares the fate of non-criminal slaves in the United States and criminal convicts in Australia, and demonstrates that 'during the nineteenth century, Australia was transformed from being a high crime frontier society to a low crime society, while the US was transformed from a low to a high crime society.' He explains the Australian transformation thus:

> When one shares an identity as a citizen of a just legal order, there is a willingness to comply with that order. To realign the identities of convicts to those of law-abiding citizens, convicts need to be persuaded that they are now in reach of a society where the rule of law is something that offers practical protection to them and is therefore worthy of being honoured. Brutality is more bearable when its end can be imagined and seen and when its excesses can be challenged by fair procedure. Neither Australian Aborigines nor American slaves could imagine its end in the same way the white Australian convicts could.

One should not over-romanticise this story. Much of the law was extremely harsh, and in any event the rule of law was not the only inheritance with which the convict settlement endowed us. For example, as it grew, as Braithwaite has shown, so too did a robust tradition of police corruption that stems from the first convicts-turned-policemen (including Kable again) who quickly came to participate in the government of this penal colony. And of course there are the legendary traditions, or myths, of Australian distaste and disregard for law and authority, which, though they might seem far-fetched to a visiting Romanian, or Indonesian or Fijian, are among our most resonant myths.

But they *are* myths. Compared to most contemporary societies, at any rate those I know and know of, our distaste and disregard for law is far less striking than our remarkable routine obedience and invocation of it. We are a strikingly law-filled society. Rather British, as a matter of fact. The law provides many of our symbols, highest office-holders, Governors-General galore, investigators of all manner of contentious issues, whether or not they involve breaches of the law, and until recently a frame for industrial bargaining viewed, indeed, as 'a new province for law and order'. That frame, the industrial conciliation and arbitration system, was intended to answer the question put by its author and first President of the Conciliation and Arbitration Court, Henry Bourne Higgins, in his famous *New Province for Law and Order*: 'Is it possible for a civilised community so to regulate these relations as to make the bounds of the industrial chaos narrower, to add new territory to the domain of law and order?' That recent governments have decided it is impossible, or at least unprofitable, does not diminish the significance of law in our history, even if it cuts back the legal imperialism so prominent in Australia's development. Indeed one author, Alastair Davidson, complains that law has so dominated our polity that it has altogether squeezed out popular sovereignty in favour of sovereignty of the judiciary. I find that argument over-heated and implausible, but the mere fact that it can be made seriously and at punishing length suggests something of the weight of law in our polity.

The moral of this story is that – notwithstanding initially autocratic institutional structures of frequently indifferent quality, subjects with an unhappy relationship with legal and political institutions, and harsh and difficult circumstances – the settlers of New South Wales laid the foundations of a free and law-governed society in a very brief span of time. One of the most important assets they had was the institution-alised cultural baggage that they brought to the colony; baggage which, unlike the Kables' parcel, could not easily be stolen. As Neal remarks:

> Neither the imperatives of a penal colony nor those of a military out-post had displaced the principle that English people, even convicts, carried with them such of their rights as were not forfeited. Hence, New South Wales experienced the paradox of the rule of law in a penal colony. However, in the Antipodes, where strange creatures abounded, one having fur like an animal but a bill like a duck, paradox was plentiful.

**No**

> 'Do not shoot me. I'm a B-b-british object.'
> – David Malouf, *Remembering Babylon*

The Kables' victory did not mean, of course, that nothing could be stolen in the new colony. Indeed a whole continent was, under cover of law. Nor is the paradox Neal describes the only one to accompany the introduction of the rule of law to the colony. Another is a direct result of the same process that Neal describes, but it is a very different result, for it led to the dispossession and decimation of scores of thousands of people and hundreds of peoples.

When Governor Phillip landed, he brought with him instructions that required the colonists to:

> endeavour by every possible means to open an intercourse with the natives, and to conciliate their affections, enjoining all our subjects to live in amity and kindness with them. And if any of our subjects shall wantonly destroy them, or give them unnecessary interruption in the exercise of their several occupations, it is our will and pleasure that you do cause such offenders to be brought into punishment according to the degree of the offence.

For the first part of his term, Phillip appeared genuinely in sympathy with these aims. Instructions to later governors were similar, but already by the later parts of Phillip's rule and increasingly thereafter, they had less and less to do with what was happening here. By 1835, when Lord Glenelg had taken over as Secretary of State with responsibility for the colonies, such instructions had taken on a disconcerting mix of piety with impotence. Writing to Governor Stirling of Western Australia, he directs:

> It will be your duty to impress upon the settlers that it is the determination of the Government to visit any act of injustice or violence on the natives with the utmost severity and that in no case will those convicted of them remain unpunished. Nor will it be sufficient simply to punish the guilty, but ample compensation must be made to the injured party for the wrong received ... whenever it may be necessary to bring a native to justice every form should be observed which would be considered necessary in the case of a white person and no infliction of punishment, however trivial, should be permitted except by the award of some competent authority.

In his *Black Australians*, Hasluck drily records that Stirling, who was at least in part the object of this lesson, printed extracts from the despatch in the Government Gazette, and also 'Without comment, but with obvious satiric intention, he republished above it [his] despatch of 1832 which told settlers to protect themselves.'

Whether Glenelg believed he would be obeyed or was merely writing for the public or history, his injunctions were of little effect. Of course, had they and the earlier instructions to governors been successfully enforced, or indeed enforceable given the lack of financial and administrative commitment to support them and the mysterious complexity of the encounter, we might have been able to say that the first goal of the rule of law, protection from arbitrary exercise of power, had purchase in the colony. But, for two reasons, that was extremely unlikely from the start.

First was the contradiction, well expressed by Henry Reynolds in *An Indelible Stain?*, inherent in the imperial government's position in the early years of New South Wales (and Tasmania): 'Governors were exhorted to treat the tribes with amity and kindness while according no recognition to Aboriginal ownership of land. They counselled peace but sanctioned the use of military force and declarations of martial law when the Aboriginal tribes resisted the incursions of the settlers and their flocks and herds.' If occupation of land is non-negotiable, resistance can be assumed to follow. Civil relations are inconsistent with the combination. To insist on the primary goal and affect surprise at its readily foreseeable (and very soon visible) consequences can seem disingenuous.

Second, as Hobbes understood, protection from arbitrariness requires a government with a monopoly over the imposition of force, and in the early years of settlement in New South Wales there was no such government much beyond the limits of Sydney. Thus on the relentlessly expanding frontier, restrictions on the use of force by settlers (and natives) were not enforced, and given the nature of white settlement could not have been. This was what prompted the despair of James Stephen, expressed in a memo to Glenelg, at a problem which would 'set all legislation at defiance': 'how to provide for the Government of persons hanging on the Frontiers of vast pastoral country to which there is no known or assignable limit ... To coerce them by Statute of any kind would I should conceive prove in the result a vain undertaking.'

Even when public officials arrived, in the form of police and magistrates, they were often too few and too weak to stop established practices and often had no interest in doing so, but collaborated with settlers who were, after all, their own people. Rowley points out, for example, that governments have only been able to check the depredations of settlers in colonies when the governments led and the settlers followed. The standard pattern in Australia was the reverse. In *The Destruction of Aboriginal Society,* Rowley identifies the logic of the situation thus:

> The problem of a cultural frontier in the colonial situation is basically the same everywhere. If the frontier is expanding, law and order depend on the government leading the way and taking charge of the

processes of trade, settlement, recruitment of labour; and establishing by use of superior force the best approximation to a rule of law possible in these very difficult conditions. This has happened only rarely in colonial history ... In any case, more 'development' is necessary for more revenue. Development involves the taking of land: and in spite of legal theories about certain lands being 'waste and vacant', practically all land is the object of indigenous claims to ownership. There may be violent resistance, and reprisals by the settlers taking the law into their own hands. Efforts by police to keep the peace tend to come later. In practice, the police will go where there is 'trouble'; and the nature of the trouble will be described for them by the settler community. So the first contact of the Aboriginal with the police has been characteristically in the role of an avenging force.

Settlers were often isolated, frightened and, in the nature of things, on the make. And what they were intent on making, pastoral success, involved them in taking Aborigines' land, waterholes, killing their game as pests, killing them, too, for a variety of reasons. This is precisely the sort of situation Hobbes envisaged, and that stems from a truth often enough manifested and noted: *homo homini lupus* (man is a wolf to man). Often nothing more high falutin' is necessary to explain it. In the nineteenth century, not always but often, it was as basic and shabby as that. Sometimes it was better, and not infrequently it was worse, helped along as it was by the weakness of restraints on the frontier, the superior power of the settlers, the fact that real interests were at stake, and beliefs that Aborigines were barbarian, not quite human, anyway nothing like us, and, by the late nineteenth century, doomed to die out.

What was the government to do? Rowley contrasts the policy of J. H. P. Murray in New Guinea with what typically occurred in Australia. Murray formulated 'Australia's only really humane frontier policy', that officers act only as civil police and only use force where necessary for the purpose of arrest. The policy was often 'in violent contrast with the facts', but Rowley observes that 'There is a difference, nonetheless, between the practices that arise from a policy based on reprisals and those that arise from the breakdown of a principle based on the rights of the person ... No matter how inapplicable the law may be to the circumstances, once it may safely be assumed that the law does not bind the officer and settler on the frontier there can be no barrier against the worst tyranny and crime.'

The tyranny was not primarily state-imposed, though, and the crime not state crime. State protection was largely absent, and officers of state were often complicit, but settlers were the motors of the action. At least this was the observation of a visitor in the 1820s, quoted in Reynolds' *Frontier*, who investigated the position of the Aborigines for the Methodist Missionary Society. Blacks, he wrote, were in a 'state of exposure to caprices and wanton punishment … exposed to the caprice, interests and whim of everybody, they are cast on the mercy of all and find protection from none. They are exposed without any fair means of redress to the ill treatment of all … The White assumes within himself the power of punishment, and inflicts it upon the black just as the feeling of the moment impels.' Ultimately, however, from the perspective of the Aborigines and of the rule of law, it does not much matter whether it was the state directly, or the settlers on their own account, who acted 'just as the feeling of the moment impels'. Either way, where the reach or scope of the law ceases, so too must the rule of law.

Numerous authors, among them Neal and Reynolds, mention the ambivalent way Aborigines were looked upon in the beginning, sometimes enemies with whom settlers were at war, sometimes British subjects entitled to the protection of the law. The first interpretation might have justified lawlessness on the frontier, and, whatever the law, it was the most plausible gloss on the dispossession that was the basis of white history here. However, by the 1830s, it was unambiguously not the official interpretation: Aborigines were British subjects, in principle protected by and able to make use of British law. However if it is hard to see how they were or could have been protected by that law in the circumstances I have sketched, it is even less clear how they could make use of it.

In the first stages of contact, this was not primarily or even significantly a result of the character of the formal law. With a few exceptions, law had yet to be devised specifically for Aborigines. The 'law in the books' was generally that which applied to convicts. But contact brought out in the most dramatic and extreme forms the depth of those truisms of sociology of law that stress the distance between 'law in books' and 'law in action', or between official law and what the legal sociologists Ehrlich and Petrażycki, respectively, call 'living' or 'intuitive' law. Those distances exist in every society, however familiar and obedient to law. But some societies are not at all familiar with it, and among those who are, not all are obedient. In this connection, I would repeat an observation I made, reflecting on Eastern Europe, which is even more dramatically applicable here:

> for the rule of law to *count*, rather than simply to be announced or decreed, people must *care* about what the law says – the rules themselves must be taken seriously, and the institutions must come to matter. They must enter into the psychological economy of everyday life – to bear both on calculations of likely official responses *and* on those many circumstances in which one's actions are very unlikely to come to any officials' attention at all. They must mesh with, rather than contradict or be irrelevant to the 'intutive law' of which Leon Petrażycki wrote, in terms of which people think about and organize their everyday lives. None of this can be simply decreed.

Whatever the formal law was like, Aborigines did not and for a long time could not know it, or understand it. If Poles under Russian or Prussian or Austro-Hungarian rule throughout the nineteenth century, or under communism in the twentieth, took the law to be alien and imposed, were reluctant to enlist the legal system and not much used to doing so, then early nineteenth-century Aborigines, assailed with the finest fruits of the common law tradition, were astronomically less well placed. And how could it have been otherwise? As Hasluck comments:

> These new British subjects did not know British law and they did not believe it was a good law, and even if they had known and believed, their situation and condition meant that the law was not accessible to them and that they were not amenable to it. They knew nothing of the process of sworn complaint, warrant, arrest, committal for trial, challenging the jury, pleading, legal defence, recovery of costs, suit for damages, summons for assault, evidence on oath, and so on. Those

living in the bush did not know that it was wrong to resist arrest or hinder a policeman in the execution of his duty and they also frequently refused to stop when called upon to do so.

The notion in such circumstances of Aborigines *using* the law makes little sense. That is dramatically true of criminal law, where the process was in the hands of whites, and it was even more true of the sorts of action that led to Henry Kable's ascent. For, as Hasluck again notes, 'in any civil relation ... the move for redressing injury or maintaining a right rests with the wronged person'. It takes a great deal to imagine crowds of avid Aboriginal litigants in the early years of settlement. Still less the far more important service that the rule of law is supposed to provide in informing and supporting the relations of citizens who never go to court but act on understandings of the law in countless routine individual acts, accidents and forms of co-operation in daily life. None of this 'tacit knowledge' was or could quickly be available to the Aborigines upon which the penal colony had been inflicted. In the long meantime, at so many levels in so many ways, British law contradicted exactly that 'living', 'intuitive' law that legal sociology has shown to be fundamental to people's ordinary lives, and to the structures, roles, culture, and expectations that underpin them.

The rule of law, then, presupposes a lot to be effective and a lot to be good. In early contact with Aboriginal society its presuppositions did not exist even where the will to adhere to it did. And as we have seen, that often did not exist either.

What of the values of the rule of law? If we accept these to extend to 'respect for the dignity, integrity, and moral equality of persons and groups', then they were denied from the beginning in ways already mentioned, and most momentously, by the denial of indigenous rights to land. This was not merely one legal choice which happened unfortunately to underlie the decimation of whole ways of life. After all that could just be an unfortunate accident; 'the operation was successful. The patient died.' However, at least after it was realised that Australia had been long inhabited 'from coast to coast' by people who depended upon, and had deep spiritual attachments to the lands they were losing, the denial of any prior rights to land presupposed a deeper, if not always conscious, commitment, sustained till 1992: denial of the full humanity of the land-holders. It was the extreme example of a point that Raimond Gaita has made in his *A Common Humanity*. Gaita regards the High Court's recognition of native title in *Mabo* as:

> a belated recognition of their [Aborigines'] true humanity, because it is the recognition that they are beings with inner lives of the same depth and complexity as 'ours' and that therefore they can be wronged as seriously as we can be ... For many of the settlers, the Aborigines were not the kind of limit to our will, to our interests and desires, that we mark when we speak of respecting someone's rights, or treating them as ends rather than as means, or of according them unconditional respect, and so on.

Henry Reynolds, who in less philosophical fashion has made this the point of his life, makes a poignant observation in *Frontier*:

> The injustice was gross regardless of whether the Aboriginal circumstances were compared with those of the settlers or those of indigenous people in other Anglo-Saxon colonies of settlement ... whose native title was recognised ...
>
> The contrast between the respect accorded Aboriginal property rights and those of everyone else in early colonial Australia was even greater [than the latter] ... Convicts – and marines as well – were hanged for theft while Sydney was still only a few moths old. Hangmen and flagellators continued to enforce the sanctity of private property for the first two generations of settlement. A community with such priorities could not find a more decisive way to illustrate its fundamental disrespect for another society than to ignore its property rights. Even an enemy beaten in battle might receive more consideration.

Even if we limit the values inherent in the rule of law to such things as (formal) equality before the law, the right to a fair trial, and allied process values, early Aborigines were severely handicapped not only in fact but in principle. If in our own societies there are strong internal structural reasons why 'the haves come out ahead' in court, this was a result massively augmented in the rare encounters between whites and blacks which came to court. All the procedures and values were totally alien to the latter and quite literally out of their hands, and these practical difficulties were not eased by the facts that, for a long time, as heathens, blacks could not testify in court, and that long after emancipated convicts won their battle to serve on juries, Aborigines could not. But perhaps one should not harp on legal discriminations in this period. Apart from the quite fundamental problem of denial of rights to land, they were not systematic in the formal law, but occasional. That, however, was not where the action was. In another example of the difference between the law in books and the law in action, we have Rowley's reminder, in *Outcasts in White Australia*, that 'there was very little legal discrimination against Aboriginal British subjects at the time when their annihilation was in full swing.'

This attempt to apply British law to Aborigines was, then, a remarkably sustained failure, if serving the interests of Aborigines was any part of its aim. By the 1860s, a new phase of our history began, however, that of self-government, which was established by then in every colony apart from Western Australia. By this time, governmental authority had spread much further within the individual colonies. And one could imagine that the situation might markedly improve: Aborigines could be protected, since the sway of government had grown; knowledge and understanding of British law might have penetrated deeply enough to facilitate Aboriginal interactions with each other and with whites, they would by now be better placed to make use of it, and the values of the rule of law would infuse the law that they dealt with. On the other hand, self-government meant that power was now in the hands of precisely those settlers whom the British had ineffectively tried to restrain. That proved fateful.

The bulk of the Aborigines who did not die of disease or dislocation or guns were reduced to dependency on Europeans, typically in degrading settlements and conditions, because of the eradication of their own bases of food and life, physical and spiritual. In these circumstances, the increase in the hold of governments might indeed have curbed the Hobbes problem – unrestrained encounters between individuals – but it did so by raising the issue that Locke raised: who will protect us from our protectors. And in this phase, that was quite literally the problem Aborigines faced, for in the new regimes established by legislation devoted to this purpose, authority over Aborigines was in the hands of so-called Protectors of Aboriginals. As Pat O'Malley remarks:

> in general Aboriginal people through most of Australia have been subject to an extraordinary degree of regulation, perhaps being one of the most governed people on earth. Legislation such as the *Native Administration Act 1936* of Western Australia (for which parallels existed in other states) gave the Chief Protector of Aborigines direct control over Aboriginal peoples' sexual relations, social relations, marriage, geographical mobility, residence, employment, income, property ownership and management, education, custody of children – even over where they could camp and what the law referred to as their 'tribal practices.'

Victoria established the first comprehensive system of Aboriginal administration under the *Act to Provide for the Protection and Management of the Aboriginal Natives of Victoria 1869*. It was amended in 1886 by what came to be known as the 'merging of half-castes Act' and they together formed a regime which lasted for ninety years. In 1897, Queensland passed the most influential such Act, the *Aboriginal Protection and Restriction of the Sale of Opium Act*, which was the model for the Western Australian *Aborigines Act 1905* (amended in 1936 to exclude, *inter alia,* 'quadroons' and 'persons of less than quadroon blood') and two South Australian Acts (one for the Northern Territory in 1910; one for South Australia in 1911). There were differences between these laws in matters of emphasis, policy and detail, but the similarities are striking and considerable. All depended on racial classifications, many of them inconsistently applicable to the same individuals; all gave awesome power over individual lives in their most intimate details – residence, marriage, correspondence, movement, rearing of children – to Protectors and other officials; all gave great and largely unreviewable discretion to the Executive officials in charge. Of the Queensland Act, for example, Chesterman and Galligan observe (in their *Citizens without Rights: Aborigines and Australian Citizenship*) that 'The most extraordinary aspect ... was the breadth of regulatory power it ascribed to the Governor in Council ... and ... such was the breadth of discretion afforded to the superintendents over their reserves, and the protectors over their districts, that the Act provided very little restraint on their exercise of power.' From the time of Federation, and especially in the 1930s, these regimes became increasingly discriminatory. They were only dismantled in the 1960s.

At Federal level, similar classifications were used to exclude 'aboriginal natives' from the vote (*Commonwealth Franchise Act 1902*) and from pensions (*Invalid and Old-Age Pensions Act 1908*) and other social services (*Maternity Allowance Act 1912*). In the Northern Territory under Commonwealth Ordinances beginning in 1911, the Chief Protector is given power of 'care, custody, or control of any aboriginal or half-caste if in his opinion it is necessary or desirable in the interest of the Aboriginal or half-caste for him to do so'. Under the 1918 Ordinance he was to be the legal guardian of every Aboriginal and half-caste child, notwithstanding that the child has a parent or other relative living. Aborigines could not go into towns or travel from one reserve to another or from one part of the Territory to another without permission, and a female Aborigine could not marry a non-Aborigine without permission. As Robert van Krieken notes, the Chief Protector could depute these powers 'to any other official designated a Protector, which included all police officers, and from a contemporary perspective constitutes an extraordinary governmental intrusion into the everyday lives of a particular section of the population'.

What, from the point of view of the rule of law, is wrong with any of this? One might object to its *content* on the basis of other values, though one might defend it too, as many have. However one feels about that, it is commonly agreed that the rule of law is not of itself the rule of *good* law. So, whether or not we consider the law to be bad, it is a separate question whether it is a denial of the rule of law.

If one tries to identify the rule of law with particular attributes of legal rules, as is commonly done, the problem might escape you. Thus, some accounts of the rule of law would automatically attack the race- and 'blood'-based classifications on which all this and other legislation is based, as necessarily in conflict with the rule of law. For on these accounts, among them Rousseau's, laws must always be general in scope, applying in the same way to everyone and in no distinctive way to anyone in particular. If that is what equality before the law requires, however, it is impossible to achieve since, as Barney the dinosaur tells our children, everyone is special in his own way. And law-makers have many purposes. In consequence, law continually classifies and must do so.

So other writers distinguish between classifications which of their nature do not violate the principle of equality before the law and those which do. On the one hand, for example, those which admit candidates to higher education on the basis of 'relevant' considerations, such as test scores and, on the other, those which rely on characteristics which are irrelevant to the purpose in hand, such as race. The latter are said to be of their nature discriminatory. Were this so, then we could read the violations of the rule of law from the face of the hundreds of pieces of legislation which use classifications such as 'Aboriginal native' to bestow or, more usually, withhold benefits available to others. But this simple distinction also will not do. The notion and the grounds of a judgment of 'relevance' needs to be unpacked and defended. Many people who oppose racial discrimination, for example, believe that some references to race, for example, are relevant to proper purposes of legislation, among them some rectificatory purposes. There are issues of justice here which will not reduce to simple mechanical invocations of the rule of law.

Another deceptively simple approach is to seize on the discretionary nature of Protectors' powers as the characteristic that distinguishes the laws granting them from the rule of law. However, many modern pieces of legislation grant large discretions to administrative officials. So even though Justice O'Loughlin is right to observe, in *Cubillo* v. *The Commonwealth*, that 'The powers of the Director under the 1918 [Northern Territory] Ordinance were exceptionally wide,' wide discretion would not categorically distinguish this legislation from many other modern effusions of administrative and regulatory states in which the rule of law can still be said to exist.

Yet there is still something deeply wrong, from the point of view of the rule of law, to say nothing of other points of view, with the classifications and powers which proliferated in State and Commonwealth legislation. What is wrong can be seen if we focus less on the details of particular rules severally and for their own sake. Rather we should consider what in combination they reveal about the extent to which the law applying exclusively to Aborigines embodied the underlying aims and assumptions of the rule of law; the extent to which, in other words, the rule of law was institutionalised in those legal regimes.

The failure or lack of institutionalisation is betrayed less by lawyers' discriminations among forms of law, than in what they reveal about rulers' discriminations among subjects or, rather, between subjects and objects. Where classifications based on (arbitrarily drawn) racial characteristics define particular groups of persons *comprehensively* in ways that form the basis for withholding a whole range of benefits available to others, where they allow a regime of deep and systematic and unreviewable authority over, intrusion into and regulation of the lives of people on one side of the classification, which are applied to no groups (except in response to their acts) on the other side; where they are coupled with the grant to those who make such intrusions of extremely broad discretions in the exercise of their power and *subject* their objects to them without escape, then they deny comprehensively and profoundly the protections, facilities and values that the rule of law is supposed to embody. For where power-holders are deliberately left free of legal restraint in relation to Aborigines, Aborigines themselves are in no position to avail themselves of many of the legal facilities law provides the rest of the population, and inherent values of the rule of law are denied them, then we witness something closer to a Dual State, in Fraenkel's sense (though not, I would stress, to the Nazi state which Fraenkel had in mind when devising the term), than a rule of law regime.

In all these regimes, Aborigines were largely and legally disempowered objects of law and regulation, whether it be for their 'protection', 'management', 'merging', 'welfare', 'civilisation' or merely control. They were not its subjects. They were manifestly not authors of the law, but neither were the original convicts. On the other hand, by this time white Australians had advanced to being that, as well as what they had always been regarded to be: authors of their lives. In regard to the most basic, central, aspects of their lives, however, Aborigines were not regarded as authors at all.

*Law*, of course, is compatible with all these and other terrible things, but the rule of law is not. For, to recall, the rule of law is a *particular* conception, to do with restraint on arbitrary exercise of power and based on an underlying conception of human interaction as it is and should be. Each of the characteristics of the legislation mentioned above militates against such restraint and such a conception. All the more since they deal, not merely with professions, trades, licenses for business etc., but with people's whole lives. So they militate against the rule of law. (It is one mark of progress made that our contemporary laws lack these characteristics. How adequately they ensure the rule of law to contemporary Aborigines is a complex matter that I won't touch on in this essay, except to say that many of the most egregious aspects of the law that I describe have been removed. One related sign of progress is the extent to which Aborigines have come to be able to *use* the law, rather than merely be affected by it.)

This is not just a matter of moral evaluation of the purposes of these laws – whether humanitarian or genocidal, benign or malign, civilising or barbarous. Clearly the intentions of some of these Acts and regulations were protective, or thought to be; others, in particular in the 1930s, arguably something else. Those purposes are important to understand and historians have begun to enlighten us about them. But I am not a historian and I have no privileged insights on those large matters. And there is a level worth capturing where they do not make a difference. Whether intended to be benign or malign, the purposes of this legislation lend characteristics incarnate in its form: it is that sort of legislation which, by the power it gives officials, the discretions it arms them with, the unreviewable breadth of those discretions, and above all – more important than these matters of legal form – in the profound power they give officials over the lives of Aborigines, renders those subjects no subjects at all.

Too often today, debates hinge solely on judgments or claims that the intentions of such legislation were well or ill-meant, as though the former would deliver a clean bill of health. But though that is an important debate, it is not one with which I am engaged in this essay. For there is a deeper issue, identified in W. E. H. Stanner's laconic observation, as late as 1964, 'Our intentions are now so benevolent that we find it difficult to see that they are still fundamentally dictatorial.'

Seen in this light the policy which has most spurred the modern popular interest in relations between whites and blacks in this country – child removal – is not out of character, and should hardly have caused the surprise (though it has appropriately caused the discomfort) that has been visible in the last several years. I have not discussed that policy in this essay. Yet it might well stand as a fitting concluding example of my theme.

Robert van Krieken sums up the legal aspects of this policy thus:

> The strategy adopted here was simply to remove Aboriginal parents' common-law rights over their children and to make the state the legal guardian of all children of Aboriginal descent, to be removed at will and sent to a mission, a child welfare institution or to be fostered with a white family if sufficiently light-skinned. The legislation enabling this was introduced in relatively weak form between 1905 and 1909 in all Australian states, strengthened around 1915, and further reinforced in the 1930s.

Legislation and regulations in several states allowed officials to deem 'any child born of an aboriginal or half-caste mother' (*Industrial and Reformatory Schools Act 1865*, NSW) to be neglected, and so be sent to reformatories or boarding schools. Many other legal ways of removing 'half-caste' children from their mothers have been documented. Parental consent was not required. Such practices continued until the 1960s and thousands of children were removed, commonly without parental permission and without specific evidence of neglect, to foster homes and institutions of various sorts. The consequences were frequently devastating for the parents and children involved. And one might have thought that was predictable. Certainly it should have been predicted by readers of *The Norfolk Chronicle* of 11 November 1786, which noted, when the Kables received permission to take their child to Sydney:

The laws of England, which are distinguished by the spirit of humanity which framed them, forbid so cruel an act as that of separating an infant from its mother's breast … it cannot be but a pleasing circumstance to every Englishman to know, that, though from the very nature of the situation of public Ministers, they must, on most occasions, be difficult of access, … when the object is humanity, and delay would materially affect the happiness of even the meanest subject in the kingdom, the Minister himself not only attends to complaints properly addressed, but promptly and effectually affords relief.

## Conclusion: Institutions and Moral Imagination

That our ideas are different today does not mean that we are better people. They might, though, be better ideas. For however one characterises the motives of those who so degraded Aborigines, and they were doubtless various, there appears to have been all along a failure of moral imagination, that imagination which sees *all* persons as, in Raimond Gaita's words, 'the kind of limit to our will, to our interests and desires, that we mark when we speak of respecting someone's rights, or treating them as ends rather than as means, or of according them unconditional respect'. For reasons that historians can explore, social theorists understand and moralists evaluate, this otherwise most humane of societies failed to register Aborigines in this way for a very long time.

I began with Chief Justice Gleeson's endorsement of Sir Thomas's horticultural world-view, so I will end with it: 'The imagery of the law as a windbreak carries an important idea. The law restrains and civilises power.' There is little doubt that the institutions of law can contribute to doing that, but not simply by being law. The values institutionalised in the law must conspire to that end. In the case of convicts they did. They need not, however, and with regard to Aborigines they did not. Law, as we have seen, might just amplify or undergird unrestrained and uncivilised power. Or it might aid power in a mission to 'civilise' not power, but *people* thought of as barbarous, or in some other deep way uncivilised.

Once that mission is embarked upon, there is no simple way to go back to the beginning or abandon the undertaking, nor, for that matter, is it easy for disruptive and destructive invaders to act well, even were they to wish to. A comprehensive moral assessment of that enterprise is beyond me, though it nags away, for it is at the same time pressing and daunting. Tragedy was almost certainly written into our national history, as soon as whites decided to come here, and whatever we did. Nevertheless we did come here and we did some things and not others. There are, and have been, different ways of proceeding. I have tried to sketch some of our ways.

*2002*

# The Character of the Nation

If, as Cyril Connolly and George Orwell both alleged, within every fat man there is a thin man struggling to get out, we might ask if this also applies to works such as Keith Windschuttle's *The Fabrication of Aboriginal History*. This portly if handsome volume on the history of relations between Europeans and Aborigines in Tasmania is apparently to be followed by two more dealing with the rest of Australia. The result is to add up to some 500,000 words. But what is this tubby tome about?

The author's own answer is unequivocal: History, the job of which is to establish Facts. This is why much of the book is occupied with sieving and separating facts, no-longer-facts, not-quite-facts, never-were-facts, about the nature of frontier violence in Australian history. Much of its size derives from the painstaking detail of its examination of a range of accounts of frontier violence in colonial Tasmania.

Windschuttle regards 'orthodox' historians of these matters much as a somewhat obsessed ferret might regard rabbits: as nothing but prey. He hunts for incompetence, sloppiness, ideologically driven false-hood and fantasy, and he reckons he finds them everywhere. He seems convinced that the British just weren't the massacring sort, so wherever there is an account of a massacre, the hunt is on to show either that it never occurred, that there weren't very many Aborigines killed, or that it was all a mistake. In almost all cases these are the conclusions *Fabrication* shepherds us towards.

However, you don't just need to get the facts right, which the 'orthodox' apparently never do; you also need the right attitude, which they never have. That attitude is one of 'detachment'. Windschuttle has it, his 'orthodox' quarries lack it. What mars their work, apart from living in a 'black armband' fantasy land, is that they have 'overt political objectives' and fail to 'adopt the traditional stance of the academic historian and profess at least a modicum of detachment from their subject'. Here they are true to the spirit of the 1960s that spawned them, a spirit that 'turned the traditional role of the historian, to stand outside contemporary society in order to seek the truth about the past, on its head'. The errant results, Windschuttle informs us, follow necessarily from their (misguided and insidious) political motivation.

There is a problem here. These methodological strictures actually serve as an embarrassment for Windschuttle: the more they convince us, the more they weaken *Fabrication* itself, because whatever the outcome of the disputes between him and his targets, it soon becomes obvious that this book is not a politically disengaged pursuit of facts at all. As his own introduction observes, correctly, 'the debate over Aboriginal history goes far beyond its ostensible subject: it is about the character of the nation and, ultimately, the calibre of the civilization Britain brought to these shores in 1788.' These are matters on which members of any nation are generally not detached, and rightly so.

Most of us *care* deeply about both the character of the nation to which we belong and the calibre of the civilisation we embody. It is because we care that discussions of Aboriginal history under settler-colonialism have evoked the attention, not to mention the passions, sometimes hatreds, often pain, which they have in this country. The historical understanding of issues like frontier violence is never going to be detached, because history lies at the heart of identity, a point pursued in 'Neighbours', below.

When we consider the history and character of our nation, we do not immunise ourselves against either emotions or politics, we are thoroughly *engaged*, as is, of course, Windschuttle. Thus he opens his book with a denunciation of the previous Governor-General, assorted journalists and judges, and indeed anyone over the last 200 years who has worried that the character of the nation and its civilisation might be sullied in any way, and this is clearly his own version of such an engagement. If Windschuttle were less shy about the role of the subtext that fuels his narrative, he would not have to suggest, implausibly and unconvincingly, that he is Ranke to his opponents' Marx. Rather, he could recognise that there are better and worse ways of engaging in debate, important debate, about the 'character of the nation', and that proud boasts of detachment are neither necessary nor sufficient to distinguish those who participate well from those who do not. Historians participate in these debates without being disqualified by their vocation from doing so, and without making them any lesser historians.

Much more can be said about the fat book. For example, Windschuttle is keen to be a revisionist historian, to turn the accepted approach to his topic upside-down, and this can be a thoroughly honourable occupation. However, he pursues this aim with such a heavy hand that it threatens to turn into, or at least invite, self-parody. It would not be entirely misguided to treat the accusations it levels at others as an excellent guide to understanding the inner logic of *Fabrication* itself, it comes so close to being comically self-referential. But the fat book has already been the subject of much criticism. Our focus is different: the other, slimmer volume contained within, which embodies a particular style of thinking about the meaning, bearing and significance of our shared history for understanding and appreciating 'the character of the nation' and the 'calibre of British civilization'. For just as many of us are driven most by what we acknowledge least, it is this subtext that provides the motivation, rationale, the indefatigable energy and the spine of the larger work.

### Black v. White Myths

*Fabrication* presents debates over our past as a highly scripted Manichaean drama. In such drama, and so in such historiography, there are always two major mythical characters, negative images of each other, locked in battle. The drama is heightened by certain rules of the genre: each character is portrayed in starkly contrasting tones: black–white, no shades of grey. They must be mutually exclusive: no combination, no partly this partly that, will do. They must exhaust the field: no other possibilities, nothing else, nothing more, and they must be opposites: what is white can be inferred inversely from black, and vice versa. In *Fabrication* itself, the protagonists are, on the one hand, what we might call the 'black myth' generated by 'orthodox' historians, on the other Windschuttle's 'white myth', although of course he calls it truth. Only one of them can be allowed to remain standing: gunfight at Suicide Bay.

Not only is the black myth itself a homogenised, identikit mélange, but so is its collective author, the hydra-headed mythologist of 'orthodoxy', whose many mouths apparently all speak with one voice. It includes historians who do make strong claims about massacres and violence, others who do not but still see the tragedy involved in white settlement; journalists and media figures, some of whom, like John Pilger, seem to believe that in talking about our past, worse is better and worst is best; others who simply want to try to understand and then come to terms with that past; political figures; parties to current legal and political disputes. These are all mixed up to give the impression that, in the last analysis, as Marxists used to say, they all believe the same, that our past was an unqualified Hell populated by white demons and black angels. Having everyone agree with everyone else is convenient for an attacker in a hurry, since any criticism of one 'orthodox' historian will also do for all of them. Those who pursue a complex argument about the possibility of a genocidal 'moment' in the twentieth-century policies of child removal involving no killings are thrown in the mix with those who use the word to describe killings in the nineteenth, and with others who do not use the word at all. All of them end up among the 'orthodox' and all are then taken to be purveyors of the black myth.

The result, attributable to the malign influence of leftist historical orthodoxy, is that the story of the nation is shrouded in guilt, deriving from calumny, in turn supporting a perverse desire to hand over most of the continent to a handful of Aboriginal people clearly unable to do anything with it under the name of 'native title'. Whites, according to this myth, were bent on nothing other than exploitation, dispossession and extermination; blacks were skilful guerilla warriors defending their land, usually heroically; systematic and large-scale carnage of the latter by the former was the order of the day. Most odious and despicable of all, we appear to have been led to think of our history as on a par with Nazism. Although Windschuttle does not appear able to find a historian who actually said as much, the orthodox are nevertheless culpable for the views of those journalists who do. We must not underestimate how cunning the orthodox school is, for, writes Windschuttle, 'While the historians themselves might not have overtly used the Nazi comparison, they have created a picture of widespread mass killings on the frontiers of the pastoral industry that not only went unpunished but had covert government support. They created the intellectual framework and gave it the imprimatur of academic respectability.' One might note in passing that the Nazis did more than give covert support to frontier massacres, but this bagatelle passes Windschuttle by.

Once the black myth is delineated, the contrary position generates itself on automatic pilot. Such a counter-myth constitutes *Fabrication*'s deep structure, its underlying grammar, burrowing into Windschuttle's prose, the epithets he chooses, the targets of his anger, the structure of his arguments, the mirror-image symmetry between what he denounces and what he insists upon. He explains that it is true that white settlement provoked black violence, but not for any of the retaliatory 'political' (still less military) reasons suggested in the black myth, and certainly not out of resentment. European settlement simply 'gave the Aborigines more opportunity and more temptation to engage in robbery and murder, two customs they had come to relish'. Where particular Aborigines indulged in violence, not only were their actions 'not noble: they never rose beyond robbery, assault and murder'. Those alleged to be 'warrior patriots' were 'simply outlaws ... bushrangers who happened to be black'. They gave 'no evidence of anything that deserved the name of political skills at all', and as for military organisation, which might have 'elevated Aboriginal violence into something more than criminal behaviour ... [it] is conspicuous by its absence'.

In response to these venal representatives of a sick civilisation just teetering for 30,000 years before collapsing in forty, far from seeking to exterminate them, whites were desperate to civilise the blacks. Notwithstanding the 'agonising dilemma that the continuation of Aboriginal violence created for the settlers' (others' 'agonising dilemmas' are not recorded), killings of blacks were not systematic, they were merely 'sporadic'. Since not everyone agreed even then with this picture of generalised benevolence occasionally thwarted by its benighted beneficiaries, the ones who don't agree are denigrated throughout the book. That is true of the historians who are its imme-diate targets, but it is also true of *anyone* who purported to 'protect' blacks (with the implicit suggestion that they might need some protec-tion). Thus missionaries, thus George Augustus Robinson, thus anyone over the past couple of centuries, who experiences a 'whispering in [their] hearts'.

There are other ways of doing this. If there are indeed mythological elements to the currently dominant approach to Aboriginal history, it is possible to show that such a myth is historical caricature without lurching towards an equally flat, monochrome counter-caricature. As many historians, among them Henry Reynolds, have shown, the story is altogether more complex, both factually and morally, than either car-icature allows. A worthy job for a historian might be to probe and reveal some of those complexities, but it is precisely *Fabrication*'s poli-tical concerns which prevent it from doing so.

A favourite writer among those who pursue the approach to history represented by *Fabrication* is Paul Hasluck, who remains today the leading intellectual of the anti-self-determination, assimilationist posi-tion, with its current proponents a mere pale shadow of his much more sophisticated understanding. *Fabrication* approvingly quotes this pas-sage from Hasluck's *Black Australians*, a history of Aboriginal policy published in 1942:

> There have been two colossal fictions in popular accounts of the treat-ment of natives in Australia. One suggests that settlers habitually went about shooting down blacks; the other, framed as a counterblast, is that every settler treated natives with constant kindness. There is no evidence to support either statement in Western Australia.

Fair enough: it would be hard to find anyone who would explicitly argue with this point. But, perversely, most of *Fabrication* effectively does: we get Pilgerism *à rebours*, in the form of Windschuttle's own counterblast. The only *un*kindness he is willing to acknowledge is that of *misguided* kindness (the protectionists), but everyone else who sought the civilisation of Australian Aborigines appears unable to do much wrong.

Yet even Hasluck, who might be accused of constructing another fiction that every *assimilationist* 'treated natives with constant kindness', was much more prepared to acknowledge complexity. He observed, for example, that the reluctance of 'civilised' white Australians to incorporate Aborigines into their communities was as much a barrier to assimilation as anything to do with the policies pursued by governments or church agencies, or the characteristic capacities and inclinations of Aboriginal people themselves. On the question of frontier violence, what he called the 'direct action' pursued by settlers, Hasluck was able to argue in favour of the *character* of the men who engaged in such violence without finding it necessary to deny its morally problematic features:

> That policy of direct action on the frontier did not come from any peculiar viciousness in individuals, it arose out of the nature of contact. Men who if they had been in England on those days or in an armchair in the present day would probably have abhorred the shooting down of natives, were brought by fear, rivalry and exasperation to kill men or to condone the killing by others. It was recognised as a means of establishing order and peace.

His point was that one should see frontier violence as a product of a particular situation or structural context rather than of character flaws, without denying the reality and damaging effects of that violence. Hasluck's plea was not to attribute all frontier violence to Aboriginal criminal tendencies, but to ask ourselves 'why it was that men of decent habit and usually of controlled passions were moved to a tolerance of violence and even to its commission'; in other words, to investigate what it was about the frontier situation that led apparently civilised people to behave in barbaric ways.

Some commentators, including Peter Coleman and Ron Brunton, have said that *Fabrication* lacks a sense of the tragedy of Aboriginal history. This is an observation at the same time perceptive, incomplete and not completely accurate. It is *perceptive* because this is a disturbingly heartless book, even about the deaths and miseries (attributed to 'the dual weight of the susceptibility of its members to disease and the abuse and neglect of its women') that are acknowledged. It is *incomplete* because it sees this inattention to the tragedy of the end of a civilisation and its human carriers in the space of a few decades as an independent, accidental blemish, rather than an integral component of the white myth embodied by *Fabrication*. But it is also *not completely accurate*, because there are some points in *Fabrication* where tragedy is acknowledged: for example, Windschuttle thinks it was a tragedy that that 'the Aborigines adopted such senseless violence' during the Black War in Van Diemen's Land, of which they were themselves the primary victims. Later we are also informed that the 'real' tragedy was 'not British colonisation *per se*, but that their society was, on the one hand, so internally dysfunctional and, on the other hand, so incompatible with the looming presence of the rest of the world'.

What is wrong with this? If you call someone a Nazi, unfairly, it is indeed right for them to deny it and show that they are not. But what of those such as Stanner, Elkin or Rowley, who talked not of Nazism, but of a colonial history, inevitably fraught with tragedy though not only that, better than some worse than others, peopled with good people and bad, good motives and bad, events of which we can be proud and others of which we should be ashamed, yet a history which, with both its achievements and its calamities is *ours*, and which, for all its real factual and moral complexity, had comprehensively catastrophic consequences for the original inhabitants of this country, not all of them unintended?

And what of a view less concerned with individuals and their motives than with situations and their imperatives? The settler-colonial situation has had tragedy written into it for a very long time. It is hard for settler-colonists to behave well whatever their intentions, because of power-imbalance, contradictory interests, cultural distance, condescension built into the missionary impulse and the 'civilising mission', cluelessness, carelessness and many other things. One can very easily do harm without meaning to, even when meaning to do good, not because like Windschuttle's missionaries and historians, one is hopelessly captivated by a romantic ideology of noble savagery, but because the situation is good for some and bad for others, and good for some because bad for others, all at the same time. *Fabrication*'s approach to history is not concerned about even this small level of complexity, because its myths and counter-myths are all equally simple. It is defeated by real complexity and ambiguity, unable to grasp the distance between what a debunking detection may have revealed and what really needs to be shown to make out the counter-myth.

One way this conceptual inability is manifested in this particular book is the talismanic role, sometimes bad sometimes good, it gives particular words. The bad are massacre, genocide and Aboriginal self-determination; the good are (some versions of) Christianity, civilisation and the rule of law. Let us briefly consider them.

### Genocide, Civilisation, the Rule of Law

If deliberate massacres characterised our history, the character of the nation bears deep scars and we have reason to think more deeply about the calibre of our civilisation. If it turns out that what happened in particular circumstances cannot fairly be called either a 'massacre' or 'genocide', that is good news. The Europeans who came to Australia certainly did see themselves as aiming to civilise the blacks whose condition they 'pitied' – to begin with, at any rate. This meant, suggests Windschuttle, that notwithstanding the 'agonising dilemma that the continuation of Aboriginal violence created for the settlers', they were only provoked to kill blacks occasionally, and therefore, his narrative suggests, such killings were of little significance. Certainly not worth wearing a black armband for. How could it have been otherwise, since the whites were Christians *and* carriers of the Enlightenment *and* of the rule of law. 'It was this rule of law', writes Windschuttle, 'that made every British colony in its own eyes, *and in truth*, a domain of civilization.' (emphasis added)

### *Massacres and Genocide*

If massacres cannot be unequivocally shown to have occurred, according to rather strenuous conditions of proof, then the verdict in *Fabrication* is not the Scottish 'not proven' but 'non-existent'. If no extermination or extirpation, then the only harm done was that effected by those 'humanitarians' – missionaries and others – who purported to be saving Aborigines from non-existent threats of extermination, and by initiating 'separatism' did them in with their fraudulent ministrations. Yet even the settlers whose voices we hear in *Fabrication* itself had a more complex understanding of where the blame for the violence lay.

In any event, does our understanding of the character of European civilisation really begin and end with massacres, with whether we 'exterminate all the brutes', and should we set settler-colonial dispossession aside as an issue unless it is organised around killing? However many deliberate murders occurred, and various historians have already cast doubt on the ubiquity of massacres while still insisting that killings were widespread, they do not exhaust the pain of the encounter, and they are not the only things that can be done to colonised peoples about which later generations of settler-colonists might feel uneasy. Many of those who have written about settler–Aboriginal relations have been concerned with aspects of these encounters besides massacres, and those aspects too must be registered in any appraisal of the character of the nation. What of all the slights, humiliations, hurdles, obstacles involved in the colonial encounter? Moreover, even if there had been no massacres at all in Australian history, the violence of colonial dispossession itself does not count for nothing.

In his masterly book *The Decent Society,* Avishai Margalit points out that apart from the degree to which the institutions of a society are 'bridled' so as not to inflict physical suffering without restraint, societies differ in the degree to which they are what he calls 'decent', using that word to mean 'non-humiliating'. The essence of humiliation is rejection, and two general ways in which people are likely to be humiliatingly rejected by social institutions generally, and by colonial invaders typically, is, first, when they are not treated as human by them, and second, when they are denied control over their vital interests. Where such rejection occurs, the humiliation exists no matter how noble the motives of the colonist might be.

We do not have to go to extermination camps, then, to find systematic and humiliating disrespect. That can happen whenever we are 'human-blind', and that, as Margalit points out, does not mean failing literally to see people, bumping into them as if they were invisible, or thinking of them literally as machines or dogs. It means seeing them 'under a physical description without the capacity to see them under a psychological one'. It commonly involves *overlooking* them, that is 'not paying attention to them: looking without seeing … [it] does not strictly mean seeing them as things, but rather not seeing them fully or precisely.' Many colonial regimes, Margalit points out, were:

> often more restrained in their physical cruelty than the regimes they replaced. Nevertheless, the colonial regimes were usually more humiliating, and more rejecting of their subjects as human beings, than the local tyrants, who considered their subjects their fellow nationals or fellow tribe members and thus equal to them as human beings.

Apart from massacre and humiliation, what of the small matter of dispossession? It is conceivable, we concede, that that could be done without killing a flea, even with the utmost politeness, but it is hard to conceive it being done without injury to those dispossessed. And the injustice of that injury, as emphasised in the passages from Gaita and Reynolds that I quoted in the previous essay (at pp.82), goes well beyond 'simple' loss of land. The taking is an injustice in itself, and a profound one.

Whenever *Fabrication* touches on dispossession, by contrast, it fudges the boundary between reporting and endorsing, with some actors' perceptions being subject to no critical scrutiny at all, but presented as 'fact':

> … when British eyes of the eighteenth century looked on the natives of Australia, they saw nomads who hunted but who had no agricultural base, and who therefore did not possess the country they inhabited. In contrast, the British colonists took up the land and 'improved' it – a term persistently employed by the first settlers. By 'improving' the land, the colonists thereby regarded themselves acquiring right of possession. They were not dispossessing the natives. Instead, colonisation offered the indigenous people the gift of civilization, bringing them all the techniques for living developed by the Old World.

Again the binary logic: either one is dispossessing the native, or one is bringing the gift of civilisation. One of the more central points, however, of understanding the impact of European civilisation on the rest of the world is grasping the ways in which 'civilisation' is, as the German sociologist Norbert Elias suggests, precisely the 'watchword' of colonisation: it is through 'bringing the gifts of civilisation' and effecting the changes in the behaviour and dispositions of the colonised necessarily accompanying those 'gifts' that colonisers execute and above all legitimate their dispossession of indigenous populations.

*Fabrication* appears to find it difficult to subject the cognitive and moral universe of the settler-colonist to very much analytical scrutiny at all. More precisely, the assertions and the motives of any colonist who suggests that white violence was a problem are always mercilessly cross-examined and usually pilloried. By contrast, when settlers give justifications, whether theological or legal, for dispossession of Aborigines, we are simply invited to understand their *Weltanschauung*. A good example of this is the use made of Anthony Pagden's work on the distinction between Spanish and British discourses of colonisation, *Lords of all the World: Ideologies of Empire in Spain, Britain and France c. 1500–c.1800*. *Fabrication* makes much of Pagden's contrast between the Spanish concern with the conquest of peoples and the British focus on the governance of things, particularly land, constructing the British approach as not 'really' constituting colonial dispossession of the indigenous inhabitants of the Australian continent. Instead of the Spanish inclination to conquer indigenous peoples in order to extract their gold and silver, there was an alternative type of explanation for why British settler-colonists were entitled to the use of lands inhabited by indigenous peoples, one which American settler-colonists found extremely congenial, as did Australian settlers. In this construction, land which had not been cultivated through human labour did not 'really' belong to the people that used and lived on it, indeed it was the solemn natural duty of cultivators like the British and the French to put such 'virgin' land to use for the benefit of all humanity.

In *Fabrication* this account of some of the features of British colonial discourse is presented as an effective *defence* of 'the calibre of British civilisation' against critical analysis of its dynamics and impact. Since 'the British *regarded* their settlements as peaceful exercises, mutually beneficial to both colonist and native,' and since 'the early British *objectives* towards the indigenous people were primarily to trade useful products and to demonstrate by example the benefits of the civil and polite customs of Europe,' (emphasis added) for Windschuttle this becomes how things actually were and it immunises British settlement of Australia against criticisms of the legitimacy of colonial dispossession. Apart from a range of comments one could make on the logic of this position, it is also a mischievous misreading of Pagden.

His book, *Lords of All the World*, emphasises the *shared* historical roots of both Spanish colonial ideas and practices on the one hand, and British and French on the other, in Ancient Roman imperialism, so that they both remained different translations of an essentially similar 'will to empire'. If the British and French ended up emphasising commerce and trade rather than conquest and exploitation, this was not because of the calibre of their civilisation, as Walter Raleigh's conquistadorial ambitions show, but more because the Spanish had got to most of the gold and silver first:

> It was only when it became obvious that there was no new Mexico or Peru to be conquered, that both Cartier's 'Suguenay'; and Raleigh's 'Large, Rich and Beautiful Empire of Guiana' were fictions, that the British and the French turned, half-reluctantly, to regard their colonies as sources not of mineral or human, but of agricultural and commercial wealth.

The British emphasised domination over things (land) not as an *alternative* to dominion over people, but as a *means* to such dominion. Property and the argument concerning the cultivation and improvement of land was, to the mind of the English administrator, both at home and in the colonies, precisely *how* one governed a people. In the colonial situation, how one effectively conquered them without having to call it that, thus gaining a particular rhetorical advantage of being able to claim that it was only the barbaric Spaniards that did such a cruel thing. Pagden cites Arthur Young reminding his readers in 1772 that the distinction between occupation and possession of land was not one which held any meaning for that land's indigenous people themselves, and 'since ... they were unlikely to accept the colonists' claims without protest, any attempt to displace them would become *de facto* a conquest'.

What *Fabrication* presents as a detached description of the inner nature of British colonisation and its actual consistency with humanitarian values, is in Pagden's book an analysis of the rhetorical strategies pursued by the British (and the French) to legitimise colonisation so as to *render* it consistent with those humanitarian values. The various rhetorical strategies concerning the legitimacy of colonial settlement were also, we have to remember, pursued primarily in relation to the competition between the different European powers over their property rights vis-à-vis each other, not in relation to the persuasion of any indigenous populations, whose ultimate fate was largely to endure, with greater or lesser degrees of resistance, being elbowed out of the way by the Europeans.

Like other contributions to these sorts of debates, much of *Fabrication*'s argumentation also revolves around the appropriateness of applying the concept 'genocide' to the Australian settler-colonial context, and works with a simple dichotomous opposition between genocide and extermination on the one hand, and civilisation and modernisation on the other. However, the problem with talking about genocide is that there are a number of unresolved, and possibly irresolvable, disagreements about what it means and refers to. The concept is possibly most 'essentially contested' when it comes to the treatment of indigenous populations by European colonists and settlers, with the divergence of views organised around a distinction between physical and cultural destruction.

There are certainly strong and persuasive arguments in favour of saying that if it is not a case of deliberate *physical* extermination, like the Armenian genocide, the Holocaust, Cambodia, Rwanda and so on, then we should not be using the word genocide. Michael Ignatieff proposes, for example, that rather than operating as a 'validation of every kind of victimhood', the concept of genocide should be reserved for 'genuine' horrors and barbarisms. The United Nations Genocide Convention was written at a time when just about every member state of the United Nations would have presumed that assimilation of indigenous populations was generally unproblematic and that it was

desirable that 'primitive' cultures be modernised, making it very difficult to argue that the UN convention was intended to include the concept of non-physical, 'cultural' genocide. The remaining problems with
'forced assimilation' were meant to be dealt with in another arena, that
of the protection of minority populations. Any legal action based on
the UN convention also generally fails on the convention's requirement
of a demonstrable *intention* to destroy a cultural group, making it virtually impossible to pin down any state or administration that is not
silly enough actually to declare this intention. This is why the person
who first drew our attention to the fact that Aboriginal people often
regard the destruction of their social and familial life as 'genocidal', Hal
Wootten, in the report of the Royal Commission into Aboriginal
Deaths in Custody, also regards the 'finding' of genocide in the *Bringing
them home* report a 'quite unnecessary legal ruling' which has generated
'pointless controversy'.

However, this does not exhaust the discussion. It is also worth
recalling that the word was coined by the Polish jurist Raphaël Lemkin
*before* Auschwitz, and a core concern for Lemkin was not simply
'obvious' examples of killing but the whole colonising regime of the
Axis powers in the occupied countries, a very particular kind of legal
order based on a variety of 'techniques of occupation'. For Lemkin,
such techniques of occupation constituted 'a gigantic scheme to
change, in favour of Germany, the balance of biological forces between
it and the captive nations for many years to come', aiming 'to destroy or
cripple the subjugated peoples in their development' so that Germany
would be placed in a position of 'numerical, physical and economic
superiority' regardless of the military outcome of armed conflict.

'Genocide' was thus 'effected through a synchronised attack on different aspects of life of the captive peoples', in the realms of politics,
society, culture, economics, biology, physical existence (starvation and
killing), religion and morality. The concept was intended to capture:

> a coordinated plan of different actions aiming at the destruction of
> essential foundations of the life of national groups, with the aim of
> annihilating the groups themselves. The objectives of such a plan
> would be disintegration of the political and social institutions, of

culture, language, national feelings, religion, and the economic existence of national groups, and the destruction of the personal security,
liberty, health, dignity, and even the lives of the individuals belonging
to such groups. Genocide is directed against the national group as an
entity, and the actions involved are directed against individuals, not in
their individual capacity, but as members of the national group.

Outright killing was one, but not the only, part, of a multi-faceted
political rationality and a multi-dimensional set of legal and administrative forms and practices, and Lemkin was keen to point out the het-
erogeneity of ways in which the destruction of human groups could
take place.

Although one can argue about what constitutes a 'national group', it
remains unsurprising that those peoples subjected to colonialism in all
its forms have come to recognise their own experience in these words,
and that they experience the well-intentioned modernisation and civilisation of their ways of life as something other than 'bringing the gifts
of civilisation' to them, indeed as an often violent and destructive
process. Even if we agree that for the most effective use of the concept
of genocide, we should exclude its application to this sort of question,
this does not dispose of the issue: it simply generates a need to find
some other word and idea.

Rather than assuming that the only kind of violence and destruction which challenges the character of the nation and the calibre of our
civilisation is that of massacres and physical genocides, it is important
to give some consideration to the various other ways in which it is possible to 'destroy' a human group. For example, we could reflect upon
the remark in *Democracy in America,* of Alexis de Tocqueville, that
great observer and admirer of American civilisation. Of the contrast
between the approaches of the Spanish and the Americans to the peoples they colonised, he observed:

> The Spanish, with the help of unexampled monstrous deeds, covering
> themselves with an indelible shame, could not succeed in extermi-
> nating the Indian race, nor even prevent it from sharing their rights;
> the Americans of the United States have attained this double result

with marvellous facility – tranquilly, legally, philanthropically, without spilling blood, without violating a single one of the great principles of morality in the eyes of the world. One cannot destroy men while being more respectful of the laws of humanity.

It is not just a matter, then, of deciding whether it is true or false that relations between Europeans and Aborigines could be described as genocidal, but also one of choosing between different perspectives on colonisation and state formation. Although there is some support for the position represented by *Fabrication*, that genocide should be narrowly conceived, this does not in any way diminish the need to recognise what remains problematic, violent and destructive about otherwise civilised settler-colonisation in the name of the rule of law. Certainly these are not issues to be decided merely by contemptuous fiat.

### Civilisation: British and Christian

Not all the words which fascinate Windschuttle mark out things to be avoided. On the contrary, some – particularly Christianity, civilisation and the rule of law – do sterling service and are lavishly commended. If settlers were Christian, how could they mean to do harm? Similarly with civilisation. If the government did not intend extermination, perhaps even felt a mission to civilise, how could anyone – least of all the putative civilisees – complain? If it was charged to establish the rule of law, how could one talk of lawlessness on the frontier?

Christianity has two roles in Windschuttle's dramaturgy. On the one hand, its official representatives are accused of all sorts of self-aggrandising lies about massacres, and essentially blamed for all the ills of Aborigines that flowed from regimes of 'protection' that bred separatism and were the real source, apart from their self-inflicted wounds, of the misery of the Aboriginal peoples of this country. On the other hand, the fact that settlers were Christians is supposed to render spurious the allegations that they were involved in anything terrible.

There is no doubt that many of the leading colonists were indeed believing Christians, children of the Enlightenment, earnest 'civilisers' and avatars of the rule of law. But is this all that needs to be said? Bringing salvation or improvement or civilisation to those believed to lack it is commonly an intrusive business, most of all if you are really convinced it is as good for them as it has been for you, particularly if they are unconvinced. Sometimes it doesn't even depend on your motives: the very attempt has consequences, many of them irreversible, some tragic, some salutary, some both tragic and salutary at once and for the same reasons.

One of *Fabrication*'s sources for the settlers' beliefs is John Gascoigne's *The Enlightenment and the Origins of European Australia*, but the representation of that book is highly selective. Not only were Christianity and a civilising mission not inconsistent with dispossession and harm, Gascoigne notes, they could often allow the harm done to be ignored, or even done with an honest and clear conscience. These are points that Gascoigne makes several times, all the while recognising the complexity of motivation and effect, not trying to reduce it to *Fabrication*'s binary moral repertoire. He observes the tendency among nineteenth-century social theorists to relegate the Australian Aborigines to 'an increasingly lowly position', a mode of theorising 'invoked to justify dispossession and white supremacy'. Unlike Windschuttle, Gascoigne is prepared to use the word domination, and is able to note that Australia was '*regarded* as a piece of waste land writ large requiring to be brought into productive use' without suggesting that this is how we today should also regard it.

> The traditional inhabitants of these 'waste lands' were seen as rather like the squatters on the commons who were obliged to make way for improvements which were for the greatest good of the greatest number. Some hoped that, like the British squatters, they, too, would benefit from the increased and more regular employment that agricultural improvement brought but, ultimately, tradition had few rights in the headlong rush to transform the land as it gathered momentum, so the belief in improvement began to permeate the society more generally.

This analysis does not condemn Christianity or civilisation as base, still less demonic, but it does acknowledge that they come at a price which its exactors are not generally well situated or disposed to recognise.

Is this to demonise our ancestors, to put them on trial and find them guilty? Not at all. We're not a court, still less a kangaroo court. Some people do bad thinking it good. Others do good, but with terrible consequences. Many sad results were not intended, and few people who did evil thought that was what they did. People rarely do, but what does that tell us? Lots of otherwise decent people do otherwise indecent things, because they believe what everyone believes or do what everyone else does. And what everyone believes is rarely anyone's specific invention. To understand systematic historic injustices, individual motives are rarely decisive. They don't explain patterned and structured behaviours, and that is what later generations typically need to understand. In any event, what individuals thought they were doing is not decisive on how we now should regard what they did.

We are members of a nation, seeking to come to terms with what our inherited culture made available and our forebears did. Of course, interpretation of the past must exhibit tact and humility, depends on thoughtful, sensitive appraisal of the facts, and should avoid simple all-purpose characterisations of complex matters. And morality is not the only relevant register. Tragedy was almost certainly written into our national history as soon as whites decided to come here, and whatever we did. Nevertheless we did come here and we did some things and not others. We must come to terms with what we did.

### Rule of Law

One thing we did, according to Windschuttle, is bring the rule of law. There is deep truth in that. As we saw in the previous essay, there is no way of understanding the convict story in Australia, for example, without appreciating that convicts were not merely prisoners but prisoners with legal rights, who knew that, demanded respect for their rights, and did so from officials who were not at liberty to ignore them. What happened to convicts, however, was only part of the story, and could not, in the nature of the colonial encounter, represent the whole.

It is a complicated matter to assess the extent to which the rule of law exists in any society at any time, though these complications do not appear to delay Windschuttle at all. It is enough for him to cite the colonial governors' commitment to the rule of law to move to the conclusion that Aborigines were regularly safeguarded by it. But how could that be?

The rule of law requires, at a low minimum: systematic restraint and channelling by law of the activities of officials; equally systematic restraint and channelling of the power of powerful citizens; law that is knowable and generally known; and the capacity of citizens, in their interactions with each other and with officials, routinely to appreciate the authority of the law and its relevance to their encounters, and to be prepared to invoke it. The rule of law must not only be proclaimed, or even endorsed by officials, for whether it exists and matters is a social matter. It must *count* in the social world. But in settlers' relations with Aborigines this could not, for all the reasons (and others) mentioned in the last essay, routinely be the case. There were frequently times when the formal law contradicted the presuppositions of the rule of law itself, but, far more significant, whatever the formal law was like, settlers would often find themselves in circumstances where they faced opportunities and temptations to flout it, and Aborigines did not and for a long time could not know it, or understand it. The pretension in such circumstances of Aborigines *using* the law on more than rare occasions is absurd.

As argued in the previous essay, 'the rule of law, then, presupposes a lot to be effective and a lot to be good. In early contact with Aboriginal society its presuppositions did not exist even where the will to adhere to it did. And that often did not exist either.' Most unsettling for ardent adherents to the rule of law, among them ourselves, is that it is hard to see how a will more concerned to bring the rule of law could have done much to alter the tragedy that became the Aboriginal story in our country. Indeed, in the context of early colonialism, and even more in the light of the relative impotence of the imposed law for much of the century, talk of the rule of law could serve to justify, mythologise and may well have blinded the perpetrators to the horror of relationships of domination and exploitation out of which, systematically and unavoidably, there could be only one set of winners. Again, this is a systemic problem, not necessarily a problem of anyone's ill will. But Aborigines might be forgiven for not noticing the distinction.

## Conclusion

In *Fabrication* we read that there is a difference between scholars who do their research in order to 'investigate' a topic and those who seek to 'vindicate' a pre-existing standpoint.

> The former usually begin with an idea of what they hope to find but are always prepared to change their expectations and conclusions in the light of what the evidence itself reveals. The latter, as the sorry example of Aboriginal history in this country reveals, only select evidence that supports their cause and either omit, suppress or falsify the rest.

This distinction is an important one, and commonly ignored in debates about the character of nations. Think of the *Historikerstreit* in Germany, the more recent Polish debate over the wartime massacre of Jews by their neighbours in the village of Jedwabne, not to mention the entrenched positions of so many participants in our own debates. So many words, so much invective, so little change to original positions. Hard though it might be to keep faith with it when the stakes seem high, what *Fabrication* recommends should be a regulative ideal, not only for Rankean historians but for all who are concerned about their nation's past.

But if Windschuttle is claiming to be an 'investigator' and not a 'vindicator', the claim collapses under any serious scrutiny. A rough guide to whether one is reading investigative or vindicatory history is the possibility of *surprise*. Vindicators leave few loose ends. Everything fits, seamlessly. Investigators, by contrast, can be puzzled and taken by surprise, led to new and different conclusions. But nothing appears to puzzle or surprise Windschuttle. Who, reading his *Quadrant* articles, written before he had completed his Tasmanian research, would be startled by how that research was going to turn out in his hands? Who expects to be taken off guard by the conclusions of Volumes 2 and 3? Indeed, who can even *conceive* Windschuttle saying after a few more years in the archives, 'Whoops! Got it all wrong. Hats off to Henry.' Unless, of course, he has yet another across-the-board ideological conversion, in which case all bets are off.

We need go no further than Paul Hasluck, again, to identify precisely one of the core psychological problems for settler-colonists and for the kind of historiography purveyed by *Fabrication*. As well as observing even-handedly that there were 'a number of cases of both white men and black men suffering death or injury at each other's hands in circumstances of gross savagery', Hasluck felt that it was important to look at the 'grim history' of frontier violence in the interest of seeing 'what it reveals of the attitude of the whites', not what it reveals about the dysfunctionality of Aboriginal society. Moreover, he wrote,

> the occurrence of a phase of violence in the early stages of contact is important because inevitably it left antagonism between the races, while some degree of shame or the need to justify what happened brought a tendency to defame the primitive defender of his soil as treacherous, black at heart, murderous and open to no instruction except by force.

In the face of this sort of historical and moral sensitivity, the impression Windschuttle's book will make most firmly on the minds of its readers may be its industrial-strength obtuseness, but we would suggest that it deserves a more careful analysis. *Fabrication* is worth reading, if only to remind us that the tendency identified by Hasluck more than half a century ago remains an integral part of the culture and civilisation characterising Australian society, and that it continues to play a real and effective role in Australian political and cultural life. Title's terrific, too.

*2003*

# Neighbours: Poles, Jews and the Aboriginal Question

In May 2000, a slim volume, *Neighbors: The History of the Extermination of a Jewish Village*, was published in Poland. It caused a seismic shock in public consciousness and spawned a vast literature of debate, polemic and public soul-searching there and, to a lesser extent, elsewhere in Europe and the United States when translations appeared a year later. The book's author, Jan Gross, is a Polish historian now at New York University. His book describes the murder, on 10 July 1941, of virtually all the Jewish residents of the small Polish village of Jedwabne by their Polish neighbours. Some were stabbed to death, others killed with clubs, stones, bricks, hooks. Two women deliberately drowned their children and themselves in a pond to avoid their persecutors. The rest were herded into a barn and burnt to death. Gross estimates that 1600 people, roughly half the total population of the village, were killed. The estimate is controversial, but that hundreds were killed, and that their neighbours killed them, is not. (The fact of the killings, though not their number, has now been authoritatively confirmed by the government-appointed Institute of National Remembrance, which spent almost two years investigating the crime.)

Jedwabne had been occupied by the Nazis throughout the preceding month, after they had expelled the Soviet troops who had occupied the region (under the Nazi–Soviet Pact) for the previous twenty months. Gross readily allows that the murders would not have occurred without the pathological disturbance caused by these two brutal and brutalising occupations and, more specifically, without the consent of the Nazi occupiers. But he insists that it was the Polish population of Jedwabne, 'ordinary men', not the Nazis, who were 'willing executioners' in Jedwabne.

The book must shock anyone who reads it. The shock stems from various sources: the horrific, bestial nature of the events described; the wrenching immediacy of the accounts Gross quotes from survivors, victims, eyewitnesses, perpetrators; the unrelenting probing character of Gross's prose, charges, questions and inferences. But it has shocked Poles in special ways. I will return to those ways.

In April 1997, the Australian Human Rights and Equal Opportunities Commission (HREOC) published *Bringing them home*, a report on the practice of removal of Aboriginal children from their parents, which had gone on for much of the last century, until it was discontinued in the 1960s. The numbers taken are controversial. The report estimates that, from 1910 to 1970, between one in three and one in ten Aboriginal children were removed, but its higher estimates are widely doubted. Robert Manne has suggested that 25,000 children were removed. The public response to the report, and controversies and polemics spawned by it, has been striking. The leader of the opposition, Kim Beazley, wept in parliament as he spoke about the report. It dominated public attention like few other issues. I doubt that anyone expected a several hundred page government-sponsored report to have such a fall-out. Certainly, the government printer did not. Like *Neighbors*, it sold out in no time and had to be reprinted. Partly, the intensity of the reaction is due to the character of the recorded testimony, which contains many heart-rending accounts, but partly, too, Australians were affected by these stories in ways that foreigners might not have been. For it matters that it was an Australian story.

*Neighbors* is a small book that profoundly shook and reshaped the moral tone and content of Polish public debate. *Bringing them home* is a large one that had a similar effect here. One-off publications rarely have such power. That in itself might be grounds for comparison between them, but are there others?

Many in Australia would say no. *Neighbors* is a book about the participation of the Poles of Jedwabne in the extermination of the Jews of

Jedwabne. That, in turn, was an early item in the Holocaust, a uniquely murderous activity with no redeeming features. The child removals that were the subject of *Bringing them home* involved no killing, were on some interpretations well-intentioned, and, some would claim, led at least at times and in parts to good consequences (education, assimilation etc.). Indeed, many participants in Australian debates are infuriated by any comparison at all between any aspect of our history, including the murder of Aborigines and the dispossession and decimation of Aboriginal societies, and anything that happened to European Jews, most of all the Holocaust. To suggest that there might be any grounds for comparison between the two histories, even while conceding that factual and moral differences between them are profound, is to invite denunciation. And in the Australian discussion, as in the Polish, there has been a lot of that.

Comparisons can, of course, be abused, for example to raise or lower the rhetorical temperature surrounding particular local events, to give factitious, fictitious drama to them by associating them with something surrounded by an aura of transcendent evil or good. And it is, of course, as important in comparison to recognise differences as much as similarities, not to confuse analogies with identity, and to choose one's comparisons thoughtfully. But to say that is not to say that phenomena which differ in important ways are 'incomparable'. The contrary is true. We must be alert and faithful to the similarities and differences, often complex and various, that we find, but we will only find them if we compare. And only by comparison as well will we find out some things about what is most familiar to us. As a Polish anthropologist has observed, 'from close up, all the more from the centre of things, certain things are simply invisible.' If for no other reason than that they might find things that seemed unique are quite common and at the same time discover real local peculiarities, people mired in local controversies should seek, rather than avoid, comparisons. And in the field of what used to be called man's inhumanity to man we are, unfortunately, blessed with material for comparison.

Moreover, whatever our view about the appropriateness of comparisons between the *subjects* of the two books, my interest in this essay is different. It is not in the subject matter of the two works at all, but in

Polish and Australian *responses* to accounts of them. In neither case was it obvious, before the books were published, that responses of such character and intensity would follow, and, in both cases, the responses had a great deal in common. Similarities in arguments used, in anxieties expressed, in forms of assertion and denial are striking and pervasive. Since these responses in Australia and Poland were unconnected, this is interesting, whether or not there are similarities between the events of which they speak. Indeed all the more so if critics of comparisons are right. For the more the subjects differ, the more intriguing become the similarities in responses to them.

Let me, to adopt a Hegelian idiom, sketch just eight *moments* of response, which are pretty well interchangeable between Australia and Poland. Each of these could be pursued in greater detail, and there are others.

## 1. Revelation
The first stage is the exposé. In both Poland and Australia, a work appears that alleges terrible things were done by members of the dominant population to defenceless members of a minority group, long considered 'other'.

## 2. Shock
In both cases the first response of many readers is one of shock, often accompanied by questions such as 'how could *we* could have done such things?' This question immediately raises further questions that don't go away, about who 'we' are and what connection, if any, there is between those, often dead, who did the deeds and those, very much alive, who are asking the questions. Another question surfaces soon enough. 'Why weren't we told?' to use the title of a recent book by Henry Reynolds. As it happens, this second question turns out to be not quite apt, either in Poland or Australia, since the subjects of discussion were not secret and had been written about before, by participants, witnesses and historians. Better questions are: why weren't we listening before; and why do we listen so intently now? I don't know the answers to either of these questions, but I believe they are more likely to be found in the domain of social psychology or psycho-sociology

than in any feature of the logic or evidence or indeed argument brought to bear in the debates.

## 3. Disputation

Once the allegations are made and, typically, before anyone has really had a chance to assess the evidence, heated dispute begins over whether what is alleged ever occurred. At the early stage, this is necessarily driven more by assumptions than facts, since it takes time to get up to speed on the facts, and many of those involved in the polemics never try. Nor, in either case, is it easy. It is easier to lean on a congenial source presumed, believed, or at least hoped to have done so. So, one frequently heard from one side, it must have happened, and, from the other, that it couldn't have. Absence of close acquaintance with the facts, though, does not make discussions any less heated or the protagonists less certain of their positions. Did the events even occur? Did the witnesses at Jedwabne actually see what they alleged? Were they telling the truth? Were the allegedly 'stolen children' who testified victims of 'false memory syndrome'? While it is possible to know something and still ask these questions, it is also possible to know nothing and ask them with equal determination.

One peculiarity of such disputes is that the *book* is commonly attacked as though particular faults allegedly found in it, say as to numbers involved, should automatically discount other (typically larger) truths to which it might have alerted us. Of course, any allegations need to be checked, errors pointed out, and so on. That is standard scholarly procedure. But in the public polemics generated by these two works, scholarship is rarely disinterested or the major motivation of most participants. Rather, the aim is to remove a tormenting sting.

There is a kind of backhanded acknowledgment that something other than scholarship is involved, in the common rhetorical form that pseudo-scholarly attacks of this variety employ. The alleged faults having been pointed out, it is often admitted that something unfortunate actually happened, but that admission gets lost in the shadow of the more prominent, often petty, textual fault-finding. Attention is focused on undermining details in the text, as though it was enough to respond to a terrible historical charge with a book review, rather than reflection on the horrors that inspired it, which is convenient for those who find those horrors inconvenient.

When, nevertheless, it becomes clear that *something* terrible did happen, the question gets broken into smaller ones: did it happen to as many people as alleged? Was someone else to blame (in Poland, Nazis not Poles; in Australia, missionaries not the government)? If the facts alleged prove hard to deny, then there is dispute over whether there were reasons that might explain, if not justify, them. In Poland, for example, many writers rushed to assume, for they had no evidence, that the murders were provoked by alleged Jewish collaboration with the Soviets, or were ordered by Nazis, rather than being unprovoked or unrequired, willing participation in murder. In Australia, removals have often been described as 'rescue' of neglected or abused children rather than 'theft' from parents who we have no reason to believe loved them any less than we do our own.

There is one necessary limit to this repackaging in the Polish case, however. Once the murders are admitted to have occurred, it is not open to Poles to suggest they were done for the Jews' benefit. It has been different here.

## 4. Generalisation and Particularisation
Part of the scandal that the original work causes derives from its suggestion that the events it describes fit within a more general and sinister pattern. Candidates in Poland have included anti-semitism widespread in Polish and particularly peasant culture, and even worse – for it flies in the face of the well-based Polish conviction that they were among the greatest victims of the Holocaust, not among its perpetrators – that Poles were on both of these terrible sides, unwilling to be victims, to be sure, but perhaps not all always averse to be perpetrators. In Australia, the suggestion that child removal was part and parcel (and not the worst part and parcel) of sustained policies of destruction of the indigenous population of Australia – not to mention the 'g' word – is also liable to cause outrage.

One standard reaction of those hostile to these linkages is to offer a counter-generalisation to explain or justify the events in question. Thus in Poland there can be found reference, familiar among East European anti-semites and occasional winners of the Miles Franklin Award, to Zydokomuna ('Jewish-communism') as explaining harsh reactions to Jews in Poland. In Australia, harsh encounters are at times drained of moral charge in a tone Charles Rowley once described as 'pseudo-philosophic melancholy'. They are to be understood as admittedly painful, but inexorable, and ultimately salutary demands of the 'civilising process'. Thus, what might otherwise appear to be plain, quite low falutin' acts of inhumanity come to be elevated and sanitised by the irresistible laws of modernity.

Another alternative, for those who do, or are forced to, recognise the events as unpardonable, is to particularise: Jedwabne had nothing to do with Poles in general but was the work, under the pressure of hostile forces, of the people of a small benighted village, denuded of elites, at a particular stressful moment, and not even all of them, perhaps only low life or those who sought to revenge themselves on 'Jewish collaborators' with the Soviets. Child removal was a particular policy of certain administrations at certain times thought then to be – perhaps wrongly, but who are we to judge? – for the benefit of its objects (for, it should be stressed, in none of this were they treated as active subjects). There is some truth in both these modes of evasion, but it is not the whole truth.

### 5. Association and Dissociation

Here everyone becomes a moral philosopher of a rather casuistic turn. If I didn't do it, what's it got to do with me? Should I feel guilt? If not that, shame? If neither, what about responsibility? If so, for what others did in the past or just for what I might do in the future? If none of the above, will 'nothing at all' do? One side sees the significance of the events under discussion as national, collective and continuing, while the other insists it is local, particular and past. Those who take the former view, in both countries, are likely to favour public apology, and perhaps compensation, of some sort. Those of the second view generally believe neither apology nor compensation is appropriate.

An interesting aspect of this stage of the argument is that the intensity of the protagonists' passion does not depend on which side of the argument they take. An arch-individualist on this matter, who insists that whatever anyone else in the world besides himself does is not his concern, is likely to participate as angrily in all the other stages of the argument as those who actually say that it does have something to do with them. Yet the intensity of such serial denials of connection tends to contradict the argument. If you were really persuaded by that argument, you might just as well go fishing and wait for the fuss to die down. The fact is that Australians of every stripe, and Poles of every type, actually do worry about what their compatriots might have done. I do not believe that this is a mistake.

## 6. Denunciation

Here we get to motives. Why are these allegations being made? Polish denouncers find Jewish financial interests and hope for reparations, plus the well-known Polophobia of Jews (particularly, it is often reiterated, New York Jews), never far from the surface. Conversely, some Jews just know that, since all Poles are anti-semites, what Gross relates had to happen, indeed was typical behaviour (there is no evidence for this claim). In Australia, middle-class lefties, do-gooders, chattering classes, together with black 'leaders' (usually suggested to lack black followers) also after money, are accused of seeking to undermine a proper sense of our past, and pride in it. People who seem to find it insuperably difficult to accommodate any allegation of fact without a thousand eyewitnesses in unanimous agreement find it very easy at this stage of the argument to attribute motives to people they have never met. I know. I've done it myself.

## 7. Apprehension

A common worry among provincial countries is: what will the world think? Here it is known as the 'cultural cringe' and it is found in both countries, usually combined with a tendency to blame the messenger, rather than those mentioned in the message. This tendency has actually figured more prominently in Polish discussions than here, perhaps because of sensitivity to American perceptions and a keenness to join the European Union; perhaps because there is no extra-territorial Aboriginal lobby.

## 8. Transformation

The strange and unpredictable aspect of both debates is that certain moral questions about a nation's past move from a periphery scarcely observed, if at all, to the centre of public polemic for an extended period of time, and perhaps for all time.

How to explain these parallel responses to two very different books and histories? They might seem natural enough to those who think there really is similarity between their subjects, but, quite apart from the differences commonly insisted on in Australia, there are others, which are not commonly mentioned, and which make the parallels all the more intriguing.

Most who emphasise differences do so in the spirit I have mentioned, to underline that contemporary Australians have no real reason to feel what might be called pained association with the events of *Bringing them home*, even if Poles today, like Germans ever since the war, might have good reasons to feel such pain in relation to aspects of their own past. Let me, then, mention some differences that might be said to point in the other direction. The Jedwabne massacre was undertaken not by 'the Polish people' as a collectivity, nor even by the Polish government on behalf of its people. It was carried out, apparently spontaneously, by the population, perhaps only part of the population, of a small provincial village (in fact, a few towns in that region: Wąsosz, Radziłowe), in a doubly (serially) occupied part of Poland, under the eye and probably at the behest of the occupying Nazis (whether or not they participated, they did not disapprove), where the Polish government had no presence at all, indeed was in exile, and where the occupation was harsher than anywhere else in Europe. One can find other particularising features of the massacre, too, if one wants to, and many Polish critics of Gross have been keen to. And it is true that though anti-semitism certainly had a long history in Poland, it was by no means the whole story of Polish–Jewish relations and, more important, it had never amounted to anything like this. This was no ordinary pogrom, and the Holocaust was in no way a Polish project. All of this is true, and yet, for reasons to which I will return, it does not render the past 'another country'. I mention it, however, to remind us that there is a lot more to be said for it than might occur to some Australians, confident that they are less entwined with tragedies in their past than Poles or other benighted middle Europeans.

For in Australia, by contrast, child removal was home-grown government policy over a long period, enshrined in law, no response to any external pressures, still less to horrific occupation by totalitarian powers. It was not a pathological *event*, but a regular official practice, decided upon and undertaken by elected governments, at their leisure, and routinely administered. And it was far from the worst of the indecencies inflicted upon indigenous Australians. Easier comparisons with Jedwabne could be found in the killings of the nineteenth century. Contemporary Poles might, then, arguably have more reason than contemporary Australians to say 'this was terrible but it was no doing of ours.'

And the Polish example is instructive in another respect. Today there are hardly any Jews in Poland, whereas there are many Aborigines in Australia. So there can be no Polish equivalent of John Howard's insistence that all that really matters is 'practical reconciliation', not fussing about the past. In the case of most of Poland's once large Jewish community, let alone those murdered in Jedwabne, there is no 'practical reconciliation' left to be done. Does this mean there is nothing more to say or do?

Apparently that is not what it means, if one reads the Australian press since 1997, or the Polish since the end of 2000. Like a sore tooth, these issues just nag away. This is obviously so among those who do feel the sort of pained connection I have mentioned, but, to repeat, it is equally so, and more revealing, among those who deny it. It is one thing, after all, for those who feel a newly awakened connection with, and shame for, aspects of their nation's past to say why, even at length. It is another for those who claim these aspects didn't occur, didn't amount to much, at least not anything bad, and, anyway, it's all in the past and has nothing to do with us, to go on at the same impassioned length.

In both cases, an observer is forced to conclude that at issue is not really, or at any rate not merely, the past *wie es eigentlich gewesen,* but the present. Or, more precisely, that the imagined past is being treated as a crucial part of the present, and it is *that* present-past that is the focus and explanation for the passions these past events still manage to inspire. This suggests that as important as the subjects of the debate, and the texts that are their vehicles, are the subtexts that fuel them. These subtexts, while on occasion amenable to correction on intellectual grounds, are typically fairly impervious to argument, drawing as they do on psycho-social sources. Only psychology or perhaps psychoanalysis can get us to the anxieties, angers, attachments and antagonisms that fuel these debates. But individual psychology will not do, for this is not an individual matter. Rather, it is inextricably interwoven with wider communal attachments and identifications; it is about groups and it occurs among groups, so it is intrinsically social.

The historian Dirk Moses has explored parallels between German post-Holocaust, and contemporary Australian, polemics. He interprets both as products of what might be called the psychology of nationhood. Participants are moved in different and commonly antagonistic ways to anxious reflection over the relationships between dark events and the mythologies of national origin and character ('cosmogenies') necessary for nation-building. Confronted with such events, some move to critique of aspects of their national past, and others respond with defence. National myths come to be disturbed by those with 'perpetrator trauma' and defended by others seeking to defend a past that one can be proud to own, or at least live with comfortably. The parallels he draws are instructive and his psychoanalytically derived explanations are suggestive. I am not adept at that level of explanation, and will leave it to him. Plainly, though, however these reactions are to be explained, in Australia, Poland, Germany and anywhere else where a tainted national past becomes the subject of current controversy, it seems clear that neither the particular histories in question nor the personal peculiarities of current controversialists (though there are some) can explain what is now going on. Something larger and deeper is at work, and whatever that is common to all three cases, and presumably others. Recognising this gives a disingenuous air to much that passes for debate in these matters. What is said to be at issue is often not what is really at stake.

Whatever the psychological mechanisms in play, however, there remain real questions, both of fact and of morals, which no amount of explanation should dissolve, and I will conclude with a couple of them. Not merely why, psychologically, does any of this past stuff matter to any of us who didn't participate in the ghastly events written about, but why should it do so? There are some general answers, and some that are peculiar to particular cases. Of the first sort is the hypothetical imperative that I and many others have insisted upon: if and to the extent that you feel proud of things done or achieved in your nation's history, it is a mere matter of logical symmetry, not to say moral coherence, that you should admit to shame for baser elements of that collective history. Since many people feel such pride, and typically those who deny the appropriateness of shame insist that it is appropriate to do so, this argument covers a lot of territory. Not all the territory – since a cosmopolitan can consistently, if not always plausibly, deny both national pride and shame – but a lot. In this country, the argument has been made prominently by Raimond Gaita and Robert Manne. Gross makes the same point eloquently, so I will quote him at some length:

> When reflecting about this epoch, we must not assign collective responsibility. We must be clearheaded enough to remember that for each killing only a specific murderer or group of murderers is responsible. But we nevertheless might be compelled to investigate what makes a nation (as in 'the Germans') capable of carrying out such deeds. Or can atrocious deeds simply be bracketed off and forgotten? Can we arbitrarily select from a national heritage what we like, and proclaim it as patrimony to the exclusion of everything else? Or just the opposite: if people are indeed bonded together by authentic spiritual affinity – I have in mind a kind of national pride rooted in common historical experiences of many generations – are they not somehow responsible also for horrible deeds perpetrated by members of such an 'imagined community'. Can a young German reflecting today on the meaning of his identity as a German simply ignore twelve years (1933–45) of his country's and his ancestors' history?

This is not, as our prime minister imagines, 'black armband' history, not a negation of the riches in the historical balance sheet, but merely due recognition of the moral complexity of a nation's past. Or, as Jerzy Jedlicki, a distinguished Polish historian, has put it: 'What then counts in the general, nationwide balance sheet? Heroism or baseness? Compassion or a lack of mercy? Both count: There is no way one can subtract one from the other or offset one with the other. There will always be two separate ledgers.'

All the more is this the case, since it is not just a question of pride and shame in *persons* – Chopin, on the one side, Dzerzinski, on the other – but in the culture that connects us with others and, indeed, contributes to what and who we are. Cultures provide connecting tissue, as it were, between individuals both in the present and the past, and the cells of these tissues are not empty of content. They carry prejudices, in both the classical and non-pejorative sense of unthought pre-judgments, and in the more conventional modern sense as well. They carry preoccupations, stereotypes, ranges of moral concern, identification and rejection; restraints, taboos, but also predispositions of thought and, sometimes, of action. And while the behaviour of people to others often goes way beyond what anyone had reason to predict, and beyond what anything in a culture can be said on its own to explain or justify, the particular targets of these behaviours are seldom cultur-ally random. Particularly when these are collective behaviours. That is why horrible events in the history of a culture often contrive to send a shock of recognition among its members, at the same time as they disgust them. Poles haunted by Jedwabne and more broadly anti-semitism, and Australians by child removal and, more broadly, dispos-session of Aborigines, are haunted by phenomena, patterns of behaviour and of thought, or at least targets of behaviour and thought, that are rarely *dictated* by aspects of that culture but might well have been *facilitated* by them. It is right for members of a culture, *bearers* of that culture, to be concerned about such things. Particularly when, as is common, that recognition is in some, often anguished part, self-recogntion as well. We are, none of us, self-constituting monads. We are, all of us, *creatures*, in part creations, of the cultures in which we are raised.

This is, of course, not a simple matter. Cultures are not homoge-neous; there are other things that influence us, we make choices. Nevertheless our cultures do, in significant ways, and to a significant extent, make us up and they do link us. They mould, they shape, and they connect. As part of our collective self-consciousness, they are parts of our individual self-consciousness as well. That is why insider-critics within a culture often have such a painful struggle with aspects of their cultural history that outsiders often don't feel or understand. To reject such aspects *simply*, is to reject part of themselves, and that is rarely easy. That is tacitly, though never explicitly, acknowledged even, or perhaps especially, by the most vehement deniers in both countries, since their counter-attacks make plain how important the sanctity of their cultural inheritances is to them.

There are two more matters to be concerned about, both of which, as it happens, weigh more heavily in Australia than in Poland. Moses points to the first of them when he remarks on a difference between the German and the Australian case. Unlike Germany and Poland, Australia is a settler society. As Moses remarks:

> Strange as it may seem, this fact makes the viability of Australian nationality more precarious than the German [or Polish] one, which long preceded the Holocaust. For in the Australian case, the very existence of the nation state and the nationalised subject is predicated on the dispossession, expulsion, and, where necessary, extermination of the indigenous peoples. This means that the customary conservative ploy of acknowledging the 'dark sides' of an otherwise salutary project is incoherent because the 'dark sides' were intrinsic to the process and cannot be split off ... The positive myth of origin is at once the negative one.

And finally, there are differences in public responses that should be noted. One has to do with the ways these matters have been discussed. Robert Manne has observed that it is difficult to speak of a public debate on the stolen children in Australia. What there has been, rather, is a great deal of public *noise*. Anger, distress, shame, denunciation, ridicule are available in abundance, but not sustained, serious argument. Anna Haebich publishes an exhaustive account of the phenomenon of child removal; hardly anyone writes a word about it. Manne publishes a powerful, forensic dissection of the claims of Australian deniers; he is greeted with sustained abuse, little argument and refusals to share a podium with him by some of his most vociferous critics. In Poland, by contrast, where tempers have run just as hot, and where vulgarity is also not absent, there have been sustained, lengthy, evidence-based articles by leading specialists and intellectuals, on every side of the issue over months in all the leading dailies, weeklies and monthlies. Anyone who wants to test their quality can just look at a sample on the websites that archive them.

And, to conclude, there is the response of public officials. In Australia, the climate of opinion in which the report was conceived and born was heavily influenced by public actors: the Minister for Aboriginal Affairs who commissioned it, former prime minister Paul Keating, who passionately advocated reconsideration of our past, the High Court, which contributed honourably to that reconsideration, and Prime Minister John Howard, who resisted it all. From the birth of the report onwards, indeed even during its conception, the reaction of the present government has been unremittingly hostile.

In Poland, discussion of 'the Jewish question' was repressed for forty years by the communist authorities, nor did public actors have anything to do with the birth of *Neighbors*. Today, however, the Institute of National Remembrance, appointed primarily to investigate communist atrocities, has had as its first major assignment an intensive investigation of what happened at Jedwabne. The results were released in July 2002. The investigation appears to have been exhaustive, relentless and completely independent of political pressures. Moreover, despite more than one moral misstep from church leaders and individual politicians, the head of government and particularly the head of state have behaved in an exemplary manner. At no time more so than on the sixtieth anniversary of the massacre, 10 July 2001, which I was privileged to be in Poland to watch.

Everyone knew that the Polish president planned to apologise, and there was controversy about that. Few, however, were prepared for the agility, but also grace, with which he vaulted over a problem which has been much debated in both countries, and which our own prime minister has seemed to find mountainous: how to apologise for terrible events which many in the population weren't sorry about. The president apologised 'as a person and a citizen and President of the Republic of Poland … I apologise in my own name on behalf of all those Poles whose conscience has been disturbed by these crimes. In the name of those who believe that they cannot be proud of the greatness of Polish history, without feeling at the same time pain and shame because of the harm Poles have inflicted on others.' This response was at the same time dignified, responsible and in no way presumptuous. Our own prime minister's responses have managed resolutely, one might even say heroically, to be none of the above.

*2002*

# The Rhetoric of Reaction

I want to discuss some rhetorical manoeuvres common in contemporary Australian debates. My focus is on debates about the history of relations between whites and Aborigines, partly because I have followed those debates fairly closely, partly because the subject is important in its own right – arguably the most important moral debate our citizens have faced, or not faced – but equally because it is a particularly fertile source of what I will call the rhetoric of reaction, which is my theme. Looking at these particular debates, I believe, can be instructive about broader issues to do with how we conduct ourselves in public polemics, and why.

My title copies that of a fine book by Albert Hirschman, *The Rhetoric of Reaction: Perversity, Futility, Jeopardy*. However he and I have different rhetorics and different reactionaries in mind, so before I get to my subject, I need to clarify the two substantive words in the title, rhetoric and reaction. I will then get on to examine the thing, reactionary rhetoric, itself.

Rhetoric was understood by Aristotle to include those many, often refined, techniques of argumentation unavoidable in domains of life, such as politics and law, where persuasion is necessary but conclusive demonstration is unavailable. So, it is unavoidable, significant, and there are good and bad forms of it. As Samuel Goldwyn might observe, however, we've passed a lot of water since then. Today 'rhetoric' is almost always spoken of pejoratively, and more often than not, dismissively: words without weight ('empty rhetoric'), that add nothing but adornment ('mere rhetoric'). If in Australia it is already suspicious to be eloquent, it is unpardonable to be rhetorical.

What I have in mind is somewhere between the refined and the corrupt. The sorts of rhetoric I discuss here are significant, but none of them is to be recommended. Certainly, they are all about persuasion. I'm not a fan of them, but they're not 'mere' hot air, or sweet words, or just style as opposed to substance. Indeed they're not *mere* anything, and they are far from empty. They have their own role and significance in public debate.

On the other hand, my usage follows the modern debased understanding in disapproving of them. For their contributions to 'the conversation of citizens', while real are of a specific, negative, sort. In particular they include ways of framing issues, resolving them and avoiding them that *block* conversations rather then further them. The sort of conversational contribution, perhaps, that the American novelist Ring Lardner had in mind in a character's response to a question from his grandchild: 'Shut up, he explained.'

And I am concerned not just with any rhetoric but quite specifically with that which I take to be the specific progeny of reaction. Other motives, other rhetorics. And though the word 'reaction' in the bad sense is itself a highly rhetorical term in public debate, I mean in the first instance something quite specific: a response, a *re-action* to claims or views which assault, or give affront to something one holds dear. Or are understood to do so.

In this sense reaction can go in any political direction. White Australians can respond in reactionary ways to attacks, or what they take to be attacks, upon what they value in their society; so too Aborigines to denigration, or what they take to be denigration, of what they value in theirs. In fact, I don't think there is anything in principle wrong with the *motivation* that fuels reaction in this sense. Though I will be focusing on its dangers, it is not necessarily ignoble. Indeed its opposite might be. Recall the French notice, sometimes said to have been seen in a Paris zoo: 'Beware! This animal is vicious! When attacked, it defends itself.' Often it happens in public debate that one feels something to which one is attached, emotionally, personally, morally, intellectually, is being attacked, denigrated, sold short, treated with frivolous lack of seriousness, respect or concern. And often that is precisely what is happening. Feeling that, one can feel *stung*, personally stung, and wish to sting back. I've known such feelings. When I first thought of this paper, I conceived of it as a polemic, attacking, as one commonly attacks, the squalid activities of opponents. I have come to realise that part of the description that follows is self-description, and part of my analysis is self-analysis.

As it happens, I was born, indeed in my particular case conceived, an anti-communist. The reasons were not only genealogical. Communism assaulted, often with ferocious intensity, almost all the values that seemed to me to matter, among them freedom, rights, civil society and the rule of law, not even to mention telephones that work. And communists did so deliberately, and typically without remorse. It is true, but scarcely adequate to say, that I thought that was a mistake. I hated it. Mine was a 'reactionary' position, in this sense, if ever there was one, defined as it was in the first instance in terms of what it rejected. And I also deplored non-communist anti-anti-communists, plentiful in Australia, who, more rightly than they knew, considered me and mine reactionaries, at least in relation to them and in the sense I have in mind. One reason for my reaction, and for its heat, was what I took to be the contempt, the light-minded disdain, so often displayed for what seemed to me precious. That is one aspect of my life that I don't regret at all. In that case it served me well to be a reactionary.

Over the last couple of years I have again recalled some of those reactionary emotions, when I felt disturbed, sometimes to the point of nausea, by what I took to be the visceral glee of some critics of the war in Iraq. For some, I suspected, the war provided a welcome release for an anti-Americanism that had been pent up with nowhere obvious to go since 1989. 'At last!' I could imagine them saying.

There are, of course, many good reasons to criticise this war, and reaction of this sort often simply misses the point in relation to them. In this case I can't disavow the emotion, but I have come – though with some discomfort – to see that it is not always reliable. Unreflected-upon, it might well lead anyone, and not only people I don't like, in the directions I will shortly describe. And so, though my particular criticisms in this paper are not intended as self-criticism, they may well boomerang.

What I take to be the motivational source of reaction, then, seems to me defensible, and I will return to some implications of that at the end of these remarks. However, what matters then is what you do with it, and here what I've called the rhetoric of reaction is not the only way to do business, though it is readily available and the temptations to use it aren't small. Unfortunately, it is a distasteful but characteristic part of Australian public debate. And, though our debates seem especially rich with it, it is not only found here. I suspect the temptation to indulge in it will occur wherever and whenever the wound is deep to attachments that matter, sources of national identity prominent among them. So one will often find it, particularly in arguments over what Keith Windschuttle has aptly dubbed 'the character of the nation'. However, the extent to which that is all one finds, that it *dominates* public debate, varies. I suspect it is a useful index of the intellectual quality, openness to complexity, space available for conversation rather than noise and fumes, characteristic of a particular public culture. Its prominence is inversely related to these things. In the debates I'm concerned with, it's been extremely prominent, and I take that to speak ill of our public discourse.

Some of what I will say retraces material sketched in 'Neighbours'. I was struck there not merely by the *existence* of similar sorts of response to allegations that shameful things occurred in two contexts separated widely by time, space and subject, but also by the close similarities in the *character* of the moves here and there. The parallels are, I'm convinced, not accidental. Though few if any participants in either controversy had any knowledge of the other, and though the particulars alleged had different causes, characters and consequences, there was a sense in which the debate was in both places over the same thing: reaction to painful unsettlement of a certain myth of national rectitude.

At the end of *In Denial*, Robert Manne asks a very simple question about child removals: 'Why has so much energy been expended in the attempt to deny … that a really terrible injustice occured?' That is *the* meta-question of that debate, and it can be generalised to the larger debate about white–Aboriginal relations. In 'Neighbours' I tried to address it. Here I am more concerned with how than why.

### 1. Let's not Bicker and Argue
You might recall the scene in Monty Python's *Holy Grail*, where Sir Lancelot is welcomed by the host of a wedding party, many of whom,

among them the bride-to-be's father, he has just dismembered. Over the protests of the survivors, the host reminds them 'This is supposed to be an 'appy occasion. Let's not bicker and argue about who killed who.' This is a gambit often associated with those who say it only makes sense to concern ourselves with forward-looking 'practical reconciliation', not to fuss about the past. As noted in 'Neighbours', that move was not available in Poland, since there were so few Jews left after the war, but it has been popular here. It's a classically reactionary move, since it is only ever heard in *reaction* to critiques of aspects of that past. No one has heard John Howard say, for example, 'Let's not worry about Gallipoli. Let's just work out how to improve the lot of the Turks.'

The rhetorical point of this move is obvious. If successful, it makes it difficult, bad form even, to express concerns about the character of a nation's past. There is a difficulty with it, though. On its own, this plea for forgetfulness can only plausibly be made by people *other* than those who actually do make it. Determined cosmopolitans, resolute citizens of the world, might really have no concern with the past doings of a particular nation. What's Gallipoli to them? But the people who make the claim in our public debates are commonly hostile to cosmopolitanism. They are patriots; proud of their past and in other, celebratory, circumstances voluble about it. As many people have pointed out, simple moral coherence requires shame for the shameful aspects of our past, from those proud of the prideful. Moreover, their acts belie their words. Much though they seek to minimise discussion of sad moments, they certainly *act* as though it matters. There is nothing to choose, in terms of passionate intensity, for example, between those who affirm the importance of the past in our present, and those who vociferously claim to deny it. For neither side, does it seem that 'the past is another country.'

## 2. Presumptive Denial

If questions about the past can't be quelled this way, the next reaction to disturbing allegations is simply to deny them. Of course, that is a legitimately available response if one has evaluated evidence and found it wanting, as Windschuttle claims to have done, but what is interesting is the *speed* with which reactors jumped to denial, of stolen children, of massacres – here or in Poland – immediately the allegations appeared. Both here and there, investigation of these things has not been easy or quick. And though Windschuttle's *beliefs* are well known, his first volume was not available for some time and later volumes aren't out yet, and his chorus of supporters didn't even wait for the first one, so quick off the mark were they after his first *Quadrant* article. So it's hard to know what the claims of his early and vociferous supporters, who had not done the research Windschuttle is still doing, were based on. Actually not so hard. Like an auto-immune system of a peculiarly hyper-active, allergic sort, if reaction to perceived threat or pain is allowed to operate undisciplined, it will simply seek to expel what unsettles it. Presumptive denial is simply sneezing in prose.

### 3. 'Crazed Positivism'

Of course, denial can't just stay presumptive, and there is no doubt that deniers do argue about evidence. Windschuttle says that is all that he does. But here a common strategy of reaction is what Dirk Moses has called 'crazed positivism', that is insistence on standards of proof which commonly cannot be met, e.g. 'the fetishisation of direct evidence to underwrite every historical conclusion', such as a demand that Hitler's signature on an order to exterminate Jews be produced, or eyewitness evidence, corroborated, of any allegation of murder, however implausible it might be to expect that. This is how Windschuttle can pretend to be so certain of his 118, now revised to 120, Tasmanian Aborigines killed, notwithstanding a later nonchalant oral admission that if we contemplate the addition of wounded Aborigines who might have died unseen, that figure might need to be doubled. No room here for murders unreported by their perpetrators, though. This sort of strategy has two appeals: first, it makes it hard to prove anything much happened, particularly in those circumstances when it was least likely to have been recorded; second, and more particularly, it makes the business of talking about the past pretty simple. No inferences necessary, no 'convergence of evidence', no room for historical imagination, like that marvellously displayed by Inga Clendinnen in *Dancing with Strangers*. Just counting of reassuringly small numbers.

## 4. Ethics and Accountancy

And counting occurs in another common rhetorical trope too. Often we are exhorted to recognise that there are more goods in our national 'balance sheet' than bads, as though to recognise one involves denying the other. This allows one to acknowledge the possibility that bad things happened in our past, which might prove on occasion to be unavoidable, but to cancel them with the undoubted many good things that also happened. But historical goods and evils are not to be balanced in this way. As I argued in 'Neighbours', to recognise one *and* the other is not to indulge in 'black armband history' or its opposite, but merely to show due recognition of the moral complexity that commonly exists in a nation's past. As Jan Gross, the author of the book that exposed the Jedwabne massacre, put it: 'simply put, after all, we are dealing here with a question of ethics, and not of accountancy.'

And there is another reason counting and ethics often part company. The bads you can count (like the goods) are often only a small part of what needs to be understood. Perhaps that is why there is so much focus on them. I am acquainted with a number of former communist countries. In recent years, there have been controversies over how many people were killed in them. There is a literature of debate about the figures in Robert Conquest's *The Great Terror*, for example, and another one around the global estimates essayed in the *Black Book of Communism*. These are important controversies, but they are also misleading, sometimes deliberately so. For they lead us away from the many ways that have nothing to do with killing, in which the communist system blighted, thwarted, twisted, stunted lives. But there are no gravestones for those injuries.

## 5. Analogy Wars

As Owen Harries once pointed out, 'comparisons may be odious and analogies tricky, but they are also indispensable.' Discussing the war in Iraq, he drew analogies with the Suez Crisis, notwithstanding that 'The analogy is not exact, of course. Analogies never are.' Though analogies can't be exact, they can be intellectually and morally useful if they illuminate a subject by drawing parallels one might not have thought of without them. By contrast, they are useless or harmful if the parallels make no sense, or the differences are so great or important as to nullify them, or if their only point is to elevate or demean one's subject by bathing it in reflected glory or gore.

Critics of contentious policies or histories will often be drawn to analogies with events the evil of which needs no demonstration, to transfer our assessment of the example chosen to what they are actually criticising. Defenders of such policies or histories will resist such analogies. All this can go on in an intellectually respectable way, since analogies are made not found, and there will often be room for argument. But analogies can be usable rhetorically, as can rebuttal of them, for reasons neither intellectual nor moral. This has often been the case in the debased ways we invoke or condemn the invocation of the Holocaust and genocide in local arguments.

### Holocaust

Analogies with the Holocaust have clouded discussions on all sides. According to Keith Windschuttle, what is despicable about the 'orthodox' historians of Australia is that they have led us to think of our history as on a par with Nazism. I agree with him that anyone who ventures such an analogy is playing with moral fire. Analogies with cataclysmic events, perhaps none more than the Holocaust, are among the rhetorical strategies which should always be handled with the greatest scrupulousness, sensitivity and care, equally for moral as intellectual reasons. For such analogies are often cheap. When so, they are inexcusable. The moral stakes are too high. This does not mean that all comparisons with the Holocaust are illegitimate. That couldn't be the case, since even to deny similarity you need to compare. But identifications of different sorts of tragedy, which dissolve massive differences of quality, quantity, intention and manner of execution are, I would want to say, not merely foolish but sinful.

The Australian story is very far from Nazism. Tragic as the history of settlement has been for Aborigines, it is not a unique or unprecedented tragedy. Not even rare in human history. The Holocaust was. When I began trying a few years ago to get some measure of our history of settler–Aborigine relations I read the so-called 'orthodox' historians, among them Reynolds and Rowley. So far as I noticed, they said nothing of the Holocaust. They talked of fear, of lack of policing and biased policing, of racist condescension, and, on occasion, of murder. What they described gave plentiful reminders, not of Nazism but of the old wisdom that man is a wolf to man. There is not much consolation in the ordinariness of that fact, but it remains true that there is little unimaginable in what happened here. Our difficulty has been to imagine that our sort had been involved in it, not that anyone could be. For we know that they often have been.

So Windschuttle is right to resist the analogy with Nazism. However, given that he does not offer up even one 'orthodox' historian who makes it, it seems odd to justify his three volumes as a debunking of it. Actually, as part of a rhetorical strategy it's not at all odd. Since he admits to having caught not one historian *in flagrante*, what is the attack on analogies with Nazism doing in such a central position here? Alienating the reader from the enemy. And that's the point.

What is needed, and what the analogy wars exclude, is an intellectually and morally complex appraisal of the character of contacts, over long periods of time, between whites and Aborigines. It is likely that there was good and bad in those contacts, as Inga Clendinnen has sensitively and imaginatively demonstrated in *Dancing with Strangers*. It is also likely that tragedy was written into the script, whatever individuals did, as soon as whites determined to stay and proliferate here, pastoral industry became attractive, and so on. And it is likely too that many shameful things occurred, among them killing, forcible abduction of children and, of course, wholesale dispossession of land which no one denies and which, even had it been done with exquisite politeness, spelt the birth of our way of life and the death of that of Aborigines.

There are many ways of behaving badly, or leading to terrible consequences, as we know since history is full of them, even though it is not full of Holocausts. Had defenders of 'the character of the nation' been less concerned to deny what no one should sensibly say, and grapple with what is, at the same time, in parts a very happy and in others a very sad story, our public conversation might be in better shape than it is.

*Genocide*

Another concept which often lends itself to inapt analogies, indeed often to the same analogies, is genocide. In some ways I wish the word had never been used in the Australian context. For it is very hard to discuss rationally, because of the passions it inflames and the comparisons it inevitably demands. It is also rarely, in my experience, discussed in good faith. Many who carelessly accuse white Australians of genocide trade on the association of the term with the Holocaust, to suggest some assimilation by analogy of the two. On the other hand, many out to deny there was genocide in our history focus on the word for a particular reason. Focusing on criticism of the analogy allows one to smear and then ignore claims that shameful, even dreadful, things occurred: it's not genocide, so we're home free. But it is not as simple as that.

The way the term figures in the rhetoric of reaction is similar to the way the Holocaust does, and for the same reason. We find it very hard, and many people see no reason to try, to think of genocide without assimilating it to its most dreadful example, where without doubt genocide occurred, but so did many other dreadful things. However, there is a sophisticated literature on genocide, much of which emphasises, as Hannah Arendt, and following her Raimond Gaita and Robert Manne do, that we need *some* concept to capture the distinctive evil of trying to do away with *a people,* which is a different aim from murderous re-settlement of them or even from mass killings without that particular aim. If 'genocide' is too linked with the Holocaust to do that work, even though the term was coined before the Holocaust occurred, then some other term is needed. The issue remains, whatever word we choose.

I fear that the concept is so drenched with Holocaust associations that it is no longer helpful to general public conversation, in contexts where that analogy is misplaced, even though the conceptual case for it is convincing. But that can be argued both ways. However even this level of complexity is never broached by the rhetoric of reaction. No matter how often people who know something about genocide insist that this does not necessarily mean the Holocaust, that rhetoric sweeps these petty conceptual distinctions out of the way, immediately assimilates genocide to the Holocaust, and thus blasts away anyone who would use that accursed word of *anything* that might have happened in this blessed land. And, since homogenisation of one's opponents is standard fare in these debates, often people who have never used the concept in relation to local events have been dismissed by extension, as it were. If they suggest shameful things happened in our past, they must be saying genocide, therefore Holocaust, therefore to Hell with them.

### 6. False Dichotomies; Excluded Middles

Discussions about real and false analogies are good ways of doing what false dichotomies are so often used to do: polarise, and therefore simplify, intellectual and moral options. Targeting extremes to avoid dealing with unexceptional but complex mixtures of good motives and bad, good consequences and tragic ones, ordinary people in extraordinary circumstances, is part of the elimination of complexity so characteristic of these debates and of our time.

Excessive simplification is often just a problem of intelligence, in moral matters at times of innocence, at others of Manichaean zealotry. But it is a rhetorical resource too. For if choices can be sufficiently reduced – preferably in Schmittian fashion to one: ours versus theirs, all you need, to leave the former standing, is to knock over the latter. And so our debates have gone.

Often this sort of polarisation takes the form of Manichaean myth-making. Nowhere more so, as we saw in 'The Character of the Nation', than in Windschuttle's *Fabrication*: if not A, the black myth of genocide, then B, a white myth of civilisation. End of story. We would do well to reject this sort of caricatured set of polarisations, and face common and often tragic complexities, where good and evil come together, as noted earlier, even involve each other, where harm can be done even by people who don't mean to (though harms were also done by people who *did* mean to), where the situation is good for some and bad for others, and good for some because bad for others, all together. Instead, a common ploy of reactionary rhetoric is to fabricate – only in order to denigrate – a paranoid construction of the 'enemy', and offer its mirror image as a substitute.

## 7. The Irish Question

A focus on prohibited analogies and false dichotomies often follows the model of the Irish question, as described by the authors of *1066 and all that*. They explained that Gladstone, 'spent his declining years trying to guess the answer to the Irish Question; unfortunately, whenever he was getting warm, the Irish secretly changed the Question'. And so, many Australians have wondered anxiously whether something worrying might have happened in the nation's past – indeed at its state-and-nation-building core – something with which we might feel some moral connection, shame, some sort of responsibility even. That is a large question, to which many events, predicaments and circumstances are relevant. If the conversation can be re-directed, particularly if a questionable part can be re-presented as the whole, then one can easily forget why the discussion began, leaving the questions which have caused many of us anxiety unanswered and unattended.

A recent example of the Irish question in operation is a warm review of Windschuttle's *Fabrication* by Neil McInnes that appeared in the American magazine *The National Interest*. McInnes explains that though, in colonial encounters 'murders were not uncommon, usually as revenge for livestock rustling or crop burning … they are not the theme of the story of settlement.' They are not, because even without them, aboriginal populations would have been decimated, mainly by introduced diseases. But it is interesting to ask, what would it mean to say they were 'the theme of the story of settlement'? Even to suggest that they were the central reason for the decimation of aboriginal populations makes no sense, at least where these populations were large. Take the Australian debate. Windschuttle, after all, takes greatest umbrage at the estimates of 20,000 Aborigines killed between 1788 and the late 1920s, suggested independently by Henry Reynolds and Richard Broome. He believes the figure was far less. But even if we stay with the allegedly gross exaggerations of Reynolds and Broome, we have an estimate of 20,000 killed over about 130 years or, on average, around 150 per year. That being only a fraction of the drop in population, it can't even begin to rate as 'the theme' of it. But by now the discussion has been hijacked. What began as a complex and multi-faceted tragedy, which involved wholesale dispossession of land and in fairly short order evacuated a whole way of life, and continued in myriad ways with catastrophic effects, is reduced to the question whether the primary cause of drops in aboriginal populations was murder. Who can remember what we started with?

## 8. Sotto Voce Concessions

Interestingly, having driven out complexity in these ways, this polarising strategy allows a bit of it back, in a rhetorically disarmed form. Thus, having concentrated one's fire on the possibility of genocide, one can then admit in a rhetorically minor key that – to be sure, no one would deny, it goes without saying etc. – some unfortunate things actually happened. Almost every reactionary rhetorician does this, some way through their polemics (though rarely at the start of them, but only when the damage has been done). That sort of concession works according to the semantic logic once identified by Ernest Gellner, when he observed that 'the English expression "to be sure" belongs to the interesting class of phrases like "I would be the last to suggest", which mean the opposite of what they seem to mean.' More simply, this sort of concession, coming as it always does after the head-kicking has been done, just works to establish one's credentials as a regular guy. By the time the concession comes, it is calculated to do no harm in the main game, dwarfed as it must by the rhetorical demolition of much larger fry.

## Conclusion

There are other forms of reactionary rhetoric that I could mention, but the general idea is, I hope, plain. The rhetoric of reaction is a device intended not to further the flow of a conversation of citizens, but to dam it up or re-direct it it into unthreatening channels. Where it is the characteristic mode of intervention, it should, I believe, be exposed and criticised.

And yet I began by professing sympathy with the motivation to react. It is that motivation which fuels the rhetoric I've been describing or, perhaps more accurately, ensures that whatever the motives of perpetrators of reactionary rhetoric, it doesn't always fall on deaf ears. Perhaps nothing will open the ears or eyes of the rhetoricians I have mentioned, and perhaps not all who listen to them are persuadable either. Nevertheless, I take it to be a regulative ideal of conversation, as distinct from wars of words, that the possibility of dialogue is presumed. What is needed, then, for real *engagement* in conversation?

One answer can be stated in simple, even banal, terms: a conversation necessarily has more than one party, and it is a peculiarity of their engagement, as distinct from a monologue, a harangue, a tirade, a shouting match, that participants treat each other with respect. What might that involve, particularly when passions are high and moral energies charged? I don't have clear answers to this, nor have I always behaved consistent with such answers as I do have. But my general point is this: there is a rhetoric of critique that can easily provoke the rhetoric of reaction, as a mirror does a reflection. It has nothing better to be said for it than for its opposite. It relentlessly moralises what the other with equal determination seeks to sanitise, exaggerates what the other is determined to minimise, demonises what the other sanctifies, closes off exactly the complexities which the other also denies, but for opposite ends. That rhetoric has not been my subject today, though it has in other contexts. And anyone concerned to stimulate the conversation of citizens has, I believe, a responsibility to avoid it.

*2004*

# PUBLIC VALUES

# Between Fear and Hope

It is reported that Gertrude Stein's last words, as she lay on her deathbed, were: 'What is the answer? ... In that case, what is the question?' That's a pretty good way to end a life, and it's a pretty good question. For people's disagreements stem just as much from differences between the (often implicit) questions that matter to them, as they do from the answers they give. Indeed, the questions commonly make more of a difference than do the answers. Many people who seem to disagree strenuously about answers to the same question are often really talking about altogether different things.

This is as true of questions about the character and quality of societies and social institutions as it is of any other matters. The answers to any such questions are, of course, always going to be complex and controversial. They aren't small questions, people differ on all of them, and any answer depends on many matters of fact and judgment.

But that is not all. For even if we ignore the inevitably contestable character of these matters, two very different kinds of questions constantly lurk behind debates over the worth of societies and institutions. Often though, they are not stated, recognised or distinguished by participants. Crudely put, one question is whether these societies and institutions could be worse; the other, whether they could be better. Are they better than they might be? Alternatively, are they as good as they could possibly be or, in a common variant, as we would wish them to be? Some people cherish their society and its institutions simply because they have experienced or know of much worse. Others denounce the same things because they hope for much better. They appear to disagree, and perhaps they really do, but it's hard to know for sure until it's clear what they are talking about.

Ideally we would seek both, and with equal energy, to avoid the worst and aim for the best. More than that, we would ensure that our pursuit of one of these goals didn't imperil our chances of attaining the other. It is much more common, however, to become preoccupied with one at the expense of the other.

Many people, among them those influenced by Thomas Hobbes's consideration of the perils of a 'state of nature', a society without state and law, consider themselves realists. They are disdainful of idealists who, they believe, tend to treat lightmindedly, and often threaten to imperil, precious, precarious and hard-won institutional and cultural achievements. Idealists, so it is said, ignore many of the lessons of hard facts, inexorable constraints and dark times. Often this Hobbesian disdain is warranted. Though in the face of wondrous possibilities, caution often seems dull and out of place, many of the worst things that people have done to each other have been done in the service of deeply held ideals. And the world is littered with examples of people 'seeking Rousseau, finding Hobbes', in Ralf Dahrendorf's apt phrase.

Idealists, on the other hand, complain that there is more to life than survival, and that it is worth striving for more. They accuse Hobbesians of complacency, and Hobbesian pessimism of being a good cover and resting point for jaded winners who don't want to share. The accusation is not always unjustified.

As a result of this dolorous division of labour, there are not many Hobbesian idealists about. There should be though. We have it on the authority of Lyndon Johnson that one of his opponents and ultimately a successor 'couldn't walk and chew gum at the same time'. Whether it was true in that case, it seems to be a common predicament. One underlying theme of these essays is that we often seem to find it hard to do two useful things at once: in this case, think simultaneously about avoiding evil and about pursuing good; about threat, about promise, and about their interplay. But it's worth a try.

Orthodox Hobbesians begin with fear. They keep the worst in mind. That is a good way to start, since there is a lot to be afraid of and the worst can be terrible indeed. They end with institutional recommendations intended to prevent the worst and allay the fear of it. That, too, is a crucial task, because the reduction of fear is precious – in itself and for the productive possibilities it allows. For fear is not only frightening; it is typically also degrading, humiliating and paralysing. There is nothing to be said for it. Fear degrades those who suffer it, and equally those who inflict it. We are familiar with Hannah Arendt's brilliant characterisation, 'the banality of evil', but good is also largely banal. The former needs to be restrained, and the latter equally needs to be supported. We are weak reeds.

Notwithstanding Hobbes's censure, however, one might well want more than relief from fear, and most of us do. But one should never ask for less. The Hobbesian question should never be neglected. In any event that is where I commonly begin. It is also historically where I began, with a kind of sub-articulate Hobbesianism, and it is where I still often return.

Though in many parts of the world the questions that have worried me are very familiar, they have not always been so in contemporary Australia. There is no mystery about this, for my placid, suburban home was not only full of hybrids, but intensely political as well. However it was political in a somewhat exotic sense: its perspective for thinking about Australian politics, or the politics of other relatively happy countries, was experience of, and reflection upon, what Sir Karl Popper called satanic societies – those ruled by the totalitarian regimes of Nazism and communism, which were responsible for the greatest human catastrophes of this or any other century.

For my parents this perspective was, of course, not a matter of choice but of fate. As I have mentioned, they were among the millions of victims of Nazism, privileged victims, since they survived, escaped, and landed here, together – each of these a happy accomplishment – but victims nonetheless. They were also victims of communism, again privileged for the same reasons. More than victims, however, they were witnesses, and like many of their generation and their part of the world, their witness took a particular trajectory.

About Nazism, of course, they never had any doubts. Nor could anyone of decency and intelligence. Nazism, after all, was an abominably evil system with abominably evil goals and methods, constructed by evil people for evil ends. It had no redeeming features. That it did evil is not altogether remarkable, though the scale and horror of the catastrophe that Nazism was and wrought certainly were.

However, many of the founders of communism, that other dark force of our time, were brilliant and talented people. Many of them truly believed that they were constructing something unprecedentedly beautiful. So did many of their supporters throughout the world. Instead they built something unprecedentedly horrible: a political order which was established, in one country after another, by mass murder and terror before it slid slowly from all-encompassing oppressiveness through slovenly despotism, to end in breathtakingly speedy and serial collapse and disgrace. In the process it cost scores of millions of lives, enslaved many more millions of people, and reduced once-civilised countries to dilapidated and smelly ruins.

It took many apparently decent and intelligent people a very long time to recognise the enormity of this experiment, and the connections between its fanatical forms of idealism and the barbarities it inflicted. Worse still, this recognition only became general, if rarely fashionable, among Western intellectuals well after the worst damage had been done. It was the demons, Stalin and Mao, not the mere despots, Brezhnev and Deng Xiao Ping, who were idolised in the West. It is, of course, good that disillusionment came, but it is a pity it took so long.

My parents' disillusionment came fairly early, but not overnight. As a student in pre-war Poland my mother had been a member of an illegal communist youth organisation, and my father of the non-communist Polish Socialist Party. He was also actively involved in left-wing journalism. For them the left was obviously right, and for my mother at least, as for so many pre-war European intellectuals, its beacon was the Soviet Union. She believed that an extraordinary social experiment was going on there, of relevance to the whole world, and she supported it. He was more sceptical, though not hostile. However, through the 1930s he, and later she, came to be increasing dismayed about what they learnt was happening in the Soviet Union under Stalin. (Incidentally, it is a myth that one had to wait until the 1950s or 1960s to discover what was happening there. Already by the '40s, there was plenty of information available for anyone who wanted to know. But many didn't want to know.)

In 1940, fleeing the Nazis on what turned out to be their way to Australia, their year trapped under Soviet occupation in Lithuania purged them, so to speak, of any residual communist sympathies. Indeed it did more. It made them – particularly my father – committed anti-communists. Since Nazism had been defeated, and communism hadn't, and my father was an active man, it made him an anti-communist activist.

When I came to think about politics – in my late teens and early twenties – I tried to understand what the history surrounding my family meant, and what it revealed about human possibilities, vices and virtues. That was no simple matter for me. These were possibilities, vices and virtues of which I had no direct experience at all. When I first learnt of them, I found them almost impossible to imagine and even harder to understand. I still recall the specific moment – in 1968, just before the Soviet invasion of Czechoslovakia – when it dawned on me just how little I understood of political systems and histories of which I had heard and read a great deal. Realising it was a shock then, and recalling it is still a bit of a shock now.

How does a young, comfortable, surburban Sydneysider imagine a regime which sweeps up millions of Jews from all over Europe, in order to wipe them out, systematically, meticulously, with the most advanced technology, and with almost complete success? How another which terrorises, kills, maims and imprisons scores of millions of its own and many other populations, all in the name of human liberation? And how to understand the widespread appeal of this second system, in face of the abundant evidence of its crimes?

I have worried, obsessively and for a very long time, to try to understand these things, and I still have no confidence that I do. It is hard to encounter them on Bondi Beach, and that is where much of my youth was spent. They are not readily apparent on the suburban Kensington campus of the University of New South Wales either – nestled between a famous racecourse and another beautiful beach – and that is where I spend most of my time now. Yet our century and our civilisation have been profligate in demonstrating some of the deepest evils of which

humans so far appear capable, on the largest scale imaginable: sustained terror, bestiality and cruelty, committed systematically, over long
stretches of time and on a mass scale. How such evils are generated and
how they might be avoided are questions of continuing significance.
They are worth pondering, even from Bondi and Kensington.

They are so for two reasons. First, because contemporary Australians, by and large, share practices, a heritage and institutions that
most of us have done nothing to deserve, but which have kept most of
us in a degree of security and prosperity rare in the world. Few of us
have done any more or less than citizens of less fortunate times and
places; we're just lucky to be here. This is true of almost everyone alive,
since our traditions are not our own work. It is even more true of
migrants and hybrids, since they were not even the work of their ancestors. New immigrants, not yet Australians, are often grateful for what
they find here. They often discover they *are* Australians when they feel
pride rather than gratitude. It would be useful to know what accounts
for our good fortune, if only so that we can nurture those things. They
are rare. Paradoxically, it might be easier for hybrids to identify some of
them, as well as what they guard us against. Hybrids also have a tendency to value them highly.

For the bulk of non-Aboriginal Australians, stark evil backed by
overwhelming power is hard to imagine because it is outside our lived
experience. And for us privileged members of a prosperous liberal
democracy, where institutional and cultural traditions and practices
conspire effectively to moderate the exercise of power, several such
defences – democratic institutions, the restraint of power through law,
a plurality of independent and resourceful associations, free media –
are relatively secure. So secure that we might not even notice the abyss
from which they protect us or even that they do protect us. Where such
defences are secure, it is important to realise that and why they are, and
it is important to extend them where they are not.

Keeping evil in mind *comparatively* requires us to be alive to horrors
that are part of human but not our personal experience. There are
plenty of societies which can instruct us. This should spur reflection on
the meaning and significance of the differences. It might also spur
some regard for whatever institutions, traditions, ways of life, you

judge have contributed to such differences. There is, of course, a danger that such reflection might disappoint the need that many intellectuals have for drama in their lives, since it suggests that there is far less of it here than elsewhere. But if that is how the comparison works, one might just have to live with it. Or visit Bosnia.

On the other hand, the second reason we should keep the worst in mind is to alert us to the limitations, the failures and the selectiveness of our own defences against it. For there is no reason, in theory or common experience, to believe that evil can only happen elsewhere, to others, at the hands of still others. Whatever else we do, we need secure defences against extremes of cruelty and other evils. We need defences for ourselves, and – at the risk of sounding theological – against ourselves as well.

If we can't conceive of terrible things happening here, then we should ask why. It might be a notable export. But perhaps we are complacent. It is hard to believe that such things could never occur to us, since – though Nazism and communism lead the field by a very long way – most 'civilised' countries have done terrible things at some time or other in their history, and in some places very recently. In recent years, many Australians have been ashamed to discover that, in our treatment of Aborigines, we have been among such countries. And, as I have argued in earlier essays, that shame is altogether appropriate. It is a curiosity, perhaps of the sort that Lyndon Johnson noted, that many people seem capable of feeling only one response – pride in what Australia has achieved or shame at the ways in which our indigenous population has been dispossessed, savaged, slaughtered and humiliated – but not both. Not just a curiosity but indeed a shame.

Keeping evil in mind *locally* requires attentiveness to domestic complaints of evils done and harms inflicted, paying particular heed to the perspective of the people who have been hurt. For they are likely to be not only the victims but also the closest witnesses of evils done to them. They are also likely to feel them most deeply. They might not be right on everything and one is not obliged to adopt their views of their condition and what caused it. But they have a very special claim to our attention. Both decency and simple moral consistency require that these claims of evil-doing be taken very seriously indeed. And where those who have power over them describe as *misfortunes* what sufferers call *injustice*, there is no reason to assume any special plausibility in the former view. If there is to be any presumption in this matter, it should work the other way. After all, this is a sort of corrective rule of thumb, since, as the late Judith Shklar has pointed out in *The Faces of Injustice*, 'It will always be easier to see misfortune rather than injustice in the afflictions of other people. Only the victims occasionally do not share the inclination to do so.'

Not everyone is as assiduous in pursuing both the comparative and local implications of this view, since to do so involves psychological tension, sometimes extreme. It is a tension I have felt. It is hard at the same time to feel affection for one's own country, respect for many of its institutions, and relief that it has avoided so much that is common experience elsewhere, while at the same time accommodating the notion that it has done, or been complicit in, or allowed, terrible things to happen to some of its own members. And it is galling for those who know the comparisons I have mentioned to see them denied or trivialised by people who don't know or care about them, or who have no special affection for the institutions or people under attack. And anyway, there is always somewhere where things are worse. Nevertheless, it is hard to see how anyone who takes the problem of evil seriously can draw a morally plausible line which warrants indignation about matters abroad and complacency about those at home, or *vice versa*. All the more since, as Shklar also points out, 'Often it is the very people who are supposed to prevent injustice who, in their official capacity, commit the gravest acts of injustice, without much protest from the citizenry.' Lack of protest against injustice of which we know is itself what she calls an act of 'passive injustice' and there is a lot of that about.

In any event, both the widespread absence of institutionalised evil in Australia and its particular but significant presence are grounds for us to try to think seriously about it, to keep the worst in mind. We might have experienced terrible things, we might learn of them, or we might try realistically to imagine them. However we come to it, my suggestion is that we should seek to identify the worth of what we have and should have, by reference as much to the evils we know, as to the goods of which we might dream. There is no reason to stop with our defences, but there is reason at the very least to follow Shklar's recommendation: 'One begins with what is to be avoided.'

Shklar's writings have influenced me a great deal. They deal with many things, but above all with evils and how to deal with them. In one work, *Ordinary Vices,* for example, she observes that few contemporary philosophers have much to say about cruelty which she considers 'the first vice'. She, by contrast, follows her beloved writers, Montaigne and Montesquieu, in 'putting cruelty first' when considering political arrangements, and what they must help us to avoid. Shklar advocates what she calls in an essay of the same name a 'liberalism of fear', a liberalism which 'put[s] cruelty and fanaticism at the very head of the human vices' and thinks above all about how to avoid them. There are other, sunnier, kinds of liberalism, of course, but Shklar seems to think them light-minded. For her, the first necessity of political life is 'damage control'.

Another thinker whom I admire greatly is Philip Selznick. He has a larger and more complex ambition in his book *The Moral Commonwealth.* He is one of the few contemporary social theorists to incorporate a deep recognition of evil into a moral and political outlook which seeks at the same time to strive for the good. He goes far beyond damage control but he too insists that that is the place to start. He also considers that it is a place too rarely visited by contemporary thinkers.

Selznick was profoundly influenced by the great American pragmatist philosopher John Dewey, but he voices one criticism of Dewey which can be read more generally. This criticism has to do with what he regards as Dewey's failure:

> to meet the challenge of modernity, which requires a robust understanding of evil, especially evil encouraged by the sovereignty of will … Human frailty and recalcitrance; the persistence of domination; genuinely tragic choices; the collusion of good and evil: these are theoretical orphans. They are by no means wholly overlooked, but they have no secure place in the pragmatist interpretation of moral experience.

Selznick advocates instead a type of 'moral realism' that:

> presumes a tough-minded conception of evil. It is not enough to recognise that corruption and oppression are pervasive. Nor is it enough to think of specific evils as problems to be solved or as obstacles to be overcome. Rather, the perspective of moral realism treats some transgressions as dynamic and inescapable. They can be depended on to arise, in one form or another, despite our best efforts to put them down.

I think it fair to say that this is not an insight which has flooded the Western academy. Indeed it is hard to find examples of it at all. It is no accident that many representatives of the sort of concerns I am advocating – among them such very different thinkers as the Austrian refugee Karl Popper, the German Jewish refugee from Latvia Judith Shklar, the Russian Jewish Briton, also from Latvia, Isaiah Berlin, and kindred spirits such as Arthur Koestler from Hungary and in our country Franta Knöpfelmacher from Czechoslovakia – escaped but witnessed the destruction of their societies by totalitarian powers. It is also no accident that they were devoted to some of the institutions that they found in their countries of refuge. Direct experience of their sort focuses the mind on a particular range of possibilities, which are less vivid in the experience of happier countries and times, 'among' as Shklar puts it in *Ordinary Vices*, 'people who have relatively little experience of protracted and uninterrupted fear'. Reflection on such experience might not merely focus the mind, of course, but narrow it, as I believe that it has focused and at times narrowed mine. It is important to try to hold onto the focus and resist the narrowing.

For not only must evil be taken seriously. Reflection on public values should start with it. There are several reasons for that, none of them particularly mysterious. To avoid the worst is not yet to attain the best but it is, even without more, a very precious thing to do. And this achievement is very easy to miss wherever the worst has been avoided – precisely because it has been avoided. Yet unless that happens, the best will in any case not be attained. Particularly since the pursuit of the best very often is the enemy of the good, at least when it is not tempered by a sober understanding of what one must avoid. Moreover, when it comes to evil, we have a lot of evidence to go on. Our history and particularly our century have been generous, one might say philanthropic, with evidence of the worst, of absolute evil. By contrast, we only know relative good. Finally, as Avishai Margalit has argued in *The Decent Society*, 'there is a weighty asymmetry between eradicating evil and promoting good. It is much more urgent to remove painful evils than to create enjoyable benefits.'

What, then, are some of the worst evils which people inflict and which we should bend all our efforts to avoid? I have no comprehensive list. I present the following six evils merely as examples. There are many others. The point of discussing these evils lies, in any event, only partly in the details. More important is to encourage what might be called idealism from below: thought about what we must have by reference to what we must avoid.

Physical cruelty and the constant fear of it must be among the very worst. Not only the actual suffering, but a life lived in apprehension that it could come your way at any time, even if it never does. This is the daily lot of millions of people, and over this century it has been the lot of many millions more: in Europe, Russia, China, Africa, Asia, the Middle East, Iran and Iraq. It has often been the lot of Australian Aborigines as well.

It is now fashionable, in those circles where anti-Enlightenment reaction and post-modernism meet, to talk of the impossibility of cross-cultural comparison. No one from one culture can judge the practices of another. Perhaps nothing at all can really be judged. Still, my guess is that it is hard to find people who benefit from being tortured, imprisoned, executed or otherwise done away with, who enjoy the decimation of their families, homes, societies, who look forward to being starved or bled to death, who seek out lives of unrelieved fear. A society that avoids such cruelties has to that extent accomplished something estimable, and it is hard to conceive of much else good happening in a society that has not managed to eradicate physical cruelty from occurring on a large or routine scale. Of course there will be many degrees of achievement in this regard. Each degree is precious.

Indeed simply to restrain brutality is valuable, even if standard practices are in other respects contemptible. And often they are. Thus in 'The Character of the Nation' we noted Margalit's observation that many colonial regimes were at the same time more restrained and more humiliating to their subjects than those they replaced. It is important to stress that Margalit introduces here a distinct and separate scale, according to which social institutions and practices might properly be evaluated. Apart from the degree to which their institutions are 'bridled', so as not to inflict physical suffering without restraint, societies differ in the degree to which they are decent, that is, non-humiliating. Institutions can be bridled but not decent, in Margalit's sense, if they are humiliating. They might (though this seems rarer) even be unbridled but non-humiliating: perhaps heroic combats between fairly matched opponents might be examples of this. Typically, though, unbridled institutions will threaten not only their subjects' lives, they will threaten their honour and their dignity. For they will act indecently.

The choice between these two unpalatable alternatives – unbridled or indecent – is not a happy one. I hope never to have to make such choices myself, for they are tragic ones. Social institutions should be both bridled and decent. That is, they should inflict neither cruelty nor humiliation on their citizens.

There are other registers of evil. A third, which is a central concern of the liberal tradition, for example, is arbitrary invasion of one's freedom by others, particularly powerful others. A lot has been written about freedom, so I needn't add much here, but that is not because it is not valuable. It is precious. Here too, the importance of freedom from arbitrary intervention and oppression is both best understood, and often most eloquently conveyed, by those who have known or pondered life without it, by those who know the experience of what one Polish sociologist, Adam Podgórecki, calls 'crippled rights'. As I argue in 'The Good That Governments Do', public institutions have a crucial role to play here, and not just any institutions will do. Institutions are often key instruments of oppression, but they are also necessary conditions for securing freedom from oppression. Liberals and classical republicans well understood both the dangers and the safeguards that institutions can represent. Marxists and anarchists only understood the dangers.

Institutions are, fourthly, also important in making *civility* possible in social life. That is a complex accomplishment, as we will see. However, at a minimum, a society is civil to the degree that it allows its members confidently, securely and productively to interact with people they don't necessarily love, but don't therefore hate. Routine, peaceable relations among strangers is a sign of civility. A life where the state does no harm, doesn't humiliate you, doesn't violate your freedom, but can't contribute to breaking the equivalence between stranger and enemy, has done some crucially important things, but it is not yet civil and it is unlikely to be admirable.

We should ask of our institutions, how effectively they help us guard against these evils. A bridled society might not seem like much until we confront its negative mirror image. Similarly a decent one. Decency might seem a small, cosmetic, achievement if one is only concerned with justice, but it is quite something if the alternative is institutionalised humiliation of individuals and whole groups. And we know it can be for it often has been. Freedom is better appreciated by the unfree than by its often bored beneficiaries. Civility is an apparently tepid virtue, but it is infinitely preferable to the heat that fear and hatred can generate in its absence.

It is important to grasp that these are four separate registers of social and political accomplishment. A fifth has to do with the amount of valued goods which are available in a society. A sixth with their distribution. There is benefit here, too, in approaching these accomplishments from below, in seeing what goods are worth by examining life without them, and examining justice by focusing on the experience of injustice. Poverty and injustice are terrible things to suffer, and in a good society there will be less of them.

As I have mentioned, this selection of public vices is only meant to be exemplary, not exhaustive. But even this brief sample makes some things clear. One is that it is easier for a society to be comprehensively vicious than virtuous. There are many societies which are unbridled, indecent, unfree, uncivil, poor and unjust. It would, conversely, be nice if we could point to a rich array of societies that were bridled, decent, free, civil, wealthy and just. Instead, societies vary along these six scales in overlapping but separate ways, patchily and unevenly, and rarely at the same pace.

With the best will in the world, societies will confront profound dilemmas when the conditions for achievement on one scale seem to cut across those on an other. How much safety is worth how much indignity? Is there a trade-off between increasing aggregate wealth and increasing distributive justice in a society? How much wealth, how much injustice? How much poverty, how much justice? It is appropriate to be suspicious of anyone who presses the need for such trade-offs, particularly – as so often happens – where they are likely to benefit from the choices they advocate. Nevertheless, it is only in Utopia that everything we want is compatible with everything else we want.

Even if we restrict ourselves to allaying fears, then, to asking whether *minimum conditions* of restraint, decency, security, civility, wealth and fairness have been achieved, we will have quite a bit to deal with. We can, however, also raise our sights, and ask if these things are richly in evidence, and how they might be made more so. Both questions need to be asked.

There is much to be said for the liberalism of fear and for guarding against what it warns us against, particularly where important values seem under palpable threat. But they are not always and everywhere under the same degree of threat. Political wisdom, here as elsewhere, consists in responding to differences of degree. One should not imagine that if minimum security is attained, nothing more need be sought. Nor should concern to avoid the worst become an obsession which crowds out the desire to attain, if not the best, then at least something better. Sometimes, however, it does.

It is fortunate, important and true that our society could be a lot worse. It is also likely that it could be a lot better. And responsible critics are right to insist that conditions which are necessary for a good society may not be sufficient for one. So a determination to conserve those things which provide the minimum conditions for an uncruel, unhumiliating, unpoor, relatively civil and not unjust society and polity might properly be blended with reformist and even radical impulses. They might, so long as those conditions are respected.

Here I am merely echoing a distinction that Selznick has made between *conditions of existence* and *conditions of flourishing*. The liberalism of fear speaks to the former. What are the minimum conditions without which a society is ridden with fear, humiliation, incivility, poverty and injustice? Whatever one favours in public arrangements must meet these conditions. But consideration of them should not crowd out consideration of conditions in which freedom, decency, civility, wealth and justice might be said to flourish. Rather, as Selznick insists, 'The conditions of *survival* are easier to meet than those of *flourishing*, which are more complex and more fragile. It does not follow, however, that we should fail to treasure what is precarious or cease to strive for what is nobly conceived.'

Moreover, Selznick makes a profound point which is often ignored in the thrust and counter-thrust of the fearful and the hopeful. For he observes that people, institutions, systems, communities, undergo 'moral development'. At certain stages in the development of social institutions, for example, particularly formative stages, or when they are weak, or when assailed by strong forces hostile to them, certain values need strong support – because they are not yet established or institutionalised, or because they are at risk. All the more so when there are powerful forces which put them at risk. Such values must be secured and it is dangerous to compromise them. The rule of law is one such value, and there are others to which I will return. When, however, they are institutionally, socially, ideologically and in other ways relatively secure, the balance of emphasis in our moral ambitions can change. Striving toward aspirations can more safely supplement the establishment and defence of baselines. We can even take some risks. This is not because the baselines become less important, just that they are more firmly in place and risks are less risky. Where they are sufficiently secure we should be prepared to hazard more improvement, temper fear with hope, just as in more precarious circumstances we must temper hope with fear. The reverse, of course, also applies. Values which might be fruitful where institutions are strong, might be dangerous where they are weak or absent.

There are no all-purpose bright line guides to the exact mix of fear and hope that our institutions should respect and reflect; no political and institutional recipes, stable and apt for every time and circumstance, which we should follow without deviation. Nor are there any useful fixed ideological positions which provide detailed solutions to whatever problems trouble us, particularly since these problems constantly change. Nor still a fixed range of preoccupations to be hammered, with the same tools, and always as insistently, whatever the circumstances. Rather, as Lord Keynes splendidly retorted on being accused of inconsistency, 'When the facts change, I change my mind. What do you do, sir?'

Were I fighting for my life, I might rightly look askance at a vigorous exercise programme. I would, too, find offensive people who, in advocating my improvement, ignored my condition. I am, however, in fairly robust health, but overweight and underexercised. I would hope that whatever is suggested to be good for me avoids killing me. I would also hope that my doctor knew quite a bit about what might do me harm. I would like him to be what Frank Knöpfelmacher was once accused of being, and later happily called himself: a 'threat expert'. But in my condition, it might be reasonable to suggest that I go for a jog, and unpersuasive for me to retort that my life is at risk. For if it is valuable to live, it is also valuable to live well. In social life, some values, and some approaches to matters of value, both allow us to live together with others, and make available chances to live well with them too. One such value is civility.

*1997*

# The Uses of Civility

Romeo and Juliet, perhaps we can agree, had a relationship problem. But what sort of problem was it?

It wasn't lack of love, for the play is drenched with it, requited and unrequited. Not only do Romeo and Juliet love each other with surpassing and ultimately fatal intensity, but parents love their children, aunts their nephews, cousins each other, Juliet's nurse loves her beyond the call of duty, and even her spurned fiancé loves her to death. Indeed, notwithstanding her somewhat alarming youth and her brief interval between love and death, Juliet has time to make an observation about love that is at once poignant and profound:

> My bounty is as boundless as the sea,
> My love as deep; the more I give to thee
> The more I have, for both are infinite.

Translating from the sublime to the academic, love is not a zero-sum game where, if one wins the other must lose. Instead, both win. Indeed love matched with love forms an ever-replenishing virtuous circle, not the destructively vicious one that comes from hate matching hate. How terrible, then, when the two – love and hate – combine inextricably, as they do in the play.

Why do they? Well, of course, there's a limit to how many people we can love passionately. Or so most of us find. One currently fashionable response to that, and to the artificiality and emptiness of many modern forms of social connection, has been to advocate the virtues of *community.* Communal attachments are usually somewhat broader than passionate ones but they are commonly deeper than, say, contractual ones, valued more in themselves rather than as instruments to something else.

But Shakespeare's Verona doesn't need more communal bonds; it is full of them. To be a Montague or a Capulet is not merely to have a name, but to belong to a densely communal world. All those intense and deep connections, whose passing is lamented by modern communitarian philosophers, knit together the Montagues on the one hand, and the Capulets on the other. Indeed there is, almost literally, no place – no neutral space – where they can be avoided, except in secret or out of town. And that precisely is the tragedy of Romeo and Juliet.

For what was lacking in Verona was not the deep bonds of community, but something far more pallid yet crucial: conditions enabling smooth, routine, secure relationships between members of different communities, or, for that matter, no communities at all. That in turn depends upon a delicate and complex combination of attitudes, and institutions which sustain them. The attitudes are, on the one hand, a sense of some sort of common belonging; on the other, a particular sort of trust between citizens, which I will call 'civil trust', and – at a minimum – tolerance of differences. These attitudes are not merely accidents of individual psychology. They depend significantly upon the existence and adequacy of supporting and sustaining frameworks, among them certain political and legal institutions, about which I will have more to say in the next essay. Taken together, a society in which these attitudes are displayed and these institutions do their jobs, displays civility. Particularly in large modern and complex societies, that is a precious thing to display.

It would have been useful in Verona as well. For in such a society – a civil society – Montagues could mix peacefully and productively with Capulets, without ceasing to be what they were or demanding that others all become the same as them. And they could still both be Veronese. Their children could, if they chose, marry and live happily ever after. They might even come to produce hordes of happy hybrids: Montague-Capulet-Veronese. Or they might not.

There are two other ways in which carnage-engendering communities might be avoided. One would be for Verona to have no significant communities at all. One could after all imagine a city inhabited solely by free, self-directed individuals, with no attachments that they had not chosen for themselves. This might perhaps be a doctrinaire economist's dream – *homo economicus* writ large – and for the same reason a communitarian's nightmare. Then it wouldn't matter to anyone that Romeo was a Montague and Juliet a Capulet. Such names would merely be useful for addressing mail. We would all be abstract, mobile, rootless individual atoms, eyes on the main chance, bouncing about and doing deals, here and there as it suited us. But with that would come a real loss, an emotional loss and a spiritual loss as well. Our attachments, affections, sentiments, loyalties, identities and responsibilities are crucially important to us, and many of our deepest are unsought. Why else would it matter to so many of us where we happen to be born and to whom? Or who in particular is born to us?

Not everything that counts or should count is or should be entirely a matter of our free, unsentimental decision. This is a central insight of communitarian philosophy, and an important one. Communitarians defend what Philip Selznick calls:

> the virtues of particularism. These virtues include loyalty and piety, especially accepting responsibility for children, parents, and others to whom we owe special obligations. Particularism arises from the experience of connectedness, which makes us aware that we are implicated selves, bound up with lives that we have created and that have created us.

Apart from the many ways in which uncontracted attachments enrich and give meanings to our lives, let any ageing parent consider their position in a society which had no unnegotiated attachments of that kind. Some are uncomfortably close to it as it is.

Another solution to the problem might be for Verona as a whole to form one single community – One Nation we might perhaps call it – which overrides all subordinate loyalties: no more Montagues, no more Capulets, and no foreigners. Just Veronese. That vision, of an all-embracing community without internal differences, has appealed to many people on both the political left and the right. Unfortunate but true.

In a cosmopolitan internationalist form, it appealed to the left, among them Karl Marx, whose ideal was an international community of humanity that overrode all differences. Marx was driven by a passion for emancipation of the human species from whatever it was that kept them apart. In place of its multiple separations and divisions, he fantasised the breaking down of all significant boundaries – national, ethnic, traditional, religious and, of course, class. (He had less to say about gender.) When communism was achieved, old borders would disappear under a calm and inviting sea of unthreatening human community, connection and co-operation. No one would drown; or at least no one would need to worry that anyone was out to sink them. Marx thought that communist internationalism was inevitable and he thought it would be wonderful. He was wrong, profoundly wrong, on both counts.

On the one hand, there is nothing in human history to suggest that his ideals are realisable, let alone inevitable. On the other hand, there is a great deal of evidence that the pursuit of precisely these ideals unleashes – at the very least authorises – merciless destruction of anything or anyone who gets in the way. For there are many precious values – among them, individual liberty protected by law – which have no place in such a vision even in its ideal form, let alone in the forms in which it has in practice been pursued. For such values get in the way, and Marx saw no reason why anything should get in the way. It is thus no accident that Marxist devotion to the emancipation of the human species typically came at the tragic expense of millions of human individuals.

Notwithstanding the devoted allegiance of many for a very long time, this vision of undifferentiated humanity has waned in its appeal, particularly after the spectacular, and somewhat pathetic, collapse of the communist project. Marx's internationalist fantasies find some echoes in modern exaggerations of the effects of globalisation, but this is not the same. It's some distance, after all, from the Second International to McWorld.

On the other hand, and somewhat surprisingly, antipathy to difference has a nationally reduced, shrunken counterpart in the thinking of what appear to be the left's bitterest foes: national chauvinists, usually of the far right. Of course, chauvinists have no wish to swim (or even take a dip) in any sea of humanity, and they reject every form of cosmopolitanism including Marxism. On the contrary, they consider that their own nation – whatever it happens to be – is in every way superior to any other. Where Marxists exhorted workers of the world to unite, since they had 'nothing to lose but their chains', chauvinists rally their fellows to an exclusive national community, which could plausibly boast that it had nothing to lose but its humanity.

Yet, like Marxists, chauvinists also hate division. It's just that the scale of their preferred unity is more modest. In their case, the divisions to be eliminated are not those between nations (unless by conquest), but any which occur within a nation state. In Poland, for example, such few Jews as remain after the Holocaust, in a country they have inhabited for centuries, learn from Polish chauvinists that they are not 'true Poles'. Those many Poles who strive to make Poland an open, tolerant, civil society are, on this view, not true Poles either. Hungarians who have lived for generations in what is now Slovakia (but was once Hungary) find plenty of people ready to tell them that they are not true Slovaks; in what is now Romania not true Romanians. For good measure, Hungarian nationalists claim to speak for 'Greater Hungary', in a threat directed precisely against the states of Slovakia and Romania. Of course, Jews in Hungary are, on these views, not true Hungarians, nor in Romania true Romanians, either. Gypsies are nowhere in Europe 'true' anything but rather – in the words of Miroslav Sladek, an ex-communist censor and later leader of the far right Czech Republican Party – 'inferior', 'animals', 'subhuman'. And I have not even mentioned what Serbs say of Croats, Croats of Serbs, or either of Muslims, in what is left of the former Yugoslavia.

It is a mistake to think that similar ideologies will have similar significance and consequences wherever they are found. That significance and those consequences depend on many things other than their partisans' beliefs and fantasies. And so, the strength of chauvinistic politics varies enormously between the countries I have mentioned, and between any of them and Australia. There are many people opposed to them, and in many countries successfully so. Moreover, notwithstanding the best efforts of the One Nation Party and its supporters, chauvinism is much weaker here than in any of the countries I have mentioned. I trust it will remain so.

Quite apart from the prospects of such views, however, there is the question of their character, and of their claim on our thoughtful allegiance. In my view, and fortunately not only mine, their character is bad and their claim nil. It is notable that the structure of ethnocentric claims is everywhere the same. On the one hand, the chauvinists' own nation, in each and every case, is quite remarkable and exceptional – indeed, uniquely so. All one need do is fill in the name to find out which particular nation we're talking about at the moment. One also needs, of course, to know the identities of the particular pollutant peoples who threaten to dilute its pristine purity, though there are some useful multi-purpose candidates, such as Jews in the northern hemisphere, Asians in the sourthern, and indigenes wherever they have been conquered.

Patriotism, which involves love of country, can be a humane and welcoming emotion, just as love of one's family can. Even more so, since patriotism extends one's sympathies to millions, in the present and the past, whether one knows them or not. Jingoism is a perversion of patriotism, not its natural corollary. Patriotism does not require or imply such monolithic and exclusive perversions of love of country, and the implications of such distortions are simply repulsive.

National chauvinism, if ever it moves beyond words to realisation, has terrible consequences, and naturally so. For unless one's society is and remains naturally homogeneous, homogeneity has to be imposed. and very few societies are or today can be homogeneous, whatever their jingoistic press releases might say. Still less, young immigrant societies like Australia. And in modern, large and complex societies – outside Iceland, which is not very large though it is very cold – homogeneity is not to be found. So the point must be to live lives *in common but with differences*. That is a challenge, but unlike the challenge of eliminating differences, it is a noble one. It is to that challenge that civil society is a response.

The phrase 'civil society' has emerged from obscurity in recent years, to become remarkably popular, indeed ecumenically so. It is as hard today to find anyone against it, as not so long ago it was hard to find anyone who spoke for, or even about, it. In fact it is now so popular that we might justifiably feel some suspicion, if only on Groucho Marx's principle that you should never join a club which would have you as a member. Though that is a fine principle, I will ignore it in this case for the civil society club is a good one to join. Apart from anything else, it welcomes many people that other clubs exclude, and doesn't treat them badly. So I recommend it.

I should stress, though, that any term which has become so popular among so many people is likely to be doing a lot of different jobs. Whoever appropriates the phrase is doing something with it, not just echoing a dictionary definition. And I am no exception. What follows is what I understand and think important about civil society, not necessarily what 'it' naturally is.

In civil society according to me, then, both words – adjective and noun – are significant. In the most popular recent stream of writing, the noun – society – is typically what is stressed. The point, made in a multitude of ways, is that society matters. Apart from top-down, vertical links from governments to citizens, partisans of civil society draw attention to, and advocate, horizontal links among citizens themselves and bottom-up connections from citizens to government. They point to salutary consequences of joining, of voluntary associations, of informal institutions, of co-operation, trust, 'social capital', of activities that build up from society rather than trickle down from governments. Some lay stress on what governments can't do, some on what citizens can. Either way, attention is directed to social networks and socially generated initiatives, most commonly by contrast to projects initiated by government.

This theme was central to the resuscitation of the term by dissidents in communist states, particularly Poland, who sought to recover the possibility of social links among citizens, independent of the strangling domination of the communist state. The rebirth of interest in civil society is a paradigm example of the 'idealism from below' that I have commended in the previous essay, of the worth of something becoming evident to those who understand the vices of life without it. For it was dissidents in communist states who sparked the renewed interest in this old idea. They observed that they lacked something that seemed normal in the West: social relations which were not pulverised or distorted by a state which knew no bounds, relations which had their own agendas and rhythms. In civil societies, people went about much of their business in activities and associations which they, not the state, chose and which they and not the state directed. There was no need to ask for permission. They rose and fell at the initiative of their members, not as a result of political command. That seemed an extraordinary possibility among those to whom it was deliberately and systematically denied; however prosaic it might appear to those who have never known it to be questioned.

In Molière's play *The Bourgeois Gentleman*, M. Jourdain expresses his astonishment on learning from the philosopher he employed for edification, that though he didn't know it, he had been speaking prose all his life. Somewhat similarly, from the communist East the West discovered that it had civil societies. It did so when communism ceased to be charming or even interesting in the West, and anti-communist dissident movements became popular there. Propelled by those dissidents, the idea of civil society bounced back from the East which lacked it but wanted it, into the West which discovered it had it but hadn't thought much about it. Many Westerners, particularly intellectuals, had not even liked it much. Since then, Western enthusiasts have taken a shine to it and sought to improve it. Often they have been so struck by the newfound 'significance of the social' that 'civil society' is simply a contrast term, to point to what is not governmental but social. The adjective does no work. In this usage, it would be enough just to speak of society, but that seems old-fashioned now, and 'civil society' is more in vogue. And so it should be. For the adjective – *civil* – matters too. There are many different sorts of society, and many different types of relationships within any particular society. Only some are civil.

Perhaps the most perceptive modern student of civil society, the late Ernest Gellner, makes the point in his *Conditions of Liberty*, that while a society not dominated by the state is a necessary condition for a civil society, it is not enough. And it is not enough since there have been plenty of societies where, as he puts it, though kings didn't dominate all aspects of life, *cousins* did. Kingship and kinship. These are the two traditional options, though they were often combined. Most agrarian communities were of this sort, and Shakespeare's Verona certainly was. For better or worse, this is not the character of a modern commercial society, nor can it be a happy solution when such a society is at all large and heterogeneous. For then the space is full of non-cousins, and one has to decide what to do with them.

One can, of course, try to kill them. This – what might be called the Karadzic–Tudjman contribution to political morality and social relationships – is a commonly recurrent pattern in much of the world. It was also common, apparently, in Verona. If that is unavailable, one can always be rude, hostile, suspicious and unco-operative. In many societies that is a reasonable option, even the only reasonable option, since in these societies there are many good reasons to be suspicious of anyone one doesn't know well, and no good reason not to be.

This was the option widely practised in most communist societies, as citizens responded to the attempt by the gigantic communist state to infiltrate and control all social relationships. A natural and widespread response was for citizens to band together with those whom they had specific reason to trust. This trust often flowed from shared and illicit complicities when so little that anyone wanted was legally available. It produced what the Polish sociologist, Adam Podgórecki, called fellowships of 'dirty togetherness'. But it also encompassed fine and noble bonds of loyalty and generosity among friends who needed each other in hard times. Excluded from these tight groups was the rest of the world, those many whom there might be very good reason to distrust.

Where the state is weak, on the other hand, and distrust of others is widespread, a market develops for entrepreneurs of violence and protection. That market is serviced by the original Mafia in southern Italy, and what are derivatively and appropriately called mafias in post-communist Russia. Similar markets are booming, though they are the only ones that are, among the warlords who roam and terrorise much of the former Yugoslavia. As Michael Ignatieff observed in his *Blood and Belonging*, of the warzone of Vukovar: 'Every man goes armed. No one ventures beyond the village. No one trusts anyone they have not known all their lives.' And, tragically but wisely, many people distrust people they have known all their lives.

Another social option altogether, somewhat rare, is for non-intimates to be nice to each other. No one will do this if the costs are prohibitive, or the benefits illusory. A civil society is one which contrives to keep down the costs and spread the benefits, so that it is reasonable to be nice.

There is a Romanian expression which bureaucratic climbers will understand: 'kiss the hand you cannot bite.' It is common to find inferiors in organisations conforming to this maxim when cultivating their superiors. A corollary might be 'bite the hand you needn't kiss' and that is the way bureaucrats often treat their subordinates. Often the same people behave in conformity with both maxims, depending on whether they are looking up or down. But there are other things one can do with hands than kiss or bite. One alternative is to shake them. That is a civil alternative.

In a civil society, relationships of a particular texture and temperature can flourish, and since not all relationships in any society can have such texture and temperature not all relationships can be civil. Civil relationships are not especially close and they are not hot like love and hatred. They are cool, tepid, lukewarm or at least they can survive at such temperatures, though they don't necessarily shrivel with warmth. As Selznick has observed in *The Moral Commonwealth*, 'in civility respect, not love, is the salient value.' Civil relationships are not intimate, but nor are they hostile. They are the character of relationships among members of healthy voluntary associations, not of close families, on the one hand, nor of opposed troops, on the other. They are ones in which the opposite of my friend is not my enemy but, say, my acquaintance or colleague or neighbour. I can do business with him, and I do not necessarily betray anyone by doing so. In politics, too, even opponents inhabit a common, or at least overlapping, moral universe: competitors within some common frames of reference, however unspoken and superficially denied; not mortal foes. A civil society is, then, a common society, though it may not in any strong sense be a community.

Apart from their relationships with Aborigines, Australians have traditionally displayed more civility to each other than any other society I have spent time in, though they have not always loved each other. They have also often been civil to newcomers. Not necessarily inviting, but civil. That is to be valued, for it allows confident and reliable communication and co-operation at distance, and we have need of that. Not only that, of course, but that as well.

I have described civility in deliberately understated terms, so as not to gain allegiance by false pretences. Love, of course, is easier to promote. Who is against it? Radical feminists such as Catharine MacKinnon, perhaps, but not most feminists, and hardly anyone else. Community is more controversial, but it also has many adherents. Civility has fewer devoted partisans, at least among those who are its beneficiaries.

For civility is not one of those ideals that quickens the pulse, but then nor should it be. It might, however, steady it. Some of our most fulfilling relationships must be on the way out, if all we can say is that they are civil. The feelings for each other of Romeo and Juliet are not adequately described as civil, though they were not uncivil either. Civility is simply not enough for love. It is not to die for. A healthy society supplements and enriches it in all sorts of ways. But a civil platform is a secure place to stand. It is infinitely preferable to hatred, suspicion, hostility and vengefulness. And that, it appears, is what our heroes' families felt for each other. The terrible predicament with which the play is concerned is that, in Verona, love and hatred were the only available alternatives. Civility was nowhere to be seen. And that is not only a problem in Verona.

It is plausible that civil society is not a prescription for every society at all times. However, there is more to be said for it many times, and particularly in modern times, than for its polar opposite. Civil societies maximise the chances of having non-predatory relationships among strangers, and there is a lot to be said for that. A large and complex society, full of strangers or at least non-intimates, is a terrible place to be if the alternatives to intimacy are hostility, suspicion, distrust. And so civility is a negative virtue of a very precious sort.

But it is more than that. For civil societies can do far more than neutralise the environment. If we move beyond what is necessary for a society to survive to what might make it thrive, civil association is central. When civil societies are vital and active they will be full of chosen engagements among people, associations, clubs, partnerships. People will band together to take initiatives, to hold governments accountable, to constitute something more robust, articulated and energetic than the 'sack of potatoes' which Marx once derided. Recent studies, such as the now famous book by Robert Putnam, *Making Democracy Work: Civic Traditions in Modern Italy,* show the character and importance of such strong and healthy voluntary social associations and the contribution they can make both to social health and to government performance.

More generally, not only is civility better than incivility, when non-intimates meet, but it is immensely productive. For it affords a particular and salutary way of dealing with a predicament in which all members of modern and large societies find themselves. That predicament has been stated most succinctly by the eighteenth-century Scottish economist Adam Smith in his *Wealth of Nations*: 'In civilised society he [man] stands at all times in need of the co-operation and assistance of great multitudes, while his whole life is scarce sufficient to gain the friendship of a few persons.' We live in a world where many people we meet cannot be our friends. It is a better world when they are not therefore automatically our enemies.

A central condition for 'co-operation and assistance of great multitudes', much discussed these days, is trust. Families and friends learn whom they trust and whom they don't over long and direct periods of exposure to each other. But great multitudes do not have the same opportunities. Their co-operation depends on the possibility of trust among people who don't and can't know each other intimately but still must make judgments, however abstract, about the extent to which they can rely on each other. What that depends upon, and what it engenders, are major subjects of academic research today, among psychologists, social theorists, economists and political philosophers.

For my purposes, it is important to distinguish, more clearly than is common, the kinds of trust that might tie together members of the clan of Capulets or Montagues, respectively and in opposition to each other, from that required in a modern civil society, where individuals can pursue their self-chosen purposes in co-operation, but not necessarily in unity, with fellow citizens – and where outsiders are yet not horribly outside.

As a going concern, civil society depends upon an extraordinarily complex meshing of the activities of strangers, or at least non-intimates, who co-exist in routine co-operation and interaction. This certainly depends upon trust but that is not enough to say. Some kinds of trust are found in any form of human association. Some are of particular relevance to relationships among intimates; others to relationships among strangers. Some forms co-exist more easily than others. For many societies are decidedly not civil, even though in most societies, someone trusts someone. In some, trust among intimates tapers gently into the cooler trust of acquaintances or even strangers. In others, there are sharp boundaries to the former, and the latter is in small supply. Some are more conducive to civil society; some less. Indeed, all societies depend upon trust, but many forms of trust are quite inimical to civility; indeed as inimical as many forms of distrust. What is distinctive of modern *civil* societies is a particular, and historically very rare, kind of trust among non-intimates; what has been called 'social' or 'impersonal' trust, and what I will call civil trust.

Civil trust does not require love, nor even necessarily friendship, but it does require the ability, routinely and undramatically, to make presumptions of confidence and reliability about people one doesn't know too well.

That trust might be mistaken, and sensible people will worry about that. Therefore it is never clever to trust everyone, whatever the circumstances. Nor is it socially healthy. Nor does civility require it. If – as we know occurs – hostages come to trust their murderous captors, or slaves their exploiters, they should be freed, and then they should see a doctor. Less extremely, it is often appropriate to distrust people who have amassed a great deal of power, or offer to sell you a used car or teach you Hungarian in five easy lessons. As the American political theorist Stephen Holmes once pointed out to me, in an attempt to temper some of my fashionable enthusiasm for trust: 'a distrust-less society is sick.' Perhaps that is why we have the expression 'healthy distrust'. But not every sort of distrust is healthy, and in the context of civil society some sorts of distrust are pathological.

In civil society, it is reasonable to trust people who one reasonably believes will behave civilly. This is rarely everyone, but if it is no one the society is in very bad shape. Indeed if it is really no one, there is no society. That was Thomas Hobbes's point. And if it is just those who are part of your real or extended family or ethnic group, where there is more than one family or group, there is a divided society. That was Shakespeare's point.

A society cannot just ask people, and it certainly cannot order them, to trust each other. Well, it can ask and it can order, but it is unlikely to be successful. People need reasons to trust others, and on a macro-scale, where we don't know all the others, those reasons are generated by the large frameworks of social life. Civil trust is conditional, and in a large and complex society the conditions are themselves many and complex. They include social traditions, mores, 'habits of the heart'. They also have to do with the level and distribution of wealth and poverty, urbanity in every sense, education, and, crucially, with the nature and quality of public institutions, such as the state and law.

So one issue, to which the next essay turns, concerns the institutional underpinnings of civil societies and the trust on which they depend. This raises questions of social and political theory and explanation which are as difficult as they are important. But the question of how we treat others in our society also bears a moral dimension.

Civility already has a strong moral implication, which has been nicely captured in the remark of the sociologist Christopher Bryant that it 'remains a fundamentally democratic idea. Courtesy was for the court; gentility was for the gentry; civility is for all citizens.' One might add that it is very far from servility, which is apt, if at all, only for servants.

*1997*

# The Good That Governments Do

According to Yogi Berra, that celebrated baseballer and sage, when you reach a fork in the road you should take it. A recurrent theme of these essays has been that this is wise advice. Too often we are pressed to make false choices between alternatives which are both attractive and compatible with each other. Among those I have discussed are realism and idealism, fear and hope, survival and flourishing, individual and community, ethnics and Australians, symbols and practice, pride and shame. There is room for them all, and an important place for each.

Another dichotomy falsely deployed in many guises today is that between society and the state. The problem does not lie in the distinction itself. For central to that package deal we call modernity is precisely the differentiation between public institutions – with their own offices, procedures, personnel and ethos – and societies made up of ever more far-flung but interconnected citizens. Public bodies are linked institutionally and also – if we are lucky – by a real or ideal ethos of public service; members of a society needn't be. The former make and enforce the laws; the latter make use of and obey them, more or less. The former raise taxes, the latter pay them. Of course, the former and the latter are intimately interwoven, but in principle and to a large extent in practice they can be distinguished. Or so observers of the centralisation of states and unification of societies over the last two or three hundred years have claimed.

No, the difficulty lies elsewhere, in two related tendencies of much modern thought. One such tendency is to disdain what the state does and must do. The other is to represent society and the state as locked in a sort of zero-sum game in which one gains only at the other's expense. Each of these tendencies is readily understandable and occasionally appropriate. In general, however, both are dangerously misleading.

I believe that these ways of thinking about interrelationships between societies and states should be resisted or at least rethought. Perhaps, in the Australian manner, they should be turned upside down. For the state is indispensable for many of the things we value most in society. And relations between society and the state are not properly viewed as zero-sum encounters at all, at least not when they are in good shape. On the contrary, power, state, law and civil society are entwined in mutually reinforcing virtuous circles – or so they will be if things are as they ought to be. Our circumstances are not always happy so we must always be on the watch against pathologies in the relationships between society and state, but we should not take the pathology for the norm. Otherwise, our prophecies will threaten to be self-fulfilling and mutually reinforcing, and pathologies will become normal.

States protect us from terrible evils and so they should be valued. They have potential to do special evils of their own, so they must be restrained. And there are goods that only they can do, and these should be encouraged. None of these propositions is inconsistent with the others, so one can respect them all. But not everyone does.

There is no difficulty in understanding why the state should have become such a prominent target of hostility. States are huge today and involved in heaps. In the past couple of centuries they have become increasingly so. Over millennia, for example, the political lexicon had a stable collection of -*archies* and -*ocracies*: monarchy, oligarchy, anarchy; democracy, aristocracy, plutocracy. In the mid-eighteenth century, *bureaucracy* was added by an enterprising Frenchman to whom the phrase *laissez faire, laissez passer* is also attributed. In no time, both the word and the phrase swept into vogue in almost every European language, the former usually as a term of abuse, the latter as a counsel of good sense. The trouble was, critics repeatedly complained, bureaucracies never stopped growing and the last thing they were inclined to do was *laisser faire*.

Bureaucracies increased vastly in size, activity, scope, power and ambition throughout the nineteenth century, and exponentially in the welfare states of the twentieth. In the West, states do more, employ more, cost more, give more, take more, than any preceding states ever have. For much of this century, the communist East was dominated by states wielding unprecedented despotic power. In neither the West nor the East, it may be euphemistically observed, have all citizens been completely happy with the quality of their societies. One convenient, and often appropriate, explanation for their dissatisfaction focuses on the quality of their states, or, more generally, of states as such.

All the more since one can always ask what on earth the state has ever produced. That is not a foolish question, but the answer to it is less straightforward than it seems. Many people think the answer is obvious and short: nothing much. My own answer is only slightly longer: more than you think.

We are still in the throes of reaction against two forms of state-centred optimism which have dominated public life for much of this century. One of them, the communist experiment, failed ignominiously, and people have drawn from that certain lessons, about societies and states. The other, the Welfare State, failed to live up to some extravagant expectations of those who built it, and parallel lessons have been drawn here. The confluence of these two less-than-success stories of state-focused transformation has produced a remarkably confident belief that the state does little that is good and much that is bad. If we cannot do without it, we should at least not do much with it. All the more since the civil society movement has rediscovered society. That's where the money is made, and that – so many people believe – is where we should put our money too. In liberal democracies such as our own, many influential people have come to believe that the Welfare State has loaded the wrong sort of objectives on the wrong sort of institutions with the wrong results. They call for the state to retreat. I think these are the wrong lessons to draw from these histories, but they are not contemptible lessons. They are, as is so often the case, examples of real insights being pushed further than they can or should reach.

In the communist world, aversion to the state was profound, understandable and appropriate. Communist states were the only example in history to combine what Ernest Gellner brilliantly described as 'Caesaro-Papist-Mammonism', that is, the ambition to control the whole of politics, thought, and economy. For a long time they went a good distance toward achieving this ambition. Communism, dissidents came to argue passionately and correctly, had been an attempt – more or less successful – to crush civil society. Both as a matter of ideological principle and in practice, the communist state was distinguished from any other by its relentless hostility to the existence of spheres of social life independent of the state, and by its consequent determination to subordinate all such spheres to state control. No other system of government sought so completely to obliterate institutions and activities independent of the state and to fill the space with itself. This absence of empty social space made the state at the same time very hard to escape and to resist. Among other things, it meant that sources of social strength and diversity could not develop, while state-imposed sources of social weakness and uniformity flourished. One response to that incubus – sometimes terrifying, sometimes simply surreal in its obstructive incompetence – was to think of how to liberate society from it. And so arose the ideology of civil society, which was pitted directly against the communist state.

Dissidents rightly believed that in what they called 'normal' countries, things were different. Relations among citizens were – if not absolutely then to a very great degree – legitimately innocent of political significance and interference, or they could be if participants chose. Their shape and purpose were matters of decentralised social choice and not centralised political command. Not everything was the state's business, and to a considerable extent the state minded its own business. *Solidarity* in Poland, we were told, was a movement of the restoration, rebirth, perhaps even creation, of civil society. But this wasn't civil society on foundations provided by the state but was pre-eminently a movement of 'civil society *against* the state'.

The discourse of civil society that emerged from these movements came, as we have seen, to sweep the world. It is a discourse for which I have the highest regard. The contrast between a society independent of the state, and one which is chewed and swallowed up by it, is indeed crucial. But independence can be understood in two very different ways: on the one hand, as a distinction between parts of an organism – bone and muscle, say – or as a distinction between hostile forces. When a civil society is in good shape, and the state provides indispensable support for it, the distinction is of the first sort; when the civil society is weak and/or the state is seeking to crush it, the second sense applies. Though in practice the situation will often be mixed, it is important not to blur the distinction in principle.

But it has been blurred, and not only by those who speak of civil society. Welfare states have not collapsed, but they have often disappointed the expectations of their supporters, and encouraged the hostility of their critics. Often they have worked on the assumption that government responsibilities should be fulfilled by government provision and delivery of services, and such provision and delivery have often, and notoriously, left a lot to be desired. A common response has been to deny not merely that government is an ideal agency for the delivery of all things, but also that governments have significant and indispensable responsibilities over what should be delivered and how. The common lesson drawn from weaknesses in the welfare state is that the market not the state should rule.

As the failures of the Soviet dictatorships became impossible to ignore, many on the Western left turned their hopes away from the state toward 'new social movements', such as the Greens, or citizen actions of various sorts in civil society. Many of these people, sometimes more in sorrow than in anger, started to explore non-state options since the state often seemed not to deliver what they wanted and to deliver what they didn't want.

On the right, the failure of the Soviet project seemed only to confirm what they already had concluded about the welfare state: one should put one's faith in markets not states, 'spontaneous' activities from below, not 'planned' ones from above, the 'productive' private sector not the wasteful and parasitic public one. More in glee than in sorrow, economic rationalists have devoted great energies to filleting governments and trying to get what remains out of the way. The main task of government was to 'get off our backs' and clear the space for the free market. Like Thoreau, many today start with the motto, 'that government is best which governs least,' and some would doubtless

sympathise, at least with the spirit of his extension to it: 'That government is best which governs not at all.' Both versions seem to me deep
and dangerous nonsense.

The lessons the twentieth century has to teach us about the state, as
Tony Judt puts it in an important essay, 'The Social Question
Redivivus', published in *Foreign Affairs* in 1997, are essentially two, and
neither of them is new. Rather they are:

> simply an updated version of Lord Acton's dictum: absolute state
> power destroys absolutely, and full state control of the economy
> distorts fully … We now know that some version of liberalism that
> accords the maximum of freedom and initiative in every sphere of
> life is the only possible option.

It is a pity these lessons have taken so long and so much pain to
learn, and it is good that liberal insights into the power and importance
of freedom and of markets have been relearnt, but it is important to
understand what the lessons really are. For as Judt emphasises of the
two lessons he distils, '*that is all we know,* and not everything follows
from it'. In particular, no reason to reject the state, root and branch, follows from it at all.

States differ. That is important to remember, both in the post-communist world, where attempts to build non-despotic states are currently underway, and in the democracies, where states are not despotic
but are often not full of charisma either. Since 'the state' is not one
thing, indiscriminate opposition to 'it' is as foolish as it is in some quar-
ters popular. One way of discriminating is to ask what, if anything,
states might be good for, and what sorts of states are good for that. As
always, I begin with fear and move on to hope.

First of all, as Hobbes taught, a state is necessary for minimal peace-
keeping, for without internal peace nothing but fear grows. Curbing
individual or group cruelties needs a state with the resources and
power to overwhelm anyone who might try to inflict them, and strong
enough also to resist being co-opted. That is not controversial among
devotees of the market, but they say nothing about how to achieve it
and rarely evince an appreciation of what an achievement it is, or how

much it depends on a strong state. For it is no small job. Anyone who thinks it is might enrol as an adviser to the troops trying at present, with the greatest difficulty, to keep peace in Bosnia. Try to imagine – and unfortunately we may not have to imagine – what will happen when these foreign forces go home. The bare peace that has been established is one in which people with large guns try to tell people with smaller ones what to do, or rather some things not to do. A civil peace, a liberal peace, demands by contrast, as the American liberal theorist Stephen Holmes puts it, 'that people without guns be able to tell people with guns what to do'. We are fortunate in Australia that this happens routinely and unremarkably, yet it is a remarkable and complex achievement, difficult to engineer. Australia was part of attempts to develop both sorts of peace in Somalia and in Cambodia. Notwithstanding our best efforts – and these were truly good efforts – these attempts failed, and as a result Somalians and Cambodians are not fortunate.

But there lies another notorious problem. For states that are powerful enough to do good are also powerful enough to do ill. And if that power is not restrained, odds are that they will do ill. This is Lord Acton's lesson about absolute power. Given the possibilities that modern technology makes available and modern ideologies can be deployed to justify, that can be great ill. As countless republican and liberal responses to Hobbes insisted, and as millions around the globe experience every day, such a state can prove to be everyone's everyday everpresent nightmare. It must be restrained. Central to the republican and liberal traditions are institutional measures designed to tame and civilise state power. That is common ground. But after this point there is division.

How are we to interpret these modes of constraint and restraint on public and private power? One way, which has been very influential, is in line with the widespread suspicion of states of which I have spoken. This is to interpret constitutions and law in exclusively negative fashion, as curbs on state power, guardians against despotism, shackles on the state. This tradition of what Holmes calls 'negative constitutionalism' is the most common way in which we articulate the point of such institutions. It speaks, of course, a fundamental truth of the liberalism of fear: unrestrained power, despotism, tyranny, are terrible.

They are to be avoided at all costs and constitutional restraints are key ways in which we seek to avoid them.

Liberal institutions – constitutions, bills of rights, separation of powers, the rule of law, elections and the supervisory role of courts, and so on – are, then, commonly interpreted in exclusively negative terms, as constraints on whatever they are associated with rather than as constituents of them or resources for them. And that is certainly part of the story. But to rest here is to ignore a less obvious but fundamentally important aspect of these institutional devices which is revealed in the less familiar approach to them that Holmes calls, in his book, *Passions and Constraint*, 'positive constitutionalism'.

Positive constitutionalism is concerned to stress the enabling and facilitating role of constitutional and legal institutions. The insight of this tradition, as Holmes describes it, is that:

> Limited government is, or can be, more powerful than unlimited government. The paradoxical insight that constraints can be enabling, which is far from being a contradiction, lies at the heart of liberal constitutionalism ... By restricting the arbitrary powers of government officials, a liberal constitution can, under the right conditions, *increase* the state's capacity to focus on specific problems and mobilise collective resources for common purposes.

And, as he goes on to show:

> constitutions not only limit power and prevent tyranny, they also construct power, guide it toward socially desirable ends, and prevent social chaos and private oppression, immobilism, unaccountability, instability, and the ignorance and stupidity of politicians. Constitutions are multifunctional. It is, therefore, a radical oversimplification to identify the constitutional function exclusively with the prevention of tyranny.

This regard for the positive significance of states, and for the positive point of constraints on power, needs to be brought to bear in the design and appraisal of public institutions, for its opposite – the strictly negative attitude to state power – certainly is. Just as many people distrust states in general, so people involved in institutional design often seek to implement that distrust through legal and constitutional means. The danger of this approach is that it will thwart whatever good the state can do, and that without an effective state cannot be done. For to the extent that state power can be harnessed to valuable ends, we will want not only to limit the ability of the state to do harm but maximise its ability to do good. Our institutions, just like everything else that these essays have discussed, will have to be looked at not just from the perspective of reducing our fears but also from that of securing our hopes.

The first, negative, view starts with a general suspicion of state power and sees institutional design as a way of dispersing, diluting, braking, that power. The second, positive, view is not in principle hostile to the state or averse to its exercise of power. Indeed it thinks that the state must do many things that otherwise can't be done. It is suspicious of arbitrary states, particularly those not subject to strong and regular institutional constraints, not necessarily all states. It will indeed want to strengthen state power in certain forms for certain purposes. On this second view, like an athlete who learns disciplines to marshal raw energy, so a state is at the same time and in many of the same ways, restrained and strengthened by the same limitations.

Though it has often been passed over in liberal thought, this was a point well grasped by some of the great liberal and republican thinkers about institutions. One of the greatest of them was the eighteenth-century French thinker Montesquieu, whose *Spirit of the Laws* had a profound effect on the American constitution makers and on both the liberal and republican traditions. As one of the purest exponents of the 'liberalism of fear', he insisted that moderation and restraint were primary virtues in government. Not ultimate but primary, since they are necessary conditions for the achievement of other values. Given moderation and restraint, one need not fear power, though one can hope for more than one often gets: honesty, wisdom and virtue come to mind. And one is often disappointed. Nevertheless, power which is immoderately used and abused is terrifying. And so it is better to be disappointed by moderate, than to live in fear of immoderate, exercise of power.

The whole of *The Spirit of the Laws* was bent to investigating the sources of moderation of government and recommending institutional ways to ensure it. Not, it should be emphasised, that government should be weak; only that it should be effectively and reliably restrained. Indeed Montesquieu emphasised – with profound if counter-intuitive insight – that although restrained government was not fearful, as despotism was, it was in a crucial sense stronger than any despot could be, for:

> A moderate government can, as much as it wants and without peril, relax its springs. It maintains itself by its laws, and even by its force. But when in despotic government the prince ceases for a moment to raise his arm, when he cannot instantly destroy those in the highest places, all is lost, for when the spring of the government, which is fear, no longer exists, the people no longer have a protector.

Montesquieu died in 1755, thirty-four years before the French Revolution. Yet he understood that the French king's position was in effect weaker than that of the English monarch, notwithstanding that, as Hilton Root has observed (in his *Political Foundations of Markets in Old Regime France and England*),

> At every step the absolutist ambitions of the English Crown were thwarted: consent of Parliament was needed for taxes; consent of the law courts was needed for legal enforcement of alternative revenue sources; and, most important, consent of the gentry was needed for daily implementation of monopolies.

Nevertheless, appearances were deceptive. As the same author explains,

> legislation enacted by Parliament was usually implemented, whereas the will of the much stronger executive in France was less frequently carried out. A significant implementation gap existed under absolutism ... there were no legal limits on the French king's power or, by extension that of his ministers, yet time and time again his

ministers succumbed to cabals within the court ... Despite the legal
limits on the Crown's power imposed by Parliament, the English
king managed to maintain his position and policies. It seemed to
many contemporaries that George III's ministers were more powerful and more likely to be obeyed than the unaccountable and
theoretically stronger ministers of the French king.

Not only was English government more effective than French, more
able to raise taxes, more deeply embedded in society, but the English
economy was more powerful than the French, and the people of
England were freer than the people of France. This is not an accidental
combination. And, though France had an apparently far more powerful
system of centralised rule than England, the French *ancien régime* was
swept aside in 1789, while the English system has survived with only
evolutionary change since the seventeenth century till today. The
French head of state had enormous discretionary power, which proved
worthless when his own head was removed. The English kings – after
being forced in the seventeenth century to accede to legal limitations
on their personal power – regularly died in bed.

Montesquieu's insight into the relative strengths of moderate and
despotic governments was even more prophetic than this comparison
between England and France suggests. The most dramatic recent evidence of it is the the house-of-cards collapse of the Soviet Union and
its dominions. This was one of the most despotic empires the world has
known, and almost no one apart from Montesquieu predicted its collapse. But it was not the first occasion when apparently overwhelmingly
powerful despotisms have wilted before forces which hardly seemed up
to the task. Like the collapse of communism, the French and Russian
revolutions, the end of the Marcos regime, the fall of the Shah, all
seemed overdetermined – overly supplied with causes – after the event.
But they revealed that extraordinary fragility of despotisms which
keeps taking us by surprise. It shouldn't.

Nowhere was this more true than of the collapse of communism.
In the truly epochal contest of this century between the apparently
overwhelming power of totalitarian states – fascism and communism –
and the liberal societies which they opposed, the totalitarians fell – this

second time almost without even being pushed – and the latter didn't. Fascism and communism collapsed in turn, in defeat and humiliation. By contrast, as I argue in 'Conservative-Liberal-Socialism Revisited', liberal democracies, 'have kept plodding on, in their prosaic, tepid way, becoming over the century wealthier, stronger, freer, and, in most cases, more just'.

One familiar way of interpreting this difference is in terms of the stark dichotomy between society and the state, which I have been criticising. On this view, Soviet society and economy were smothered by an excessively large and strong state, and ours were relatively free because our states were smaller and weaker. There was less they could do wrong just because there was less they could do. It is only the fact that we had markets and thus a strong economic base, one might argue, that allowed us to perform better than the Soviet system which didn't have them. So, the differing fates of liberal and communist states only prove that markets are powerful, not that liberal states are. If our states were smaller and weaker than they are, our markets would be freer, and we would be even stronger.

Such a view ignores the simple fact that markets themselves, not to mention civil and decent societies, depend upon strong, not weak states, though on states which are strong in a particular way. When I first heard this argument, from Stephen Holmes, I found it hard to accept for it contradicted what I had long thought obvious. Now, however, reading the 1997 World Bank World Development Report, which makes the same point at length, only the messenger, not the message, seems surprising.

I had learnt to value civil societies by observing struggles against the overwhelming communist state. Surely the difference was that that state was awesomely strong (while it lasted) and ours was not. So how could anyone favour a strong state? This remains the view of many economic rationalists and libertarians who distrust any but the most minimal of states. Nevertheless, there are good theoretical grounds and both positive and negative evidence for supporting strong states.

States are not simply bigger or smaller; stronger or weaker. Their capacities differ qualitatively. Some states can pulverise subjects without resistance; others can't. On the other hand, some states can contribute to and draw upon the resources of hugely productive societies; others would love to, but no matter whom they shoot, the societies are still weak, unco-operative and unproductive, and ultimately so are the states. For it is important to stress that it is not only at moments of ultimate crisis that despotism is weaker than restrained government. In a major and distinctive way it is always so. This has been pointed out by a number of historical sociologists, prominent among them Australians Linda Weiss and John Hobson, who have written an excellent book, *States and Economic Development*, which demonstrates the crucial significance of state strength for economic development. They draw upon a distinction introduced by Michael Mann, in his *Sources of Social Power* and elsewhere, between what he calls *despotic* power – 'the range of actions which the elite is empowered to undertake without routine, institutionalised negotiations with civil society' – and what he calls *infrastructural* power – 'the capacity of the state to actually penetrate society, and to implement logistically political decisions throughout the realm.'

For the release and development of social and economic energies, as well as for political decency, it is infrastructural power that is crucial. Despotic states combine arbitrariness and lack of political or legal limits with chronic incapacity to mobilise social energies and make use of social potential. As a colleague of Mann's, John Hall, puts it in his *Powers and Liberties*, they sit like capstones atop the societies they dominate; they do not penetrate organically and effectively into the social structure. They dominate from above, but do little to contribute from within.

The connection between despotic strength and social weakness is not accidental. Though despots can repress effectively for a time, and mobilise for limited specialised purposes such as war, they have proved very weak in the capacity to penetrate, mobilise and facilitate energetic and resilient social forces. On the contrary, they typically seek to block them, and they stunt their development. In other terms, despotically strong states go along with weak societies. And this is centrally because of the arbitrariness and unpredictability with which they exercise power. These states are predatory and their societies are prey. They are not productive, and neither are their societies.

On the other hand, as Weiss and Hobson put it,

strong states are not only those which are able to control the population within their boundaries and thus extract the necessary material and human resources. They are also those which rely least on arbitrary and unstable forms of control such as terror or physical force.

They provide predictable, reliable frameworks of laws and trustworthy undertakings. They co-operate with major social forces in ways on which both sides can rely. They can penetrate the society without fraud and force, and extract resources from it without coercion. Rather than exercise power *over* society, strong but limited states exercise it *through* society. This had a great deal to do with the English advantage over France and most of Europe from the eighteenth century. There may, as Weiss and Hobson suggest, be a lot more that states need to do to foster strong societies in present times than once, and it may be that contemporary Britain has not kept pace precisely because its state is less adept in these new tasks than it was in the old. But what they demonstrate, in my opinion convincingly, is that the infrastructural role of states, whatever it might involve in detail in different circumstances, is indispensable for the existence of strong modern societies. Strong societies, in turn, can provide the economic base for strong states. So, power restrained is power, in crucial infrastructural senses, strengthened. It is also, of course, altogether nicer to live with.

This distinction between despotic and infrastructural power goes a long way to explaining the extraordinary development of capitalism in England under a monarch with far less despotic power than many others, but far more infrastructural embeddedness in the society. England was a despotically weak but infrastructurally strong state, certainly stronger than earlier states and stronger in crucial respects than any of its contemporaries. And the English state did not just sit around. This was true in the eighteenth century, as we have seen. More interestingly, it was even more true in the nineteenth-century heyday of British capitalism which occurred, not when the state did nothing, but when it did unprecedentedly much. As Judt noted in the piece I quoted above, in the earlier part of that century, English governments listened to *laissez faire* arguments, many of which would be familiar today. However:

after a brush with revolt during the economic depression of the 1840s, British Governments adjusted their sights and enacted a series of reforms driven in equal measure by ethical sensibilities and political prudence. By the later years of the century the erstwhile minimalist British state had set upper limits on working hours in factories, a minimum age for child employment, and regulations concerning conditions of work in a variety of industries. The vote had been granted to a majority of adult males, and the labor and political organizations that the working population had struggled to establish had been legalized – so that in time they ceased to be disruptive to the workings of capitalism and became effective sources of social integration and political stability. The result was not planned, but it is incontrovertible: British capitalism thrived not in spite of regulatory mechanisms but because of them.

England is a remarkable positive example of the importance of the contributions of powerful but limited government. We do not need to look that far back, however. For there is an exemplary negative lesson available to us today, all the more so because it occurs exactly where we learnt the very opposite lesson yesterday. The Soviet Union taught many people like me what was horrifying about totalitarian despotism. And the post-Soviet Union, as Holmes has demonstrated in an important piece on 'what Russia teaches us now', can teach us a lot about what is horrifying about weak states. Anyone who doubts the importance of state strength should give some thought to the consequences of state weakness in contemporary Russia and many other societies where the state is too weak to be much more than another front for dirty business or worse. And, as Holmes points out, 'Today's Russia makes excruciatingly plain that liberal values are threatened just as thoroughly by state incapacity as by despotic power. "Destatization" is not the solution; it is the problem.'

Russia today has a government which cannot govern. It cannot collect taxes, both because it has an enormous black and grey economy and its tax collectors get shot. It cannot defend individual rights because its officials are so poorly paid (or not paid), its laws so ignored, its courts so jammed, that no arm of state can insist on respect for rights, even if there was a will to do so. Often there is not. The state is a vast resource for private-public entrepreneurs to exploit, and it has little capacity, nor its officials much incentive, to resist such exploitation. Power is not in it, though there are times when one *mafioso* or other can augment his own power through it. Many of those *mafiosi* are in positions of political power; others don't bother. And that is not only the state's problem. It is everyone's. The government no longer persecutes its citizens, but it cannot do much to stop others from persecuting them, or to help them if they have been persecuted, or cheated, or evicted or ... There are many reasons for this, but one overwhelming one is that the Russian government is broke. To quote Holmes again:

> The Russian government cannot protect basic rights for the same reason that it cannot provide such elementary public goods as a nontoxic environment, books in elementary schools, x-ray film in public hospitals, veterans' benefits, a nationwide highway system, railroad maintenance, and potable water. It cannot protect rights because it cannot target extracted resources to the provision of public goods. Courts are working, it is true, but judicial dockets are chronically backlogged because budgetary outlays earmarked for the judiciary are pitiful and often do not arrive. The dependency of basic rights on tax revenues helps us see that rights are public goods. Far from being walls bricking out the meddlesome state, even the so-called negative rights are taxpayer-funded and government-managed social services designed to improve collective and individual well-being.

The good news is that Russian markets are free and spontaneity rules, OK. Before we applaud that, however, we should ponder Holmes's question:

> How should we reassess the celebration of 'free markets' and 'spontaneous exchange' when we observe totally unregulated markets in ground-to-air missiles and other lethal leftovers of the Soviet arsenal? And what about 'pluralism', 'decentralization',

'countervailing powers', 'private associations', and the 'independence of the society from the state'?

The point of all these examples is not to attack the Russian government, nor even to sympathise with it. Still less to hanker for the old
regime which left this decaying, disorganised and demoralised mess. It
is to remind us of the frivolous superficiality of much of our contemporary anti-state rhetoric. The proper contrast with a despotic state is
not a minimal state, for any liberal state has a lot to do, and certainly
not a weak one, but one whose power is infrastructural – strong and
limited and in part strong because limited. Institutionalised channelling of power, rather than its emasculation, is, thus, a key to both
strong *and* decent political orders.*

What governments do well is a complex question, and there is no
one-size-fits-all answer to it. Certainly 'nothing much' is not that
answer. And the stakes are high, for as the World Bank has recently
observed, 'good government is not a luxury – it is a vital necessity for
development.' It is clear from the evidence in the report that governments have extensive responsibilities, not merely to make and enforce
laws, but also to invest in basic social services and infrastructure, to
protect the vulnerable and to protect the environment – not as a
monopoly provider of everything but as an indispensable 'partner, cat-
alyst, and facilitator', an overseer, regulator, stimulator and investor.
How these complex tasks are to be discharged is not obvious, and controversy will continue to rage over what precisely states should do, what
roles they should play, and how they should play them. What is not a
useful controversy, however, is whether they should play them at all.

Central to what states and only states can do, of course, is make and
enforce law, and since that is a matter dear to me, let me conclude with
some remarks about it. To turn this essay full circle, legal and constitutional channelling of power both empowers states by increasing their

---

* In the years since this essay was written, it appears that Russia's President, Vladimir
Putin, has got the message that Russia suffers from chronic state weakness.
Unfortunately he has interpreted that message in precisely the wrong, but typically
Russian way: he appears determined to rebuild the Russian state's *despotic* strength,
rather than tend to its infrastructural potential.

credibility, legitimacy and effectiveness, and it empowers something else which is impossible without it. That is something of which I – like those I have criticised – am very fond: civil society itself.

This significance of law is often totally ignored by contemporary writers on civil society, or is merely acknowledged in a phrase, but it was not ignored by their predecessors. Many writers have observed, from at least the seventeenth century onwards, that legal institutions and legal rights are central to an established civil society: for it to be able to moderate – stably, routinely and effectively – the powers of government and the powers of each other.

Civil society is buttressed by impersonal institutions of many kinds, in particular impersonal legal institutions. Impersonal institutions are, roughly, institutions which are not 'owned' by anyone, which act with relative autonomy from other sources of social power. Impersonally reliable law and legal entitlements provide strangers with important sources of security against each other and against the state, but also with information about each other, with bargaining chips in their relations with each other, with information about the likely responses of official agencies and with assurances of the possibility of enforcement if trust proves misplaced. These are assets of inestimable value, without which a civil society cannot be imagined.

More generally, so is the rule of law, as I have discussed in other essays here, particularly 'The Grammar of Colonial Legality'. There is more to the rule of law than this, but there is at least this much: you have central elements of the rule of law when the law in general does not take you by surprise or keep you guessing, when legal institutions are relatively independent of other significant social actors but not of legal doctrine, and when the powerful forces in society, including the government, are required to act, and come in significant measure to think, within the law; when the limits of what we imagine our options to be are set by the law and where these limits are widely taken seriously – when the law has integrity and it matters what the law allows and what it forbids.

The rule of law – not merely *a* rule of law but *the* rule of law, the channelling and restraint of power by legal means – is the overarching goal of liberal political and legal institutions and practices. The rule of law requires that the exercise of power should be challengeable by law, and that in general it should be exercised according to laws which are knowable in advance and which can be relied upon to be enforced according to their tenor. It also makes it possible for fellow citizens to know a good deal about each other, though many of them are strangers; to co-ordinate their actions with them; and to feel some security and predictability in their dealings with them. For the rule of law, like the rules of chess, does not make everything predictable, but ties down much that would otherwise be up for grabs. In large civil societies, where ties of kinship, locality and mutual surveillance cannot bind, reassure or inform, the impersonal force of the rule of law is crucial. One of the major sources of wholesale (and lingering) distrust among strangers in communist states, among others, was the absence of the rule of law in this sense.

The rule of law is fragile, never perfectly attained, no panacea, and not the only thing we want from law. But the difference between on the one hand polities in which law counts, and counts as a restraint on power, and on the other hand those in which it does not, is a fundamental one. Many people who enjoy the rule of law don't know their luck. However, in large societies with powerful states, those who don't enjoy it are missing something special, and many of them know it and have fought for it.

Manifestly, the rule of law is inconsistent with arbitrary rule, and therefore with despotic license. It is not, however, inconsistent with infrastructural strength. On the contrary, in large and complex societies it is prerequisite for it, just as it is for social strength. Despots have many reasons to want to keep citizens in fear, to take them by surprise, to keep them anxious about what might happen next. A government which is able thus systematically to violate the rule of law cannot successfully provide infrastructures within which people plan and frame their expectations. Or if it does, these will be bleak plans and miserable expectations. For a civil society cannot successfully endure either such insecurity or lack of cognitive control.

Much in the Australian legal structure is imbued with, and exemplifies, rule of law values and the values of constitutionalism. There are laws that govern a great deal of political behaviour; a written Constitution which defines and sets limits to what can be legally done

by the institutions of state; a judiciary whose competence and independence are defined and enshrined in laws; and a partial separation of
legal competences, based on a kind of mini-Montesquieuan mix of the
English system he praised and misdescribed and the more strict
American separation of powers, in part inspired by that misdescrip-
tion. There are many other legally defined checks and balances, too,
among them the federal system, with legally independent states that
have their own constitutions, legislatures, bureaucracies, courts and
police. And – no small matter – there is money to pay for them. There
are rules for accession to power, rules that circumscribe the exercise of
power and rules for the transfer of power. At present there is a national
debate over whether we should become a republic, and there is therefore attendant discussion about whether to change some of the constitutional rules. A major item in that discussion is how such changes can
be accommodated within the existing rules of change.

More deeply, there are profound differences between political
orders where law counts, in popular imagination and in fact, and those
where it does not. Who, for example, thought of reaching for his
revolver when Mr Whitlam was sacked in 1975? The answer, of course,
is virtually no one at all. What an extraordinary answer that is, in a
struggle over the highest political stakes. In many countries, the answer
would – equally obviously – have been: everyone who counts. And
when we learn from Hansard that one of our leaders considers his
opponents to be vermin, no one imagines that he plans to exterminate
them, or they him. That too is not a fact of nature. Since it is not, it is
better not to call opponents vermin, but treat them civilly, because we
don't know how great the distance between calling people vermin and
treating them like vermin is. At the moment, however, we haven't covered that distance. Of course, states and societies range widely across a
broad spectrum in these matters, but if Australia is clearly close to one
end, Russia and many other states are equally clearly closer to the other.
These are differences of fundamental importance. It makes no sense to
sum them up by saying simply that we suffer from more constraints
than they do.

For law, and a culture where it is assumed to count for something,
are useful not merely in avoiding catastrophe. James Madison, one of

that extraordinary group of American statesmen who crafted the Constitution of the United States, wrote that if we were angels we wouldn't need any laws. Unfortunately, so the familiar argument goes, we aren't so we do. In similar vein, the great German philosopher Immanuel Kant wrote that:

> The problem of organising a state, however hard it may seem, can be solved even for a race of devils, if only they are intelligent.

However, even a race of angels would benefit from the rule of law. For even angels can become confused and lose their way. And even angels can benefit from knowing – and knowing in common – what they and others are entitled to do. The rule of law is important because it communicates important information about these things, and because it establishes fixed and knowable points in the landscape, on the basis of which the strangers who routinely interact in modern societies can do so with some security, autonomy and ability to choose. It can help provide a relatively stable framework within which, and on the basis of which, we can get on with our lives. Like the rules of a game. It is on this basis, though of course not on this basis alone, that it is possible to envisage a vibrant and rich civil society. The rule of law helps allay fear, and it makes the space clear in which, and provides resources with which, we can pursue our hopes.

A civil society depends upon the rule of law, since without it there are too many things to be frightened of in encounters among strangers. A decent society depends upon it, too, since a government can only treat its citizens with respect if it acts in relation to them on the basis of laws which they can know and use to guide their own acts. But decency requires that governments do more than provide a minimal legal infrastructure, and so – as I earlier argued, and as the World Bank has so thoroughly documented – does basic economic development. Moreover, decency requires that states go further even than facilitating economic growth. It requires that the special problems of those groups left behind, dislocated, bewildered and victimised by economic transformations – transformations themselves often encouraged by the state – be attended to as matters of moral, and not merely prudential (electoral), priority. As Tony Judt has stressed, however, 'What makes all this difficult is that it is a job for the state, and *that* is hard to accept because the desirability of placing the maximum possible restrictions upon the interventionary capacities of the state has become the cant of our time.'

Resolute opponents of state power can accept the facilitative account of law I have given, and often do. They would only reject my last claim, that decency requires that governments do more than stay within and support the rule of law. This is in part a substantive disagreement, and I will say something about the morality of this disagreement in 'Conservative Liberal Socialism Revisited'. Here, let me speak only to it as it bears on the nature and limits of legitimate state action. Supporters of 'minimal' states agree that some sorts of legal activity are necessary for the state to support civil societies, but these are merely protective, negative; not active types of activity. They distinguish these laudable and modest state activities from the more intrusive and immodest ones of modern welfare states. But on what ground can this distinction be made?

It is common to distinguish between classical liberal rights – so-called negative rights, rights against interference – and more socialistic welfare rights which depend on state provision. Traditional liberals are comfortable with the former, and worry that the latter draws upon the state altogether too much. However, even the most classical of the liberal rights depend on very substantial state provision. Markets and private property, not to mention contract, copyright, corporations, are products of systematic state interference in society. They exist owing to laws which enforce certain rules and not others, embody certain images of social interaction and not others, penalise certain behaviours and reward others. None of this is small game, and none of it involves simply tracking and backing autonomous social activity. What form this activity takes, what consequences it will have, what is to be tracked and what to be backed, and how, and with what implications, are all state decisions. How effectively any of this happens depends on state solvency, integrity, institutional design, trained personnel, and an ethos of office which can withstand the variety of corruptions that high stakes will, without counteraction, attract.

Think what the state must provide just to allow citizens the potential to sue each other, let alone the state itself. And then to expect, and then to get, a fair trial. And then to have a decision enforced. None of these rights is just a negative protection, freedom *from* interference by others. They are constituted by state decisions, underwritten by state provision, and made good by state intervention, on good legal cause proven by state-sanctioned methods in state institutions. They are, as Holmes insists, entitlements to state action; just as welfare rights are. And, like welfare rights, they are hollow without such action. As Holmes has observed, in yet another piece which has influenced me:

> the principal lesson of the end of communism is not that state power endangers liberal rights, but *exactly the contrary,* that liberal rights are wholly unrealizable without effective extractive, administrative, regulative, and adjudicative authorities. Rights protection and enforcement depend on state capacities. Statelessness, therefore, means rightlessness.

So, there is a lot for states to do. One needs a state strong enough to do what it must, and restrained enough not to do what it must not. Therein lies the point and virtue of long liberal and republican political traditions of institutional design, whose central aim is not to emasculate, but to limit, restrain and channel the exercise of governmental power. In these circumstances, and from this perspective, the various liberal nostrums that we know so well – limited government, the rule of law, an independent judiciary, a free press, and so on – have the twofold importance of allowing governments the strength they need, while requiring that at all points they act through channels, and in ways, and under the watch of other forces, which might institutionalise restraint on the exercise of power. Such institutionalisation makes power at the same time safer and more effective.

Too much zeal in either direction is misplaced. Certainly, the various categorical distinctions we use to keep the state at bay – society/state; small/big; negative/positive; allowing/providing; civil rights versus welfare rights; rights *against* versus rights *from* – cannot provide any sort of sharp-edged distinguishing mark between what states should and shouldn't do. The important thing is that they do good things and do them well.

Doing good is a matter of values. Doing well is a matter of detailed real world investigation of what works, how and when, and of proper comparison with available and always imperfect alternatives. And then, values again. As a result of such investigations, comparisons and evaluations, we might well conclude that states should do less or other than they presently do, but that must come at the end, not the beginning of the investigation. It is evident, today even notorious, that modern states do many foolish, wasteful and counter-productive things, and many things that would be better done by others. But one has to demonstrate that they are foolish, wasteful and so on. It is not enough to presume that they are, simply because the state is doing them.

*1997*

# In Praise of Prejudice

In 'Gypsies, the Law and Me', I recount my experience of being robbed by a group of gypsy women, in clear daylight, outside a Warsaw hotel, in full view of plenty of people, without a single threatening gesture being employed. As it happened I was listening, somewhat bewildered but unprotesting, to the telling of my fortune.

What happened, I'm afraid to say, was a remarkable example of psychological games played by experienced players at the expense of a fool. In short: they knew what they were doing and what I would do. I didn't. They bewildered and disarmed me with beguiling chatter, and played on my (predictable-to-them) wish not to give offence by showing mistrust, to get me to show them the money I was carrying. All the while, as my fortune was being revealed to me so it was to them. And then one of them relieved me of it.

When I sought help from the doorman of the hotel, he brushed me off until he discovered that I was an Australian, and thus bizarrely naive about what he imagined 'everyone in Europe' knows: be careful around gypsies keen to make your acquaintance. He recognised in me that rare thing: a person innocent of relevant prejudices and therefore ready to be taken for a ride.

The next day, I was talking to a sociologist friend about the incident and he said: 'It's funny. We spend a great deal of our time trying to disabuse our students of their standard stereotypes and prejudices. Yet, if you'd just had the normal prejudices of a Polish peasant, you'd never have got into this mess.'

Now that's not the end of the story, of course. After all, many of 'the normal prejudices of a Polish peasant' are not a pretty sight. And so many prejudices are distasteful in the extreme: ignorant, hurtful, indeed unjustifiably *prejudicial* to their often innocent subjects. Yet are prejudices always and only like that? If not, can we tell the difference? More worrying, even, can we do without them?

Prejudice has a bad press. No one, not even a card-carrying bigot, admits to it. Prejudices, everyone agrees, are bad things for people to have. Fortunately none of us has them, only others do.

Why this automatic anti-prejudice prejudice? One reason is that prejudices are taken typically to involve negative judgments of others, particularly other groups, ethnic, religious or whatever. It's not immediately obvious why this should be so.

Consider the word. If you take it apart, it speaks of 'pre-judgments', presumably judgments made in advance of concrete reasoned appraisal of the facts judged. But such pre-judgments could be about anything, not just about other groups, and there seems to be no reason in principle why they need be negative.

One could imagine pre-judgments that were neutral or positive about others; but the general assumption built into our use of the word is otherwise. And so we assume that if someone is prejudiced, she is full of pre-judgments unfavourable to others. Since they are *pre*-judgments, we assume further that they derive from general pre-reflective images of their objects or of people of their sort, *stereotypes*. And that too is a word that is assumed to be negative, though it is not clear why this assumption, or that it's a good idea.

But hostility to prejudice cannot just stem from the belief that pre-judgments are negative judgments. After all, we are hostile to convicted rapists, and with good reason. But there's the difference. Prejudices are thought not to be good reasons, both because they're not good and, above all, because they're thought not to be the product of *reason* at all. They precede and many would say supersede reason. And the modern world, if not its postmodern critics, sets a lot of store by reason.

Those history textbooks which rip the guts out of complex histories, with portmanteau phrases like 'the age of reason', are not all wrong. There is, after all, something in the label-description, if one wants to get a handle on one of the central and dominant motifs of the dawn of the modern age.

That age, a.k.a. the Enlightenment, set great store by reason, as do we, its heirs. In his short essay 'What is Enlightenment?', the great eighteenth-century philosopher Immanuel Kant characterised enlightenment as 'man's release from his self-incurred tutelage' which in turn was his 'inability to make use of his understanding without direction from another'. The release, put simply, consisted in thinking for yourself. That is *thinking*, and *for yourself*. Both elements mattered to Kant. Custom, tradition, authority, religion and so on, which had guided the unenlightened for so many generations were rejected both because they were derived from others, present and past, and therefore not exercises of our *autonomy*, and because they substituted for the exercise of our reason, rather than stemming from it. The motto he attributed to the Enlightenment, and which he adopted, was *sapere aude,* dare to know; 'Have courage to use your own reason.' And he did.

But the Enlightenment didn't have it all its own way. Compare Kant with his conservative Anglo-Irish contemporary Edmund Burke, in his *Reflections on the Revolution in France*:

> You see, Sir, that in this enlightened age I am bold enough to confess that we are generally men of untaught feelings: that, instead of casting away all our old prejudices, we cherish them because they are prejudices; and the longer they have lasted, and the more generally they have prevailed, the more we cherish them. We are afraid to put men to live and trade each on his own private stock of reason; because we suspect that the stock in each man is small, and that the individuals would do better to avail themselves of the general bank and capital of nations and of ages. Many of our men of speculation, instead of exploding general prejudices, employ their sagacity to discover the latent wisdom which prevails in them. If they find what they seek (and they seldom fail) they think it more wise to continue the prejudice, with the reason involved, than to cast away the coat of prejudice, and to leave nothing but the naked reason; because prejudice, with its reason, has a motive to give action to that reason, and

an affection which will give it permanence. Prejudice is of ready application in an emergency; it previously engages the mind in a steady course of wisdom and virtue, and does not leave the man hesitating in the moment of decision, skeptical, puzzled, and unresolved. Prejudice renders a man's virtue his habit, and not a series of unconnected acts. Through just prejudice, his duty becomes a part of his nature.

What Kant insists upon as the distinctive human virtue – the autonomous exercise of reason – is what Burke is most sceptical about. And 'sceptical' is a key word in this context. Sceptics of this sort aren't confident of the ability of reason to guide us unaided through the ways of the world, or to lead us to our own benefit. They don't believe we're that smart.

Their thinking goes like this: existing values, cultures, traditions, institutions, practices, help us make our way in a world so complex and fraught with risk that we need all the help we can get. They embody pre-formed responses to recurrent problems and circumstances. They enable some things and disable others. They are often the products of long histories, and are embedded in everyday ways of thinking, behaving, valuing and, yes, in prejudices. They are depositories of congealed knowledge, meaning and, on occasion, wisdom. They are familiar and, if we are lucky, they are good. Anyway, good enough. Those who deny or ignore them are bound to get a lot of things wrong, and waste a lot of time into the bargain.

A thinker of this sceptical disposition is likely to regard an open mind as an empty one. The fact is that we don't generally have open minds. Moreover, on those rare occasions when we do, the consequences are not always salutary. Or so my Polish encounter might suggest.

And it's not only counter-Enlightenment conservatives who are sceptical of the powers of our autonomous reasoning. As I've presented it so far, the dispute between Enlightenment devotees of individual reason, and counter-Enlightenment thinkers fond of what they see as the accumulation of wisdom in prejudices, is an *evaluative* dispute: what is a better basis for decision: prejudice or reason? But endorsement of prejudice goes deeper than merely matters of taste and choice.

Consider the observation of the English philosopher A. N. Whitehead, one of the great reasoners, that thought is the cavalry charge of the intellect. Cavalry charges are undoubtedly fine things, but you need a lot else to win a war. And we too draw on many things besides conscious thought, among them habits, customs and prejudices.

Moreover, it is not just a matter of how *individuals* get on. Emile Durkheim, one of the fathers of sociology, observes that 'a society without prejudices would resemble an organism without reflexes.' Consider his stress, and that of all sociology, on the importance of *socialisation* in every society. What does socialisation do? It fills us up with *pre-judgments*, that is quite literally prejudices, which we depend upon and without which we would be helpless or harmful or both, in any society. These pre-judgments have precisely the characteristics that Kant distrusted – we don't invent them and we don't think our way to them – but we are and need to be full of them. And when a sociologist talks of socialisation, he doesn't think societies have a *choice* whether to do it or not: all societies do it and no society can do without it. And so we're all programmed with prejudices.

So we have two sorts of arguments for not condemning prejudice, one evaluative – reason *shouldn't* be our sole guide in living a life – and a second psychological or sociological – reason *isn't* our sole guide and, like it or not, our psyches and societies being as they are, it *can't* be. There is yet a third ground: the exercise of reason itself starts with, and depends on, prejudice. According to the German philosopher Hans-Georg Gadamer, 'there is one prejudice of the enlightenment that is essential to it: the fundamental prejudice of the enlightenment is the prejudice against prejudice itself, which deprives tradition of its power.' It is, however, a false prejudice. We all begin our reasoning some time, some place. We are all situated beings, our understandings flowing from within the traditions and the prejudices of our time and place. There is no view from nowhere.

There is simply no way out of it and no simple way round it. Prejudices inform our every reasoning, give us the topics we are concerned with, the questions we ask, the answers we are likely to find satisfactory, the horizons within which we reason. They might limit what we can understand, but equally they inform our understanding, provide resources, latent knowledge and meaning, paradigms, and so on. Other times, other places, other prejudices, never no prejudice.

Just to allay your prejudices, let me assure you that I'm a nice guy. I don't like the sorts of things that others who attack prejudices don't like. But if there is anything in these three sorts of viewpoints, then what are nice people to do? Are we to appreciate bigotry, applaud anti-semitism? Well, no. Many prejudices are evil and cause evil. Whatever orientation they give us comes at great price. I suspect, though, that the bill is often sent to the wrong address. Here are three observations about where the bill should go.

First, we should be clear about what we are opposed to. I am opposed to dysfunctional families, exploitative sex and bad food, but I like families, sex and food. So we need to distinguish between prejudices that are fruitful in orienting us in a complex world, and those that are noxious.

It is the *character* of the prejudice that matters. Bad prejudices are bad because they're bad, not just because they're prejudices. But when prejudices are bad, and especially when bigots treat their prejudices as unimpeachable, their badness is, as it were, overdetermined, rendered bad by their particular character and difficult to disabuse by reason, since they are not based on reason.

One of the commonest defects of harmful prejudices is that they encourage us to be what Avishai Margalit calls 'human blind'. As we saw in 'The Character of the Nation', Margalit points out that 'human-blindness' does not mean failing literally to see people, but rather failing to 'perceive the human aspect in a human being', seeing them 'under a physical description without the capacity to see them under a psychological one', *overlooking* them.

Typically this is not an individual decision, where you size someone up and decide to see through them. More common is what Margalit calls 'mediated rejection', rejection of the groups to which people belong and through them individual members of those groups. Colonised people, servants, other races, are commonly categorised according to some general attribute they share or are thought to share. Often those attributes are furnished by commonly held and unquestioned preju-dices, that authorise us to then 'see through' countless members of particular groups, to attribute incompetence to them, to treat them at best patronisingly, at worst genocidally, but in either case and all the cases in between, humiliatingly. Racial and other prejudices are common ways in which these forms of rejection are rendered respectable, even unnoticeable.

Such prejudicial categories can, then, authorise thoughtless human blindness in those who have them, and can humiliate members of target groups, even when these individuals aren't personally being targetted. For mediated rejection to humiliate, it is enough to know that members of a group to which you belong are regarded in this way. You feel humiliation by identification with the group. Here, then, are attitudes which are bad not because they are prejudices, but because they are bad; but they are then made socially efficient, as it were, easy to propagate and to spread, and hard to counter with argument or evidence, because they take the form of prejudices. They go without saying, as the saying goes.

Second, I believe that many of the prejudices that do most harm are better approached sociologically than psychologically. People in the grip of noxious prejudices rarely think them up for themselves. They learn them. That can be true of whole nations at times, as arguably it has been in Serbia or Germany, or it can be true of particular social sectors. And so a psychological explanation of anti-semitism, say, is not to the point, where one's milieu is full of anti-semites. Or rather, we ask the question of the wrong people. The question to be asked of anti-semites in an anti-semitic society is not why, since the answer is obvious. More interesting, because less obvious, where the question can be put, is why not?

I stress the sociological aspect of this because too often we are inclined to believe that only individuals with bad motives do bad things. Thus, as we have seen, Keith Windschuttle has launched a crusade to rescue the reputation of Australian settlers who, he claims, have received a bum rap as massacrers of Aborigines. Apart from denying that most of the alleged massacres occurred, he insists on the good intentions and fine beliefs of the settlers. But, as Robert van Krieken and I take pains to argue in 'The Character of the Nation', you do not have to be an indecent individual to do indecent things, still less to do things with harmful consequences. It happens all the time, to (and by) the most ordinary, otherwise unexceptionable folk. When the cards are stacked in certain ways, most people play the cards they are dealt; they don't abandon the game because they find it distasteful, particularly when they are winning. There are limits, of course, and there are exceptions, but fewer than we often fondly like to believe.

A third point is that we often attribute terrible consequences to prejudice, when the crucial question is not why people *believe* what they do, but why they *do* what they do. Prejudice might be an ingredient in action, but not necessarily and not sufficiently. Not *necessarily*, since some of the most terrible things done in the past century were engineered by people in the grip of highly rationalised ideologies (for example, communism), rather than unthought prejudices. They believed they were doing what had to be done, precisely because they had thought about it. Bad thoughts, but thoughts nonetheless. Not every murderous ideology trades off prejudice, and it is not always a better ideology when it doesn't than when it does.

Prejudice is also *insufficient* to explain the things people with noxious prejudices do. Anti-semitism is an old prejudice, yet the Holocaust is a matter of recent memory. Again, Serbs have for some time resented defeat in a battle in the fourteenth century, but, till only a few years ago, the streets of Sarajevo were full of intermarried families, and Serb, Croat and Muslim friends of long standing, who later killed each other. To talk of triggers or powder kegs already is to assume that the horrible consequences were just waiting, sometimes hundreds of years, to happen. That is often an unfounded assumption, a prejudice even, rather than a result of good evidence or clear thought.

And another example. As we saw in 'Neighbours', in Poland there was recently a bitter controversy over a 1941 massacre by its Polish residents of the Jewish inhabitants of the small village Jedwabne. But they had lived together in that town for generations and nothing like this had ever happened before. Any explanation of these terrible events cannot ignore local and deep anti-semitism, but it also can't ignore the circumstances of first Soviet and then Nazi occupation, without which we have no reason to believe the massacre would have occurred.

Just recall those observations, that Paul Hasluck made and I quote, of the place of white violence in settler–Aboriginal relations in our own country. Prejudices were perhaps part of the story, arguably more than Hasluck admits, but so, too, were the particular situations in which people found themselves. And he is right to stress that frontier violence was more a product of a particular situation than of character flaws, without denying the reality and damaging effects of that violence.

Again, recall Hasluck's plea that we ask ourselves: 'Why it was that men of decent habit and usually of controlled passions were moved to a tolerance of violence and even to its commission?' It's a good question, and prejudice, while almost certainly a part, is at best only part of the answer.

Prejudices then are often blamed for things that are not their fault, or their fault alone. They can be praised, and whether or not we praise them, we can't escape them. So what to do? What can distinguish an enlightened prejudiced person from an unenlightened one? Is the former different from the bigot in just not having bigoted prejudices? That might be part of the answer, but it's not likely to be the whole of it, since we don't choose our prejudices.

So are we all bigots? I don't think so. I think it is the *way* the bigot believes that matters. The person 'blinded by prejudice' doesn't merely pre-judge, as we all do, doesn't only rely on things other than reason, as we all do, doesn't even only think badly of people without sufficient evidence. Most of us do that too. He does so in a way that is not *reflexive* about his prejudices. He has no wish, or no ability, to take any distance from them, to try to uncover them, to interrogate them, to confront them with experience, dialogue, criticism and revision.

He is incapable of what I would happily call, if it did not have unfortunate connotations in Australian-English, rooted reflexiveness. Such a posture acknowledges that we never start nowhere but recommends that we always be open to finishing somewhere else. In this I echo Walt Whitman's account of a moral person as one who is 'both in and out of the game and watching and wondering at it'.

*2003*

# The Price of Purity

In 1978 the Polish philosopher in exile Leszek Kołakowski published a credo for the Conservative-Liberal-Socialist International, which he described as a 'mighty International that will never exist'. Kołakowski drew out and commended particular and distinctive insights from each of the components of his credo, and pointed out that they were all consistent with each other. So it made sense to be a conservative-liberal-socialist. Nevertheless, he warned that, 'because it cannot promise people that they will be happy', the International would not eventuate. And, to my knowledge, it never did.

In 1992 I was seeking to make some sense of the ideological backwash from the collapse of communism. Where did it leave the left? Where the right? What was left? What right? Did these labels do any useful work any more? I sought to continue Kołakowski's campaign, in a slightly modified form. I published an essay, 'In Praise of Conservative-Liberal-Social Democracy', first here and then in Warsaw, in the first issue of a newly renovated, once underground, journal. It appeared there with the editorial note that 'The author's views on this subject are very close to our point of view.' So when the Polish editors suggested a fee, I proposed that they keep the money to fund a dinner for the inaugural meeting of the Conservative-Liberal-Social Democratic International (Polish section), to be held next time I was in Warsaw.

That dinner duly went ahead, at a new and rather swish Warsaw restaurant. It was well-attended and enjoyable. Still, when it was over, I recalled the nineteenth-century French pre-socialist, Henri Saint-Simon, who sought to educate himself by inviting distinguished

Parisian intellectuals to dinner. He later complained that his guests ate well but said little. The realisation dawned on me that I remained the only paid-up member of my movement.

That is not much of a surprise, of course. Conservative-liberal-social democracy, not to mention what I would now want to add, doesn't trip off the tongue, and it suggests confusion, or at least complexity, where often the desire is for clarity, or at least simplicity. It is ill-suited for recruiting. Nevertheless, I remain attached to it.

For there is one banal truth which I wish to emphasise, since it is so routinely ignored. Issues of political morality, which is what these essays have been about, are hard. They are hard because it is difficult to get the facts right. They are hard because it is difficult to decide what we should cherish and strive for, how to mesh these things with other things we value, and how to apply all of this to what we know of the facts. And they are hard because the world is not just waiting to hear what we want. The world has to be taken into account, and that is a tricky, complex and never-ending business. Nevertheless none of this is hopeless and we are not helpless. In particular we are not lacking in reflections about and experience of the play of ideals in the world, upon which people who care for something might draw. My one-man International seeks to bring some of these reflections and experiences together in what might, in the way of these lectures, be called a hybrid form. Yet, unlike its author, this form is not a hybrid of circumstance. It is a hybrid of choice.

The choice stems from a reluctance to tie things up too neatly. Partly that flows from inadequacy. Unlike systematic public philosophers, like the American John Rawls or our own Philip Pettit, I run out of steam long before all the ends of some architectonic principle have been followed through. And my head hurts pretty quickly as well. I learn from systematic philosophers, but I don't want to emulate them.

For it is not only incapacity. It is also a matter of temperament and intellectual taste. Not all of what appeals to me has a philosophically interesting lineage or argument, for wisdom and cleverness are different, and they are not always combined. And some insights, as Kołakowski saw, come out of different traditions of thought that are not on speaking terms with each other. That often matters to writers I read and people I know, more than it does to me. Even if *they* don't mix, I am happy to mix them. The result is untidy at times, but there are worse faults.

All the more so since I have no reason to believe that readers will all find what I have said appealing or persuasive. Indeed I am confident that many will not. Some won't like what I like, others the uses I put it to, and still others – or all together – may not like me much either. Needless to say, they're wrong about all of these things, but it's not much use to say that. Better to suggest some points of contact, and to try to encourage dialogue among people of differing, even antagonistic views. To do that, it is worth crossing some boundaries and suggesting how such boundaries might be crossed. It is also worth suggesting how elements from different sides of the boundaries might be joined. None of this will ensure consensus, and that is no part of my aim. But it might enable conversation. And that is a useful thing to have.

Not everyone agrees. There is a tendency, particularly common among people overtaken by One Big Idea, to reduce the tangled complexity of social life and social thought to the single register of their Idea, whatever it is. It is a bit like those machines at the end of tollways, which can only recognise coins of a particular size and shape. That will do for collecting (a limited range of) coins, but it's less appropriate for thinking. Especially when so many people of this tendency believe that their currency is at the same time uniquely precious and unconvertible. Even more so when, as so often in political debate, a difference of opinion is treated as a call to war.

Marxists, for example, *knew* that social classes, and nothing but social classes, were the fundamental actors in social life, in comparison with which all else paled. They also knew that anyone who didn't know this knew nothing much. Many followers of the French writer Michel Foucault know that power, and nothing but power, stands behind whatever it is they see, wherever they see it. Those who don't see that have missed the essence of things. There are feminists who see in gender, and nothing but gender, the same overwhelmingly significant role in society that class had for Marx. But Marx was wrong. Of that they are confident. Many so-called economic rationalists share with Marx the belief that the economy, and nothing but the economy, is the theatre of history, and share with him the confidence that they and they alone know how to deal with the economy.

Even worse than such lack of humility about what they imagine they know and lack of charity about what others believe, such idea-crats spread that conviction – as Marx himself did – to their dealings with every domain of human life. Marx, it is true, sought to show that his theory stemmed from a proper analysis of reality, but the compre-hensive sweep and dogmatic certainty of that theory, its contempt for what could be dismissed as 'merely apparent' in favour of what the theory insisted was more deeply real, was a classic manifestation of what the Greeks called *hubris* – overweening zeal – on an almost cosmic scale. On a less elevated plane, it is also what Jews call *chutzpah* and Australians call hide.

Marxism has now gone, but this spirit of certainty has migrated to other faiths, among them today some versions of economic ration-alism, or has become quiescent. There is little evidence that it has been laid permanently to rest. It should be, for it is suspect wherever it is found in thought about social and political life.

It is suspect in itself, because, given the complexity of social and political arrangements, traditions and institutions, no one has the authority to claim such certainty about virtually anything to do with politics and society. And it is suspect because of its consequences. Those who believe that they are masters of a science which offers the key to the real direction of human affairs and to the good, find it hard to tolerate people who disagree or ideas or practices which get in the way. And the consequences of that certainty can be, and in many places have been, terrible.

*Hubris* often begins from real insight, as it did with Marx. However it is typically imperialistic and will cause casualties in any domain whose rhythms and values are different from those where it was born. Moreover, in human affairs it is presumptuous. Impertinent even. The complexity of political morality deserves more respect. So does the complexity of the world. What is involved in respecting them both?

In an essay called 'The Death of Utopia Reconsidered', Kołakowski reports that, when asked where he would like to live, he always replies, 'deep in [a] virgin mountain forest on a lake shore at the corner of

Madison Avenue in Manhattan and the Champs Elysées, in a small tidy town'. Though it might reduce the charm of the location for him, I would happily live next door. So long as the coffee is good. Unfortunately, I am doomed to be unsatisfied, and he need never worry about the neighbours. Sad realities claim their due.

And so they do in life. We have that on the authority of our former prime ministers Malcolm Fraser ('life wasn't meant to be easy') and Paul Keating ('life doesn't get much better than this'), and these insights have also been, less self-servingly, confirmed by the Rolling Stones ('you can't always get what you want'). We also have the sad optimist/pessimist jokes that used to do the rounds of communist countries: the optimist believes things can't get any worse; the pessimist knows they can. Or: a pessimist is an optimist who is well informed.

Does that mean that one should never hope for more than one has, that only a pessimist can be a realist, that Eeyore rules, OK? No, it doesn't.

Hopes, dreams, ideals, utopias even, are powerful fuels of political achievement. Where hopelessness paralyses the will, hope can galvanise and sustain it; often against the odds. And, sometimes, irrepressible idealists turn out to be the only realists around. I recall, for example, an article which I read in admiring disbelief in 1985. It was written by the Polish dissident, writer and hero Adam Michnik, and had been smuggled out of gaol as he was awaiting his next trial. (He spent, in all, some seven years in gaol.) Though his 'realistic' compatriots, and armies of observers (including me), respected his apparently Quixotic sufferings, most of us – knowingly if regretfully – explained that the regime was in for the long haul. Michnik assured us, on the contrary, that 'the sociology of surprise is inscribed in the nature of the Leading System [as he ironically described communism]. Here, on a spring morning, one may wake up in a totally changed country.' And so he did. He even got the season right.

But not just any hope will do. Otherwise, Kołakowski and I could pack our bags. How, then, might we discriminate among hopes, on what basis favour some over others? As usual, I move from what should be avoided to what should be welcomed.

Some hopes, of course, must be rejected, because they are evil to the core. This was true of Nazism, and it is also true of racist and other group supremacist ideologies of all kinds. All one needs in order to find them objectionable is a commitment to the moral equality of human beings, and these days that is quite a common commitment. The fact that it wasn't always doesn't show it isn't justified. It is merely one small piece of evidence that moral progress is possible.

There is nothing evil in Kołakowski's dream, however. It is simply impossible to attain. That is so for two sorts of reasons, one contingent the other necessary. The accidental reasons are that Madison Avenue is not rich in mountains, forests and lakes, the Champs Elysées is an ocean away, and neither New York nor Paris is small or tidy. These are simply facts.

The deeper reason, however, is that the elements of Kołakowski's dream, the values they represent, are incompatible. They *could not* exist together. The idyllic unspoilt seclusion of one part could not survive the invigorating busyness of its other parts. Choosing some will mean not having others. This is not only a problem for Kołakowski's vision, however. It is a common problem among visions.

The intellectual historian Isaiah Berlin spent a long and distin-guished life insisting – rightly, I believe – that there is no way in which all of our values can be made to cohere without loss or trade-off. Rather, as he writes in an essay on 'The Pursuit of the Ideal':

> collisions of values are of the essence of what they are and of what we are … The notion of the perfect whole, the ultimate solution, in which all good things coexist, seems to me to be not merely unat-tainable – that is a truism – but conceptually incoherent; I do not know what is meant by a harmony of this kind. Some among the Great Goods cannot live together. That is a conceptual truth. We are doomed to choose, and every choice may entail an irreparable loss.

Many nineteenth-century utopians, whose ideals were not them-selves evil, brought evil into the world by ignoring or denying this nec-essary plurality and conflict among values. Either they denied that values in conflict with their own were any good, or they imagined that proper realisation of their dream would incorporate any good in them. A practical implication was that nothing that was inconsistent with the utopia could be good – movements inspired by such transformative fantasies had tragic consequences. Active pursuit of the Idea, and then the fanatical but vain attempt to impose it against any recalcitrance, conflicted with the minimum conditions of civilised life.

These conflicts were inevitable, not accidental. They flowed from the character of the inspiring vision, and from the certainty it generated in believers. And when the conflicts appeared, those conditions of civilised life were sacrificed: for a time in good conscience. The earliest communists, for example, were at the same time far more idealistic and far more brutal than their corrupt and cynical successors. The combination of idealism and brutality is fateful.

The founders were convinced – they had no doubt – that they knew the direction of history, that it was leading to a wonderful future, and that it was their duty to do anything which might help this – anyhow inevitable, and inevitably good – development along. Sacrifices would have to be made, but since the goal was so clear and so good, they were worth making. And they certainly were made.

*1997*

# Conservative-Liberal-Socialism Revisited

Under communism, adjectives and nouns had a discomfiting tendency to devour each other. And not only each other. Consider the ravenous adjective in 'socialist democracy', the gluttonous noun in 'democratic centralism'. And what of 'salami tactics'? This voraciousness is reason to be chary of such predatory semantic couplings. And so the successors to communism were, when they insisted on 'democracy [and other good things] without adjectives'.

But such things never come without adjectives, explicit or implicit, since the pure forms of democracy, legality, and so on, have yet to be realised. We should get used to that and ask questions about the *quality* of the partner and the potential success of the partnership, rather than advocate an impossible celibacy. That is consistent with St Paul's advice to would-be fornicators concerned to avoid sin (namely, marry), and it is wise advice. We should all avoid bad marriages, of course, but not every marriage is bad, perhaps not even every *ménage à trois*. One can even end up with something greater than the sum of the parts. Conservative-liberal-socialism (CLS), for example.

CLS was also a product of communism, though presumably unintended and certainly unofficial. As we saw in the last essay, Leszek Kołakowski published its credo in exile from communist Poland in 1978, though he warned that his 'great and powerful International … will never exist, because it cannot promise people that they will be happy'. More recently, however, Adam Michnik claimed that this 'peculiar coalition of ideas' actually *had* emerged among his generation of dissidents in the 1980s, since their rejection of communism stemmed from 'reasons equally dear to a conservative, a socialist, and a liberal'. The coalition 'collapsed along with communism', however, as erstwhile allies became bitterly polarised foes – conservatives against liberals against socialists – and he sees no way to resurrect it. He votes for radical democracy, 'grey' but 'beautiful'. In the meantime, the ex-foes of the coalition, the much-made-over Polish post-communists, do well[1] while its ex-members fight each other and stumble hither-and-thither.[2]

Perhaps they should re-group, and perhaps we should too, so that the 'great and powerful International' really does come to exist. For there is a lot to gain. The particular circumstance of having an enemy one hates more than one's traditional opponents has turned out to be transient, and fortunately so. But from it can come insights that deserve to endure, even where they have been forgotten or discarded, and have potential to reach far beyond the places and time of their origin. Such are the insights of CLS.

Taken individually and taken whole, each of the traditions within CLS has unacceptable elements, versions, interpretations and exemplars. None of them is without its weaknesses or blindnesses – sometimes tragic. Nor is any of them adequate, on its own, to the job of thinking well about contemporary politics. Nor are they obviously compatible, since some were forged explicitly in opposition to one or both of the others and some come to find their voice – as in post-communist Europe – directly at each other's expense.

Yet each of the component traditions is drawn to distinctive projects and styles of thought which are slighted or rejected in typical forms of the others. Not all of these sit easily together, but some do, or can be made to come to an accommodation. In combination they can augment and on occasion correct each other. For sometimes their mutual neglect or opposition is a result less of hard thought than strong feeling, less mental than visceral. It is worth rethinking. It might then become easier to digest.

Indeed my only objection to the movement is not Michnik's, that it is too colourful, but that it is not colourful enough. I would prefer a rainbow

---

[1]   No longer so (2005).
[2]   Still (2005).

coalition. In my earlier modest variation of Kołakowski's credo, I substituted social democracy for socialism, trusting that he wouldn't mind. I will take it that, since no non-democratic interpretation of CLS can be taken seriously today (something that was not always the case), it can go without saying. My current preference is for a Conservative-Liberal-Republican-Communitarian-Social-Democratic International. But asked to write on CLS, and on the principle that a bit of a good thing is better than nothing, I am prepared to commend the more muted tones of CLS (with its silent but ever-present 'D'). As did our founder, Kołakowski, I will comment on each of the component traditions in turn, and confine my observations to three aspects of each of these traditions.

## Conservatism

1. Conservatives have always maintained a distinctive view of the *methods* appropriate to politics, and of the temper, perhaps temperature, proper to political engagement and reflection. They oppose the temper of certainty in politics, stress limits to human plasticity, worry about unintended consequences, are fearful of what are sometimes extolled as 'transformative projects'. In politics they expect less light where the heat is strong, worry about radical ambitions and enthusiasms, more generally about *hubris* in public affairs. Revolutions might occasionally be justified, but they need an apology. 'Permanent revolution', so appealing to Trotsky and Mao, is appalling to a conservative.

Though communism taught many unintended lessons of this sort, none of this waited upon communism to be formulated. It was central to Burke's attack on the French Revolution, and it has been a repeated refrain. Quite appropriately, then, 'conservative' appears as an *adjective* in the International, since its role here is to qualify the way you pursue and think about whatever it is you want.

The way it recommends has two sources, one sociological and the other epistemological. First, conservatives stress the complexity of long-established arrangements, their multiple interconnections and reciprocal effects, their pervasive shaping and structuring impact on individuals, groups and the only partly-chosen environments they find themselves in. Second, they stress the appropriateness of epistemological modesty in relation to such things, a modesty warranted by the limited degree to which we understand how they work, can predict how they will react to what we do, or can even guess how some parts of society will be affected by what we do to other parts. Consequently, they regard humility in these matters as not merely more attractive than *hubris,* but intellectually better off as well.

A happy revolutionary cannot be a conservative in this sense. And the fanatical temper of certainty that revolutionary Marxism exhibited and bred was reason from the start to regard it with distaste. That would be so even if one were in sympathy with the values to which Marxists claimed allegiance. Conservatives knew that the enterprise in which the Bolsheviks were engaged – at once radically destructive and (in Hayek's sense) radically constructivist – was great folly, not simply because of what they were about but because of the way they went about it.

In principle, methodological conservatism is compatible with a variety of substantive political commitments. In his *The Poverty of Historicism*, Popper advocated 'piecemeal' rather than 'holistic social engineering', and there is little in his position to which a methodological conservative would object, apart perhaps from the unsympathetic scientism and voluntarism of the metaphor. Conservatives prefer social arrangements to be cultivated than engineered. A social democrat can be methodologically conservative, and many of the most perceptive critics of communism and other forms of doctrinaire socialism were. So can a liberal, and many have been, among them David Hume and Adam Smith. Those, however, whose liberalism is a rationalistic pro-gramme of large-scale transformation to be imposed whatever the country whatever the cost, are methodologically un- indeed anti-conservative – even where the programme is attributed to Hume and Smith. Or they are to the extent that they ignore deep truths – conservative truths – about the complexity and variety of human affairs and social action, limited understandings and the need to attend to local traditions and local knowledge.

To be more than a dogma of timidity, conservatism must acknowledge variation, both in the complexity of affairs and what we know of them. Also in levels of vulnerability. Scepticism is not the same as terror. Moreover, precisely because conservatism insists that circumstances be taken into account, it must be alive to differences in institutional strength, support and resilience. Not everything is as weak, vulnerable, mysterious as everything else, so a nuanced conservatism might well allow more risks to be taken in a good cause where institutions are strong than where they are weak (because in those circumstances the risks are less risky), allow that we know some things better than others, indeed acknowledge that some evils are so malign that radical action might be appropriate to combat them.

Methodological conservatism should not be confused with *reaction*, since it has nothing inherent to say about *restoration* of values or institutions which have allegedly been overthrown. Indeed if the overthrow was real, and restoration is essayed in too enthusiastic a manner, a conservative should caution against it.

Finally, methodological conservatism does not necessarily entail what I will call *normative* conservatism, a positive evaluation and attachment to what exists. Thus conservative liberals or democrats in a society without liberal or democratic traditions, values or institutions, might have no sympathy for what they find around them, but still recognise that these things are there and need to be *taken account of*, and that's a serious business, whether one likes them or not, whether one is out to subvert them or not. If they are simply *ignored*, there will commonly be a price to pay. That seems to me an apt posture for post-communist reformers, for example, though many enthusiasts have not adopted it. They have acted as though what existed was of no account, until faced with the disappointing results of their efforts. Disappointment might have been predicted by anyone who had learnt from methodological conservatism that there are no clean slates. Drawing on them, you must take account of what is already there. That is so, whatever you think of what you find.

Arthur Koestler describes his autobiography as 'the account of a journey from specious clarity to obscure groping,' and (though, sadly, not all his groping has stayed obscure) it is clear that he learned something along the way. For it is a deep and appropriately unintended lesson of the most celebrated emancipatory adventure of modern times, that the temper of certainty is unfitted for politics. That lesson should stay with us, so the methodological conservative warns, long after communism has gone.

2. One *could*, then, be a methodological conservative even if one loathed existing institutions. It would be enough just to register that they need to be taken seriously. Those happiest to call themselves conservative, however, are not just talking about method and approach. They have a normative commitment to what exists, which they often express as a presumption. A fundamentalist will make that presumption close to irrebuttable; a more moderate conservative will allow it to be rebutted.

The psychological and sociological sources of normative conservatism are various. Some conservatives want to hold on to what they have, which is why conservatism is often associated with privilege. Others fear what they might get, which is why many anti-communists moved in a conservative direction. Some conservatives are at ease with the *status quo ante*; others fear what might be the *status quo post*. Others just prefer the familiar to the strange.

It is not always easy to specify in general terms what normative conservatives want to conserve. For to a considerable extent, conservatism is what Huntington, in an influential essay on 'conservatism as an ideology', calls a positional ideology, 'concerned not with the substance of institutions but with their preservation'. It is invoked when values, practices, institutions to which people are attached seem threatened, whatever they happen to be. Over time, the objects of such attachment have varied greatly.

Intellectually, however, there are some common themes. First of all, while methodological conservatism does not *imply* normative conservatism, it can lead to it. Their implicit sociology persuades many conservatives that longevity is no small matter, from which some of them conclude that long-standing practices, values, institutions are worthy of respect, sometimes even reverence. Their very existence can be taken as evidence that they have got something right, which it is not easy to get right. In any event, long-lived values, cultures, traditions, institutions, practices are embedded in everyday ways of thinking, behaving and valuing. Locals understand them. They are familiar and if we are lucky they are good. Anyway, good enough. Even if they aren't, they are there. They enable some things and disable others. They offer particular constraints, and particular resources. In other places they are different and, as a result, so are the constraints and resources. They pervade and affect, even though (a crucial distinction) they do not determine, everything we do. We'd be lost without them.

Second, as conservative epistemology likes to remind us, we're not that smart. Given their scepticism about human and social inventiveness, their advice is that we do better in general (at least presumptively) to respect what has developed than what we imagine should develop, or think we can design. Combine the sociology with the epistemology, and conservatives are liable to say that some of the best features of long-established traditions are likely to be those that ambitious reformers cannot see (until, at times, after they have destroyed them). These claims, of course, have rich obscurantist potential, but they are also at times true.

Added to these methodological sources of deference, conservatives are often attracted to overarching supra-individual social institutions, such as families, religious institutions, communities, and so on, which have been thought necessary to hold societies together and to enrich our lives. Their weakening is said to threaten to sunder or at least degrade social life. This is a theme which has re-appeared among contemporary communitarians.

Such substantive claims should always be made more tentatively than conservatives are wont to make them, because we truly don't know what will happen if 'traditional' practices to which we are attached (often actually of recent invention), were to change or even disappear. It has happened often enough in the past, often with warnings of dire consequences, often without such consequences; thus Kołakowski: 'I can well imagine paleolithic nomads angrily resisting the foolish ideal that it would be better for people to have permanent dwellings or predicting the imminent degeneration of mankind as a result of the nefarious invention of the wheel.' Still there are reasons to consider certain traditional practices and institutions, such as families and larger sources of collective attachment and identity too, crucial to social, and perhaps even psychic cohesion, even though – indeed because – no one designed them and they have been around for a long time. And even though we often find, and have to survive, them in pathological forms.

3. Asked to justify their commitments, conservatives typically have less to say than liberals or socialists. And what they do say is less likely to be systematic or programmatic. For conservatism does not trade confidently in doctrines or ideologies. It is more commonly to be found in *dispositions,* to use Michael Oakeshott's term, rather than in articulated theories. It prefers traditions to recipes. If, as Oakeshott elsewhere claims, the rationalist 'is the *enemy* of authority, of prejudice, of the merely traditional, customary or habitual', the conservative is their friend.

Such dispositions can allow us to draw on socially and generationally accumulated wisdoms, where rationalism – the insistence on interrogating and judging every practice, custom, tradition or proposal by the light of one's reason – makes for cleverness, at times shallow individual or ephemerally fashionable cleverness. But since conservative dispositions are typically well disposed to the traditions which we inhabit and which inhabit us, they serve us best where these are nice. Unfortunately they are not especially good at discriminating between those that are nice and those that are not, between what we should cherish and what we should deplore.

Even Oakeshott observes that 'If the present is arid, offering little or nothing to be used or enjoyed, then this inclination will be weak or absent.' Aridity is the least of it. The present may include positively nasty traditions, of great vintage, strength, resilience and local appeal – this is a problem which even a Russian leader of impeccable democratic leanings (rare but not quite oxymoronic) would still face. It may also be empty (or have been emptied) of certain traditions which one would wish to cultivate and emulate – this is a problem throughout the post-communist world. Or it may be full of a plurality of traditions which point in inconsistent directions and have different, yet strongly committed constituencies – this is the problem of everyone in large, differentiated, modern societies. One may wish it were otherwise, but Russia's traditions are as they are, wholesome traditions cannot be manufactured overnight, and our societies are not quickly going to become small, undifferentiated or pre-modern.

History is not destiny, change is continuous, people have good ideas, and we keep being surprised. So we should never assume that what we have is what we must have. Nor necessarily what we should have. And for all their significance, traditions change and conflict, the products of foreign traditions can be grafted onto existing ones, and new things happen. Actors are influenced by many things, not only the traditions with which they grew up. Anyway, they grow up with and within many traditions. Some of those traditions are not very palatable or have unpalatable elements or dark sides, sometimes we come to realise it, and sometimes we can and should do something about it.

And new things happen. Some ideas and ideals will appeal to us, wherever and whenever they grew, simply because they seem to us good or right. We can't assume that they will therefore have success in the world, but there is no reason to reject them simply because we haven't had them before. Otherwise no one would now have a written constitution, because only 250 years ago, no one ever did. And representative democracy was also new not very long ago. Australia is one of the oldest, and it is a young nation.

Conservatives are right to emphasise the stickiness and complexity of social and political arrangements. In any particular place, dealing with the application of ideals requires local knowledge; the more the better. But it requires other things as well. And normative conservatives have less to say about those things. For apart from taking into account what exists, one needs to be in a position to reflect upon it and evaluate it, both affirmatively and critically. Here normative conservatism must be more controversial, and, since it is more often based in sentiment and disposition than argument, it is commonly less persuasive to those of different sentiments and dispositions.

The conservative presumption in favour of the way things are might give enthusiastic critics pause, but without more it does little to answer their complaints. It can only stop for long those who already share an affection for the way things are. Those who don't share that affection, or are not sure whether or why they should, might ask to be convinced. And then what?

Any answer must involve *arguing* about values, practices and traditions, advocating some, criticising others, preferring some, letting go of others. Winning an argument is not in itself a substitute for sensitive exploration (and extension) of existing traditions and their intimations.

Nevertheless there are many circumstances in modern societies where that will not do enough; where to say 'that's the way we do things here' is not to say enough. (East Europeans could say that, with justice, about anti-semitism and quite a few other deeply rooted and odious local traditions. Many do, but fortunately quite a few – particularly liberals – find that unsatisfying today.) To say more, reflectively and routinely among strangers and without guns or knives, is to participate in a liberal form of conversation.

## Liberalism

1. Many liberals have no time for the conservative disposition. Such non-conservative liberals are enemies of the unexamined life. In principle, they believe everything should be weighed on the scales of liberal reason. Piety has little meaning for them. In this they seem to conservatives to be rash – dangerously and corrosively rash. Silly too. And often they are. This is one reason why liberal chatter so commonly appears unattractive and frivolous to conservatives.

Nevertheless, there is much to be said for the liberal commitment to reasoned discussion. And it is possible for a conservative to participate in it. Desirable too. Even where the cause is good, conservatives must be able to engage with liberals once that cause is challenged. Hostile attention cannot be doused, in free societies, by demands for deference. In rational discussion one might draw attention to and emphasise the often hidden wisdom and virtues of traditions, but even if one wished to, it is hard to avoid the discussion once it has started.

And the cause is not always good. A virtue of liberal relentlessness is that it demands justifications of many established institutions and practices whose bearers and beneficiaries wrongly resist it. Not all mysteries are deep. Not every tradition is full of intimations which we would be wise to pursue. Some are just mired in obscurantism, best to eschew. The question is which is which. Once it is asked, inarticulate submissiveness is not much of an answer.

2. More than conservatism, liberalism is committed to particular substantive values. Central among these is individual autonomy. That leads quickly to hostility to arbitrary imposition, restraint or direction. An

associated value is tolerance. Since the world can be threatening and one does not want freedom to be a matter of chance, liberalism stresses rights and institutional arrangements which might anchor and safeguard them. Arrangements to guide, channel, diffuse, restrain and balance the powers of the powerful are liberal arrangements, and a great deal of liberal attention to the rule of law and constitutionalism has been devoted to the design of such arrangements. These are good causes even where, often especially where, they have not been old causes.

A crucial medium of liberal institutional arrangements is law; not just any law, but the rule of law. I have written at length about the character of the rule of law in these pages and elsewhere, so I will not return to it here. But it is a crucial liberal commitment, and a distinctive one. For it is certainly not universal, and those who lack it have often recognised its worth.

Thus, one of the major sources of wholesale (and lingering) distrust among strangers in communist states was the absence of the rule of law in this sense. Communist (and Nazi) states had plenty of laws. There was a Nazi jurisprudence and it was a horrible sight. Its aim was to make law maximally pliable and permeable to political direction. Communist law had similar aims, though with time they generally became less ruthlessly pursued. For the most part law was viewed purely instrumentally: when it came to replace (or regulate) direct terror, law was one among an array of instruments for translating the Party's wishes into action and maintaining social order. These states were not lacking in law, but the rule of law.

Among other things, the rule of law is essential for a civil society in good shape, and liberals, unlike many conservatives and most Marxists, are fond of such societies. Some conservatives, and Karl Marx, denounced civil society when it was young. The conservatives wanted to avoid entering it, preferring the more intimate (and sacred) connections that modernity threatened to undermine. Marxists wanted to transcend it. The former failed and, for better or worse, it is hard now to wish modernity away. Marx loathed what he understood as civil society. He loathed its separations, its boundaries, its individualism, its law, its private property, its competitiveness, its markets, its money, its religions, perhaps its variety. Communist society would have none of these things, and indeed it didn't. Marxists in power succeeded in destroying civil society where it had existed, and repressing it where it had not. The consequences were catastrophic. Over the past decade, throughout the post-communist world, many people have been wondering how to build or rebuild a civil society from the rubble that remained. It is not easy.

At its best, as I argue in 'The Uses of Civility', civil society is a crucial condition for non-predatory relations among strangers. Since modern societies are full of strangers, these are valuable relations to have. Civil society is also, among other things, a congenial forum for the eminently liberal activity of arguing about values. In that argument, liberals have some important things to say, and they have had some success.

3. Some of the things for which the past century will be remembered are already clear. Prominent among them is the contest between liberal democratic and totalitarian states. For much of the century it was a very uncertain contest. To almost everyone's surprise it ended as almost no contest at all.

Fascism and communism were not only horrible regimes but they also seemed, for much of the time, to be immeasurably more powerful than the sloppy, unco-ordinated, aimless, open and tolerant societies which they faced. As Orwell noticed, many people admired that power. Others feared it. Both considered it formidable, as for a time it was.

Against these monsters stood merely the liberal democracies, and whatever else could be said about them, for much of the century no one – neither friend nor foe – accused them of excessive stamina. And while liberal democracy always had supporters, until recently it had few enthusiasts. Not only did liberalism have many hostile critics, particularly among intellectuals. Even its friends did not seem to like it too much. At best, there was something second best about liberalism. Perhaps it warranted Forster's 'Two Cheers' or Churchill's ambiguous praise ('the worst form of Government except all those other forms that have been tried from time to time'), but scarcely enthusiastic ovation. It was, however, enthusiastically opposed.

Totalitarian regimes attacked virtually every sort of civilised value, but central and most explicit among the values, practices and institutions they attacked were liberal ones. The Nazis' relationship to German conservatism and conservatives was at best ambiguous. They were radical and fanatical, and they deformed conservative values, but they were not opposed to all of them. They hated and destroyed democracy, but Hitler was voted into office. They hated communists and social democrats, but they were after all National Socialists. Their relationship to liberalism, however, was uncomplicated. They violated every liberal value, not occasionally or by accident but systematically and with pride.

Communism was deeply anti-conservative, at least until it seemed firmly entrenched. But communism was not at war with conservatism in the same way that it was with liberalism. For in the Marxist understanding, conservatism was already doomed by history. It simply could not withstand the relentlessly changeful force of bourgeois modernity. But at the level of ideology, liberalism *was* bourgeois modernity. And communism – super-modernity – was an assault on liberalism, at every level. It assaulted, often with ferocious intensity, all the core liberal values: freedom, rights, privacy, civil society, markets and the rule of law. 'Rotten liberalism', as Lenin liked to call it, was a prime target.

As things have turned out, fascism and communism collapsed in turn, in defeat and humiliation. Indeed the latter fell with hardly a blow being struck – just fell apart, rotten to the core. Liberal democracies, on the other hand, have kept plodding on, in their prosaic, tepid way, becoming over the century wealthier, stronger, freer and more just. There remains a lot to complain about in modern liberal polities – problems unaddressed, unresolved and newly spawned. But there is less to complain about than among their most significant rivals, and there is a lot to praise as well. Perhaps something altogether different would be immeasurably better. Neither conservatives nor liberals will hold their breaths.

It is nice to be able to say that liberalism is not merely better but also stronger than totalitarianism. That, however, is not enough. One can still ask whether it can be better than it is. Even how it might be made better. The conservatives in our coalition should not disqualify these questions but caution us as we ask and answer them. Liberals and socialists, of course, have strong views on these matters.

## Socialism

1. Socialism has fewer methodological lessons of its own to offer than conservatism and liberalism. In the version most famously tried, we have 'seen the future' and it didn't work. Yoked to our International, however, socialists have absorbed from conservatism the dangers of unrestrained idealism and the temper of certainty in politics; from liberalism the importance of liberal discussion, values and history; and some profound and negative lessons from what came to be known as 'really existing socialism'.

Some socialists maintain that the failure of Soviet communism tells us nothing about socialism. This is nonsense. It cannot, of course, tell us that every conceivable form of socialism must be unsatisfactory. It does, however, tell us a lot about one form, and one that has the distinct (dis)advantage of having existed. And as the Russian (ex-communist) liberal Aleksandr Tsipko put it in exemplary conservative terms: 'Hope is in general not an argument in scientific debate.' It also tells us that unrestrained pursuit of some ambitions deep in socialist traditions, among them levelling and indeed 'liberating' ones, have terrible consequences, and that others, such as comprehensive planning and statism, have nothing good to be said for them. And it tells us this at every level: in economic terms, in terms of quality of life, in terms of freedom, and in terms of human dignity. Also, I believe that it tells us some deep and deeply unpalatable things about the ambitions and implications of the thought of the greatest socialist of all – Karl Marx.

From these sources CLSocialists derive scepticism about transformative projects, loathing of monopoly state control and an appreciation of civil society, with its undirected complexity, its tolerance of free and open discussion, its markets and its multiple sources of power and independence. These are things they now share with their coalition partners.

Yet they also believe that the lessons of Soviet socialism can be overextended and oversold, and that part of what is valuable about reflection on the Soviet case is to realise what are not useful analogies, rather than merely what are, what are the sources of difference as well as of similarity. There are profound differences, for example, between the pursuit of social democratic aims within a liberal democracy and the destruction of such a democracy, allegedly to further those aims. And this is so even if one can say of both that they involved a commitment to some form of social justice and they envisaged a significant role for the state in attaining it.

Some liberals (or in the US, libertarians) who spurn our coalition, for example Hayek, have predicted a slippery slope from pursuit of social justice with the aid of state intervention to Soviet-style despotism. It is therefore worth remembering that no society has ever slid down that slope. No communist state ever began as a welfare state in decline, and no welfare state has ever delivered the comprehensive political, moral, economic and ecological degradation that communist states did. On the contrary. CLS is a partisan of existing liberal polities which are among the striking success stories of the last century. Yet these polities, at the moments of their greatest success, were liberal social democracies, with government activity and welfare services greater than have ever existed in the history of the world. One can say that they would have done better if they had never been welfare states at all; but then, as conservatives know, one can *say* anything.

2. At its best, socialism was the product of a moral concern for the plight of people whose condition was a product of forces larger than them, with consequences often inescapable by them. That was true of the new class of workers formed by the Industrial Revolution, and it is arguably true of the new class that the French call *les exclus,* formed by the post-industrial and global economic transformations of the world today.

Many people will suffer, as many people always have suffered, for reasons which have nothing to do with individual worth or desert. Under no illusions that they can (or even should try to) relieve them all, CLS is concerned to address such sufferings and the indignities associated with them. They consider unemployment, for example, a matter of moral, not merely electoral, responsibility for governments. They also reject the claims of some libertarians that the very idea of redistribution is immoral, though they are not as confident as social-ists-without-adjectives once were about how it might be done.

In a democracy, we have, of course, purely prudential reasons to seek the relief of exclusion and disadvantage. After all, even the most vulnerable people vote, and continually disaffected and excluded members of a society can cause crime, violence, fear and other sorts of trouble. They might also cause moral unease among the better placed.

But the reasons go deeper. CLS goes beyond conservative-liberalism in seeking to blend liberal democracy with public social responsibility. The conditions of flourishing membership in a society should extend, as much as possible, and consistent with other values, to all its members, and those conditions can be extensive, for they include health, education, relief from poverty and potentially many other forms of support. They also include liberty under law, which is rarely uniformly spread through a society. They are among the conditions necessary for a life of dignity, for inclusion in a society, for satisfying connection and participation of citizens as moral equals in a society's affairs. Remedying conditions that disable some of us from enjoying these conditions is properly the concern of all of us, or at least of our political representatives who are supposed, after all, to represent all of us.

3. Moving from aims to means, CLS is conscious that history is rich with examples of bad things done in the sincere pursuit of what appear to be good motives. I have spoken of socialism at its best, but socialism was often not at its best and life under what used to be called 'real socialism' was commonly as bad as could be. Since it is conservative and liberal, CLS can never contemplate treating people as pawns to be moved around at will to satisfy some Procrustean fantasy. That is an offence both to liberty and dignity. In any event Procrustean social engineering has shown itself spectacularly unsuccessful in attaining its self-appointed tasks, let alone at minimising 'collateral damage'.

It has been a deep, and at times tragic, conceit of transformative projects, to believe that decent ends naturally spawn the means to achieve them and that these can be used without cost to other important values. There is no reason in principle or experience to believe that. A prudent investor would believe the opposite. At least he would hedge. Yet many optimists about the welfare state, let alone more ambitious rivals on the left, rested with just that questionable assumption.

The state has been the repository of many dubious dreams. Some social democrats were confident that, once captured, the state would work like a perfect, frictionless machine to attain the ends for which it was designed. At this time of day such optimism seems a little quaint. These are obvious truths to conservative-liberal-social democrats, but unfortunately they have not always been obvious to everyone.

And yet, they can be misconstrued, and have been in many liberal attacks on socialism. Not only do some such attacks misconstrue 'socialism at its best', but they also get liberalism itself wrong. For as I argue in 'The Good That Governents Do', liberalism, and the flourishing civil societies that CLS looks to, require strong and effective states. What they don't need is arbitrary, capricious, despotic states, or states that overreach themselves. No more, though, do they need weak or ineffective ones.

Even 'simply' keeping the peace is no small matter and in modern conditions strong and effective states are needed to do it. This is evidenced by the difficulty of restoring peace in societies whose states have collapsed or have become too weak to keep it. And if we explore what else we value that depends on a state that is effective and strong, the list becomes long and complex. It certainly includes markets, private property and civil societies, which are so often wrongly seen as alternatives to strong and effective states, though in fact they depend upon them. Moreover, recall the World Bank's reminder to us, and perhaps itself, that if economic and other social development is to be successful, there is a lot that governments need to do. They shouldn't do everything themselves, indeed there are excellent reasons why they shouldn't even dream of it, but they have a responsibility to provide many conditions without which it is simply impossible for such things to be done.

One should, then, avoid the mistake, often made by libertarians, of seeing 'the state' as inevitably the enemy of liberalism or civil society, or at best a necessary evil. The state is a heterogeneous category, and some forms of it are a necessary good. Many states do evil as a matter of course, and even adequate states commonly do much that they shouldn't or worse than they should. But the important distinctions among states are qualitative, and we are only beginning to make them. One difference is between states which effectively *own* the whole of the economy, polity, administration, and in effect society, and those which act within and alongside a civil society which contains many other and powerful actors, and which is undergirded – *indispensably* so – by an effective state, sufficiently strong to do what only it can do.

Again, as we saw in 'The Good That Governments Do', some states can pulverise subjects without resistance, but (or perhaps better, and) the societies remain weak, and so too the states. On the other hand, there are states that help generate and garner resources from co-operative and productive societies and help these resources to be put to good ends, though they find killing their citizens hard. These capacities and incapacities are related, and unsurprisingly, CLS favours those of the second sort. It was, after all, born in states of the other kind.

## Conclusion

Whoever reads this far might, I fear, have difficulty choosing between two alternatives, neither of which commends itself to me: either the combination I advance is impossible or it is banal. (It could, of course, be both, but that also doesn't commend itself.) Either it is unrealisable (or not worth realising), or so obvious that it goes without saying.

To treat these unappetising alternatives in turn, it seems to me possible, indeed sensible, to value the conservative temper and traditions, to feel some respect for complex social institutions, to participate in liberal discussion and applaud liberal values, to abhor socialism without adjectives but support public social responsibility. So it is possible and sensible to support CLS. There are, of course, tensions between an uncompromising commitment to certain elements of the position, say the conservative disposition, and an uncompromising commitment to other elements, say the liberal demand for reasoned public justification. Thus I have sought to suggest why both a conservative disposition, and liberal discussion, contribute to political understanding, though neither is sufficient on its own or at all times. That is why, though they are in potential tension with each other, we need both. So too with conservative and liberal values, liberal and social democratic values, conservative and social democratic values. Tensions are not necessarily what Marxists gleefully called 'contradictions', which can only be dealt with by systemic change. Some we can resolve, others we just have to live and deal with continuously. And if it were to turn out that no truly seamless and tension-free political theory can be made out of CLS, a *conservative* liberal socialist could live with that too.

CLS has no algorithms for practical decision. Since no one has, it is none the worse for that. At best, like conservatism, liberalism and social democracy themselves, CLS identifies and clarifies important values in play, and suggests some useful ways and considerations with which to think about them. No general complex of values can dictate how they are to be applied to particulars. Anyone familiar with law is familiar with the problem. However strong the values, they will be engaged and refracted in varying ways by the circumstances in which they are invoked, and often they will clash, either in principle or in practice or both. There is no escape from the need for deliberation, choice and judgment. That is why on any particular issue conservatives can be found arguing not just against non-conservatives but with each other, as can liberals, and social democrats. So will conservative liberal socialists.

As for banality, there is a sense in which I hope it is so. Part of my aim is to dissolve artificial or overblown antitheses, by stressing the extent to which what we already know or want overflows them. Policy choices might well be miscast if too quickly boxed into one or another allegedly distinct and self-sufficient, worse still exhaustive or exclusive, style or tradition of political thought. Each of the traditions represented in CLS has distinctive themes and preoccupations. To gauge the power of these concerns it is often good to go to the source. Even if we emerge impressed, however, we should not feel obliged either to stay there and go native, or to camouflage and strain our eclecticism to make it *salonfähig* somewhere else.

Nor should we fear becoming all things to all people. Even if the three factions of CLS come to agreement, they will still have more than enough enemies to go around. Quite apart from reactionaries, Utopians and assorted fanatics, among them will be fundamentalists, in all three camps, who feel betrayed. Of course, CLS might be accused of 'cherry picking' the congenial and compatible aspects from each of its component traditions, leaving behind just what makes them objectionable and should not be touched. I would advise members to plead guilty to this charge but not to feel guilty. After all, if the cherries are nice, why not pick them? If they go well together, why not mix them? And if some of their neighbours are rotten, why not leave them to rot? Conservative-liberalism has more to offer contemporary debate than unconservative liberalism or illiberal conservatism. Blended with carefully picked elements of social democracy, it offers a promising route back to the future.[3]

*2002*

---

[3]   On re-reading Kołakowski's credo, I (re-)discovered that in this, as in most things, he was ahead of me. His opening paragraph is: 'Motto: "Please step forward to the rear!" This is an approximate translation of a request I once heard in a tram-car in Warsaw. I propose it as a slogan for the mighty International that will never exist.' I prefer the relative optimism of my conclusion, which might be rephrased as 'Please step backwards to the front,' but its inspiration is clear.

# COMMUNISM AND POST-

# Stalemated in Poland: Life 'As If ...'

My family comes from Warsaw. They are Polish Jews, for whom the adjective is no less important than the noun. Unlike most Jews, but like many other middle-class urban Jewish intellectuals, they felt profoundly Polish – in language, culture and nationality. They have not forgotten what it meant to be a Jew in pre-war Poland, but they were and remain Polish patriots. Their Jewishness may well have influenced their politics, but it did not diminish their attachment to Poland, its poets, its past or, for that matter, its people. Against Polish anti-semites and in contrast to pre-war Zionists, they denied that – to use a delicacy recently uttered by an Australian Pole – Jews were 'guests' in Poland. It was their home and they were deeply attached to it.

After considerable time, and through a rather robust Antipodean sieve, these attitudes and values seeped into my soul more than I knew and more, I suspect, than anyone intended. (I was scarcely conscious of this until I was in my late twenties.) As I suppose often happens among the children of refugees, for whom cultural and traditional attachments cannot be simple givens, the land of my parents, its culture, language and people, came increasingly to occupy my thoughts and sense of self. Particularly over the past ten years, I came to read Polish and about Poland, to seek and enjoy conversations and friendships – some of my closest – with young Polish refugees and to think of myself, in somewhat confused but important part, as Polish. So Poland and 'Polishness' have dwelt rather vividly in my imagination for some years, as they have in my parents' since 1940.

But my parents have never been back and until September 1985, when I visited for the two weeks leading up to the 'elections', I had never been there at all. (Polish, by the way, has two words for elections: one, *głosowanie*, literally means 'voting'; the other, *wybory*, means 'choices'. One philosopher explained to me that while the regime used the second word in its omnipresent pre-'election' propaganda, Cardinal Glemp the Polish primate, in an unusually forthright speech spoke only of *głosowanie*. There was of course no choice.) My original purpose was simply to visit and absorb impressions of the land of my forebears and my imagination. I was also keen to discuss some academic work with several distinguished writers in my area. As it turned out, I met Poles at European conferences held shortly before my trip to Poland and was asked to give some seminars in a number of universities. This somewhat changed the balance of my visit. However, since there is only one subject of conversation in Poland – Poland – and since everyone participates in that conversation – taxi-drivers, passengers in lifts and trains, people in queues – my second purpose deviated from my first less than it might in countries with less urgent and pervasive obsessions.

I had apprehensions of a directly political sort about visiting Poland. I carried what the regime must regard as a suspect surname and my own comparatively few and insignificant political activities would tend to confirm any genealogical prejudice that might bear. And I was aware that communist regimes were not beyond bearing such prejudices. My family were quite anxious and sought to dissuade me from going (though as the visit approached I suspect that their fear was tempered by excitement that I would actually be staying in a Warsaw which they had not seen for forty-five years). When it was clear that I would be going my mother warned me sternly that in Poland, 'You must mince your words.' I had no heroic aspirations and I was not concerned that anything dramatic would happen. I had been assured by knowledge-able people that once I was granted a visa I would be quite safe. On the other hand, when I came to make decisions about, say, what to take across the border or what to say and to whom within Poland I realised that notwithstanding my not inconsiderable book-learning about com-munism I really had no idea of how to behave in an unfree country; particularly one in which I was intensely interested. Even my mother's sage warning did not take me very far. This cut both ways: I might rashly not mince words enough or, equally unsettling, I might mince too many words and manage to demean myself and learn little but platitudes at the same time. Similarly, though I knew well that certain things should be said and done only among those one trusted, I was not at all sure, that I would be able to tell the difference.

As it turned out, I need not have worried. I had no political difficulties at any time, at the border or anywhere else. Indeed I later regretted that I had not taken in a bagful of Western literature, of which Poles are starved for both political and financial reasons. (Instead, advised that Poles lacked fresh fruit I took a bagful of apples. This was not an inspired choice. Poland was swimming in apples when I arrived. Oranges, on the other hand, are extremely scarce and astoundingly expensive – a kilo cost 1800 złotys, about one-tenth the average monthly wage. Lemons were unobtainable).

As for mincing words, well virtually *no one* does. This is one of the exhilarating things about visiting Poland. One continually meets people preoccupied with serious matters, in fact the same desperately serious matter, and prepared to speak openly, candidly and thoughtfully about them to a stranger. And since in Poland – unlike 'normal' countries, as Poles call the West – conversations are in a sense always the same, one gains quicker and easier access into what preoccupies people than is usual in countries with the luxury of unfocused small talk. There is no small talk, though there are plenty of jokes – all of them political.

The openness with which people are prepared to speak in Poland is extraordinary, whether compared with other *bloc* countries or, as I understand it, with pre-Solidarity Poland. This is one of the profound and lingering consequences of August 1980. Timothy Garton Ash goes to the heart of what several people told me. He writes of the 'principle of As If' which has long been part of the self-definition of the Polish *inteligencja* and its understanding of its mission:

> Try to live *as if* you live in a free country, it says, though today your study is a prison cell ... But ... in the mid 1970s, the number of intellectuals who actually tried to live by the principle of As If was still tiny ... What transformed the 'dissident' minority into a 'dissident'

majority was the Solidarity revolution of 1980 and 1981. The Solidarity revolution was a revolution of consciousness. What it changed, lastingly, was not institutions or property relations or material circumstances, but people's minds and attitudes ... Behind the front line of confrontation between Solidarity's national leadership and the communist authorities, millions of people across the country – in factories, offices, universities, schools – suddenly found that they no longer needed to live the double life, that they could say in public what they thought in private ... For a few months it really was *as if* they lived in a free country.

In Poland it does not take much looking to find people at least talking *as if*. People generally are not afraid of the consequences of what they say and they say a great deal. Poland is not Russia. This is evident in the ease and speed with which strangers and chance acquaintances will move to tell you what your friends have already told you: life is terribly hard, the economic system is quite surreal in its inefficiency, and nothing better (or in a common variant, much worse) can realistically be expected. *No one* I spoke to dissented from these judgments, not even a journalist for the Party daily *Trybuna Ludu* who criticised Solidarity and defended the present government. His private comments about 'the system', however, differed remarkably little from those of everyone else. Everyone made such judgments freely, if not always publicly.

I spent an hour in a little shop run by a father and son, waiting while a cap I had bought was stretched to fit my oversized head. In no time I received instruction on the privations and *bałagan* (mess, chaotic disorder) of everyday life, the absurdity of official pronouncements, the impossibility of believing anything – particularly optimistic things – that 'they' *(oni)*, 'the reds' *(czerwoni)*, 'the communists', say. The father had enthusiastically believed 'them' when they came to power after the war. He laughed recalling the promised transformations to which he had looked forward. In a taxi travelling from Cracow to Auschwitz I received similar, though more detailed instruction, and example upon example of ways in which the system makes even the most ordinary, routine activities difficult. After about half an hour of such pedagogy, the taxi-driver paused, perhaps thinking of earlier times in his life, and said: 'Sir, I've said quite a lot. I trust none of this will go beyond the two of us.' Before I had come to Poland I would have expected such a question. After listening for two weeks to talk *as if,* I was startled. I assured him that I would betray no confidences and the lesson continued.

Before visiting Poland, and with no thought of the visit, I had written several papers, including one on my current work in legal theory and one revisiting work I had done some years ago on Marxism and bureaucracy. When invited to give seminars, I offered the former but once, largely in jest, mentioned the latter. That was taken up with enthusiasm and I felt in a quandary. Having told myself that I would be sensible, I was not sure that a critical discussion of Marx, Engels, Trotsky on Stalinism, and post-war critics of communism such as Djilas, the Poles Kuroń and Modzelewski, the Hungarians Konrád and Szelenyi, the Russian Voslensky and others, was the best way to begin. Yet the paper was conceived and written as ordinary academic work and I did not want to *start* by being a coward before I knew that it was even necessary. I received wildly different advice – some people saying that I should not even take the paper across the border, others (rightly, as it turned out) saying I would not encounter any problems. With some misgivings, which only disappeared when the customs officials evinced no interest in what I read or wrote, I took the paper in with me. (Poles, needless to say, have greater difficulties, at the border and everywhere else.) I decided to leave the choice of what to give until I had some feel for the situation. Ultimately I left the decision to my hosts wherever I visited, and gave each paper twice.

On one occasion the head of the department I was visiting preferred to hear my other talk, whether because it seemed more interesting or safer, I don't know. But some young members of the department had invited several post-graduate students and there were a number of ex-Solidarity activists in the audience (also, I later learnt, three Party members). They suggested the seminar take a vote and it was Marxism again. On both occasions, discussion of a paper highly critical of Marxist treatments of the social and political role of bureaucrats was absolutely free and unconstrained. On both occasions the discussion was fascinating to me, as much anthropologically as intellectually. Marxism, for example, has a somewhat different resonance, where it is the ideology of a loathed regime, from the one it still has in universities in the West. I met few Marxists; indeed to my knowledge none, though I met several people who had thought deeply about Marxism. Though some did, few people sought to dispute my argument that the Marxist tradition, in a rather systematic fashion, has little useful and much that was useless to say on this subject. On the contrary, several speakers warmed to the theme.

Essentially, the discussion, strikingly and poignantly un-'academic' in the pejorative sense, was about whether I or the thinkers I discussed had anything illuminating to say about Poland (and the other countries with 'really existing socialism'). On both occasions people freely expressed views which they could nowhere publish 'above ground', about the nature of their political and social system and its practices. One speaker, for example, vehemently denied that one could sensibly use the same term for Western bureaucrats and those in the communist *bloc*. The gist of his remarks was that there is a difference between a clerk and a gaoler, which it is important not to blur. The seminars themselves were ordinary university discussions, in no sense secret or clandestine, and I felt no pressure to mince words. On the contrary. Yet my paper could not appear above ground in Poland. Were it to appear underground I would be delighted and in more distinguished company than I am likely to be asked to join elsewhere.

Underground is not very subterranean. People constantly exchange illegal periodicals – of which there are allegedly over a thousand – and whole Western and banned Polish libraries can be had in underground Polish editions. Such publications are often course texts in universities. Garton Ash conveys 'the extraordinary quality of Polish intellectual life today':

> here is a communist state in which the best writers are published by underground publishers, the best journalists write for underground papers, the best teachers work out of school; in which banned theatre companies just carry on performing, in monasteries, while sacked professors carry on lecturing as 'private guests' at their own seminars; in which churches are also schools, concert halls, and art galleries. An

entire world of learning and culture exists quite independent of the state that claims to control it.

A recent article in *The Times*, reporting on the impact of high tech in the *bloc*, gives further examples:

> There is a hunger for uncensored films in the bloc. By Western standards some of this is pretty innocuous … church videos – now a very common phenomenon can draw a full house in Poland. But the challenge to the censor is usually more explicit. A film of the funeral of Popiełuszko, recorded by Solidarity cameramen who flaunted equipment bearing the sticker 'independent Poland productions', is shown regularly in churches.

The underground produce documentaries – interviews with people who claim to have been abducted or beaten in the Toruń area, the more politically sensitive of the Pope's sermons – and have started work on a feature film about internment under martial law. They also make scores of copies of banned films …

Some Polish dissidents use word processors to print out *samizdat* materials. Underground pamphlets, even books, are sometimes put on to floppy discs, smuggled into Poland, then printed at the press of a button. More playfully, there is even an underground video game called Zomo (Polish acronym of the riot police) in which a riot policeman chases a Solidarity supporter through a maze of streets.

The most solidly institutionalised pillar of life *as if* in this extraordinarily religious, now almost solely Catholic, society is the Church. One particularly poignant example is the church of St Stanisław Kostka in Żoliborz, a suburb of Warsaw. This is the church where Father Jerzy Popiełuszko preached. After his murdered body was found he was buried in the grounds of the church. He is mourned as a martyr both for the Church and for Solidarity. His church and its grounds have become a shrine in his memory (there is also a memorial to the young student, Grzegorz Przemyk, also murdered by the police, in 1983), and pilgrims come from all over Poland leaving badges and banners – huge Solidarity banners – in his honour. It is a startling and moving experience to enter these grounds from the unrelieved greyness of Warsaw. In 'official' Warsaw there is almost no colour and, it must be said, no visible sign of Solidarity, though the Church's campaign against drunkenness and the 'students' self-government' organisation both emblazon their slogans in a familiar and world-famous style and colour of print.

During my stay, in fact, the only public colour was provided by the ubiquitous and frequently glossy 'election' advertisements: 'from a wise choice come wise laws', 'we are choosing the Polish Sejm (Parliament): secure, financially responsible, just', 'do you thirst for democracy?; help develop it', 'choose! decide for yourselves who will be your representatives', 'Patriotism: a characteristic all Poles share', 'the future of the country depends on you'. (Note that all energies are in fact devoted to persuading people simply to *vote*, not to choose.) In Popiełuszko's church the contrast is complete: his grave thickly covered with constantly tended fresh flowers, the fences of the churchyard strewn with one vivid banner after another proclaiming slogans both religious and political, and naming their source, 'University of Lodz Solidarity', 'Warsaw Steelworks', etc. In answer to the election posters which were compulsorily placed in every shopfront, several of these banners proclaimed, 'Father Jerzy. We are voting only for Mary' (one of these continued, 'Solidarity. Lublin electoral district').

So, conversations are free, lively, intense and deeply serious, though the jokes are good (shortest joke I heard: 'A *milicjant* [militiaman] stands and thinks'; blackest: in Łódz the Polish–Soviet Friendship Society houses a coffee shop. The locals call it 'Katyń', after the forest in which the corpses of thousands of Polish officers, murdered by Soviet troops in 1940 were found buried). In the contrast now universally used by Poles, 'society' *(społeczeństwo)* has not been cowed by the 'power' *(władza)* and survives as a largely autonomous realm. There are dense and strong social networks beyond the reach of the state, a vast range of extra-state activities, publications and forums for debate and discussion, and in the Church a powerful institutional protector of independent activity, almost wholly intact. And one is moved and humbled, not simply because all this is happening under the nose of a state which, to put it gently, would prefer that it didn't; but also because so much of it is done on such an admirable moral and intellectual plane. I met many people for whose views and life-choices I felt deep respect. Unlike what so often passes for political engagement among Western intellectuals, in Polish discussions one finds no coquettish frivolousness about serious, usually tragic, political business, such as revolution – even among its supporters. This is not, of course, to say that everyone is wise and reasonable, but many are and as many or more are brave. It is hard not to be a little intoxicated by it all.

Yet from the beginning I was struck by how sad so much of what I saw seemed. I was ill-prepared for this. Though I had heard about most of what I will describe I had not *felt* it. The sadness of the conditions of life in contemporary Poland is so pervasive as to be palpable when one is there. Yet it is, of course, intangible and difficult to convey to outsiders. It may indeed not be reducible to its most obvious manifestations, but here are some that I observed.

I think that I, and many people, tended to think of Poland in rather vivid colours, especially after August 1980. The Gdańsk strike was, after all, a vivid event, worthy of the startling flags, banners, slogans, badges and T-shirts with which the movement which it sparked is indelibly associated. The emancipated society of which I have spoken deserves to be evoked in vibrant, lively tones, and in journalistic accounts it usually is. One of the major inspirations of life *as if*, Pope John Paul II, and its best-recognised practitioner, Lech Wałęsa, are scarcely 'grey blurs', as Trotsky used to call Stalin. And they are nothing if not Polish. On the other hand, it is of course traditional to think of *apparatchiks* as grey, and men like Kania and Jaruzelski do not let us down. Where the apparatus has crushed or dominated the society, I guess one expects greyness to permeate everything. But I did not expect that of Poland.

I was not really prepared for the overwhelming greyness of the setting of everyday life, or at least that part of it constructed in the past forty years. The image that kept recurring to me was of a curtain, not iron any more, too full of holes; but thick, drab, shabbily patched, unrelievedly grey and draped over nearly everything one saw; everything that didn't move. Warsaw, of course, had to be almost wholly reconstructed after the war and, with the splendid exceptions of the faithfully rebuilt Old and New Towns, it is done in a uniformly drab, swiftly dilapidated and 'user-unfriendly' way. Indeed, Warsaw is so drab now that I was once shocked to walk by a flower shop (as it happened, a lovely one), just to see such an abundance of brightness.

Of course other cities were less damaged and much beauty remains. The centre of Cracow, untouched by the ravages of the war, is splendid but it degenerates swiftly as you move into suburbs and it degenerates in the same monotone fashion as Warsaw. Of course too, my experience was limited and even then I saw several exceptions. In Warsaw, for example, to walk into a pre-war apartment after unleavened exposure to the typical small dingy, post-war chicken coops is like moving from night into day. And since Poland has so many enterprising people bending and finding gaps in rules, there are sure to be many more exceptions. Yet I don't believe that this impression of greyness was an illusion, and it is not simply to do with specific material things. It pervades all public space: the identical half-empty shops with identical and identically drab signs; the weary shoppers standing in the omni-present queues; the dilapidated but not old buildings; the uneven pot-holed roads; the shoddiness of cars and other finished goods; the drabness of clothes.

Even if not all that one hears about the shoddiness of domestic products, or the universal blame for this on the system, is justified, it is believed to be true. That in itself is a significant social fact. Perhaps if one tore away the curtain nothing much would change, but the contrast between the vividness and resourcefulness of the society and the sickly pallor of their conditions of life makes that hard to believe. And this contrast, like so many in Poland, is all the more poignant for being so stark.

And life is not merely grey but constantly, pervasively and wearyingly *hard*. Even the most routine things are difficult to get, and unpredictably difficult. So a shopper's life – and who is not a shopper when so much is scarce? – is a constant hunt for something that, if here today is sure to be gone tomorrow. So far as I could tell – my sample being merely three large urban centres, not the provinces – it is not at the moment a question of *poverty*: essentials can be obtained somehow – in shops if they and you coincide; *na lewo* ('on the left'; roughly 'under the table', 'on the sly'); on the black market (for more); from private sellers, some of whom are legal; or, if one has Polish gold – US dollars – at the special dollar shops *(pewex)*, where many imported goods and some higher-class Polish goods are available to those (both Poles and foreigners) who have hard currency. But if poverty was not evident to me, the constant strain of making ends meet was. Money is very short and all too often even if one had the money one cannot find what one wants to spend it on. So much routine attention has to be given for such pitiful reward.

I took three friends to dinner at a restaurant. The dinner cost about 7000 złotys, or well over one-third of the average monthly salary and the whole of a pensioner's monthly pension. (For a Westerner it is either a reasonable sum at the official rate of 150 złotys to the (US) dollar, compulsorily extorted from the tourist at $15 per day spent in Poland, or next to nothing, at the real rate of 650 złotys to the dollar.) One of my guests, a surgeon, is not well paid by Polish standards, and *a fortiori* by most other standards. He cannot make money on the side, as many doctors apparently do, because his specialty requires hospital facilities. In any event he is happy to work in the hospital because he still wants to learn from more experienced specialists. But he is angry and frustrated that facilities, equipment, conditions, drugs, are so primitive in Poland.

His wife, a vivacious and attractive woman, regaled us for some time with tales of how fortunate she is to live in Poland. She explained that it is insufferably boring to go shopping in a 'normal' country: as soon as you leave home you know where to go for what you want and you know that it will be there. Her life, on the other hand, is full of surprises. Each day is a fresh hunting expedition. She goes forth armed, like almost every Polish pedestrian, with a string carry bag – whatever your purpose, you might pass a shop which has something you want, or a queue which suggests that it might be worth waiting for whatever it is that others are waiting for. And then she stalks. She is never certain what her 'game' will be, or whether it will still be there by the time she gets to it, but she is ready to pounce. One day it might be toilet paper – a good catch – another day something else. And when she pounces she buys up all that she can or, if it is rationed, all she is allowed, because it might not re-appear for some time. (One habit which Poles who travel told me is hard to unlearn in the West, is to go to a supermarket in, say, Vienna, and buy in bulk, in case the merchandise fails to re-appear.) If there is a crush of people for a popular item she limbers her hand so that her attack is faster than another's. Each day she has the opportunity of returning home triumphant, because she has found something she thought unobtainable, or beaten the competition to something desirable. Her life is full of successes. This parable was told lightly and wittily and I laughed a lot. But of course it was not a funny story.

It is in fact hard not to laugh at the surreal consequences of an economic system so bizarrely out of touch with human needs. Thus the same woman told me of a new institution for particularly long queues which might last many days or even longer. Apparently queues for furniture are among these. The institution is stand-in queuers – usually pensioners or cripples – who for a fee hold a place for their 'clients' until the time of purchase arrives. Or an academic searching for pots and pans was rung by a friend to tell her of a set of Chinese cookware which she had seen on display as she rode past in a tram. Unfortunately, it turned out to be a display organised, if I remember rightly, by the Polish–Chinese Friendship Society, not an item for sale. For all I know, she is still looking.

The day I arrived in Poland – hot, tired and sticky in a crowded train from London – friends drove me to the apartment where I stayed for a week. Unfortunately the apartment – in a huge block in the centre of Warsaw was without hot water for most of that week. When I asked why, my friend shrugged and replied, 'Who knows? Socialism.' I was happy to take a cold shower but my friend would not hear of it. Instead he drove me to an international hotel with a sauna and swimming pool. He knew a caretaker and exchanged favours with him. Thus I spent my first hour in Poland, unexpectedly luxuriating in a sauna for well-heeled foreigners.

The system's inefficiencies and incompetency are such that it breeds a people skilled in informal arrangements – legal, semi-legal and illegal – to overcome its privations and frustrations. Such arrangements are endemic: what is unavailable can often be found, from a friend, for a bribe, *na lewo;* what is illegal is often done, and for many ordinary, mundane purposes needs to be done. One example apparent to every tourist is currency exchange. Private currency exchange is a criminal offence. However, the dollar is so valuable – both because it is worth many złotys and because *officially* many things can only be bought for dollars, no matter how many złotys you have. The natural and inevitable consequence is that people are keen to buy dollars. And the official rate is so derisory that anyone with dollars who needs złotys has small incentive to go to a bank. And if he does, he will be accosted in the street outside the bank by touts offering a handsome rate for his money. He might even receive an offer from the bank teller. So currency constantly changes hands privately; everyone does it and everyone knows that everyone does. But don't buy from those touts. Among them are provocateurs and you might be arrested.

Apartments are very small. One distinguished academic I met has an ill child who, with her husband and child, lives with her parents in their flat. There is so little room that he lives in his office, going home at about eleven in the evening merely to sleep. Currently a young couple who put their names down for a palace such as this can expect to wait about twenty years. In the meantime, unless they inherit an existing apartment or can afford what I am told are prohibitive prices to buy one, they must cram in with their parents and hope that their own children might get the benefit by the time *they* are ready to leave home. A friend bemoaned the lack of mobility among Polish academics: she occasionally dreamt of moving from Cracow to Warsaw or some other city but said it was inconceivable. I asked whether that was because jobs were tight, as they are now in Western universities: 'No, I would have nowhere to live.' When I emerged from my sauna in Warsaw, I went to the telephone operator of the exclusive, expensive, international hotel housing it, in order to look up a phone number. The operator gave me a 1978 phone book, which she said was the most recent she had: 'But don't worry; we don't move around.'

Life is a constant grind. There is nothing dramatic about this, nothing horrifying; just unending, frustrating, time-consuming and unspeakably wearying grind. Moreover the strain is not merely, nor for many people I spoke to primarily, related to such material privations and frustrations. Of course everyone is sick of queues. But their tiredness is not merely physical – though there is more than enough of that.

Even the bravest people I met, perhaps especially they, live under constant psychic strain. Life *as if,* after all, is not without risk or price.

True, it appears that the regime has for the moment given up on hearts and minds. It seems resigned to being regarded as the alien 'power' set against and oppressing Polish 'society'. And as a glance eastward shows, the regime could be more brutal than it has yet been. Yet it insists on compliance and appears to seek submission, in an increasingly repressive manner.

The shop-front organisations of Solidarity have, for the moment at least, been crushed. Extraordinary symbols of independence though they are, the shrines to Przemyk and Popiełuszko do, after all, commemorate murders. Arrests continue. In May three prominent dissidents were arrested for discussing a proposed fifteen-minute strike (which never took place) with Lech Wałęsa in his flat. In June, after a farcical trial, the three – Adam Michnik, Bogdan Lis, and Władysław Frasyniuk – received two-and-a-half to three-and-a-half year gaol terms. The recent so-called amnesty for political prisoners will not apply to them nor to anyone regarded as 'socially dangerous'. New laws which came into force on 1 July (the day protests were expected over increases in meat prices and falling living standards) increase the legal powers of the security forces and summary courts, further restrict rights of independent assembly, and increase penalties for 'public order disturbances'.

Hitherto the universities seemed, for some reason, to miss some of the more malevolent forms of regime attention. Indeed the universities were governed by a relatively liberal *Higher Education Act* of 1982, which was an only partly watered down version of drafts prepared before the state of war was declared. That is changing. In April, Bronisław Geremek, a medieval historian and adviser to Solidarity, became the first person to be sacked from the Polish Academy of Sciences. In May, General Jaruzelski told the Central Committee that 'the state could no longer afford to maintain universities that would be training grounds for dissent.' In late July, the Polish Sejm, which had passed the *Higher Education Act* of 1982, passed 'amendments' which emasculated the autonomy and self-government which that Act had allowed. The draft amendments had brought forth massive protest from university governing bodies, academics and students – in them-selves unique in communist states. The final laws are thus somewhat less vicious than they were intended to be, but they are vicious enough.

New faculty members must take an oath of allegiance to the state and pledge that they will dedicate themselves to the socialist education of students. The universities' electoral colleges, which used to elect rec-tors and deans, are to be disbanded, and this function is to be per-formed by university senates – with vetted membership – and all choices can be vetoed by the Minister of Education. The Minister can overrule or suspend decisions of collegiate bodies, dissolve them, decide on curricula, dismiss rectors, deans and other members of fac-ulty. The powers of student self-government bodies have been gutted. When I was in Warsaw it was rumoured that there was a list of eight faculty members scheduled to be sacked. Elsewhere the head of one institute I visited was told to expect an invigilation of staff in the new year, which would examine their records of loyal acts. One such act, he was told, would be voting in the October elections. On the Friday before those elections (which were held on Sunday), the male members of the one department I visited that day received letters from the army, requiring them to make appointments for interviews on the following Monday. No reason was given. My friends assumed that it was yet another 'subtle' attempt to concentrate their minds over the election weekend.

At the time of writing (early December 1985) the expected purge has begun. Over sixty senior academics throughout Poland have been dismissed from their posts, though not from their institutions, 'verifi-cation' – political vetting – is to begin early next year, and the Party spokesman has announced that 'universities had to uphold the princi-ples of socialist education and that lecturers had to be measured against these principles' (*The Times*, 11 December).

Finally, a number of academics with foreign invitations for some years have been and continue to be refused passports. Since foreign materials are so hard to get, and their sense of isolation from the Europe to which they profoundly and defiantly insist they belong, is so deep, this is a painful blow. Again, like most Polish repression, the barrier between the East which oppresses them and the West which has so much that they lack and yearn for, is not impermeable; but it is real and palpable. Many Poles do travel; professional literature sent to professional addresses (*not* to private homes) stands a good chance of getting through. But no one will be surprised if it does not, and one must take care what one sends. I am told that problems of isolation from latest developments, let alone equipment, are particularly strong in the hard sciences. They are certainly not small in the fields with which I am familiar. Apart from whisky, the best present one can bring a Polish intellectual is a good book.

What results from this unholy mixture – unique in the *bloc* 'a country', as Adam Michnik puts it, 'where the nation strives for freedom and autonomy, and the authorities try to force it back into a totalitarian corset'? Not, it must be said, terror nor even among most people I met, immediate fear. While the authorities' continuous repression appears to retain pragmatic usefulness – it stops strikes – it has lost symbolic power. And the regime's repression is so uneven – some heroes do get passports, some non-heroes do not – that it is doubtful whether even a draconian law will be enforced systematically. No one, for example, seemed to know what use the regime would make of the harsh new law on universities. No one, of course, considered it, and the huffing and puffing accompanying it, to be encouraging signs. Nor are they more likely to after the recent dismissals. However, optimists said to me, 'We'll survive. We've had to live with such laws before. Poland is still far from being Russia'; pessimists replied in effect, 'Given the continuing crisis the situation can only get worse. This law will be enforced and there may be worse laws to follow. And Poland may well become Russia.' Instead of fear one has frustration and wary apprehension. Of course good should triumph, but Polish history does not give one much reason to bet on it and Poland's neighbours are not keen to help it along. Many futures are possible; some of the most plausible are less than attractive. And no one is a short-term optimist.

In the meantime one waits, struggles, and decent people continue to behave decently. None of this is easy. Some of the most courageous people of principle I met are very, very tired; tired of the petty frustrations and idiocies of daily life in 'people's Poland'; tired of that single conversation, so exhilarating to a foreigner; tired of constantly struggling for the fate of Poland; tired of a life where so many decisions and acts – inconsequential in 'normal' societies – are moral decisions here; tired, in effect, of constantly *having* to be morally serious; drained from constant material, psychic and moral strain and the knowledge that it might go on forever and, of course, might get worse.

Living through a war must be something like this. In most ways, of course, it is easier to live in Poland now than during war. Hardly anyone is killed, no one lives in terror and though the struggle is recognised to be a long one, morale is strong. It is more like living under occupation, with rulers who won't go home. These rulers have, in their implacable overlords, a trump card which no one wants them to play; they are also well versed in what Trotsky called 'corridor skills'. For the rest state and society are in stalemate, which both sides expect to last some time, and there is no respite visible.

One morale-testing and sometimes sapping difference between the present situation and one of war is that the Polish regime is not outside the society, though it is alien to it. It holds the jobs, pay, economy, political and administrative structures. The system rests on greater and smaller complicities. As one officer of the secret police recently observed to an underground paper, 'I have the impression that efforts have been made for many years to turn Poland into a country in which it is difficult not to be a scoundrel.' The benefits of collaboration are material and obvious: foreign trips, access to dollars, job preferment, a better apartment quicker, unrationed petrol (the present ration is twenty-four to thirty litres per month), non-market privileges, and so on. Not, I imagine (though I don't know), princely fortunes – Jaruzelski is not Gierek and anyway the whole country is so ramshackle that it is doubtful whether there is a great deal to spread around. But every bit extra counts when it is denied to everyone else. And the regime is adept at encouraging complicities, even among those – now an extraordinary number – who will do nothing gross. I was told of a meeting between the Deputy Prime Minister, Mieczysław Rakowski and leading literary and intellectual figures, after the declaration of martial law. Knowing his audience well, since he had been among them for many years, he allegedly said, 'You probably think that by refusing to co-operate with us the *inteligencja* can force us to back down. That's not so.

Czechoslovakia was a cultural desert for over ten years. Poland can be the same. *It's up to you.'* I spent an evening with a young academic who berated himself and his colleagues for holding on to their jobs, though younger aspirants would have to decide whether to take the oath of loyalty or not. He quoted an author (whose name I missed): 'The Nazi occupation forced us to be heroes; this occupation forces us to be shit.' I suggested that there was a significant area of moral space in between but he, who obviously occupies that space and is no shit, refused to agree. So there is a good deal of melancholy.

People have to decide again and again: how much dealing with the regime is permissible? How much is too much? Have I gone too far? Have my friends and colleagues gone too far? The choices are not enviable and, of course, they do not affect oneself alone. I had some of my most rewarding conversations with a young academic who had been in Solidarity. She sought to explain to me some of the ways in which even one's most basic and private decisions get caught up in moral dilemmas. In 'normal' societies, she argued, you would like to bring up your children to share your values, whatever they are. But so long as this system exists, our values are the opposite of its values. Should we teach our children to believe what we do, or to believe what we despise and to behave in ways in which we would not behave?

Apart from such 'first-order' concerns – 'what should *I* do?' – this constant call on moral decision breeds a variety of second-order preoccupations, some of them wise, subtle and discriminating, some suspicious, some fundamentalist, some dogmatic and extreme. Not all of this is socially or politically healthy. It is fed by, and feeds, the traditional Polish divisions between 'realists' and 'romantics' which have bedevilled Polish politics for centuries and have made realism seem (and often be) opportunism and idealism seem (and often be) utopianism. Poland does not need these divisions to add to its list of problems, but in present conditions they seem inescapable.

Of course a great many people negotiate this chasm realistically and honourably – it is, after all, a skill they have had some practice in acquiring. One friend, for example, works in a small academic department, several of whose members are in the Party. He explains their motives without rancour: one is scared, one is a careerist, one likes to travel. Personal relations at work are civil and he does not suspect them of undue patriotic diligence. He thinks it unlikely that they will report on other members of the department and discussion, as I have said, is candid. But he will have nothing to do with them socially; they will never enter his home.

There is, however, another option, and many Poles, particularly young ones, are taking it. That is to opt out. The most clear-cut way is to leave. Poland has suffered a brain drain of enormous proportions from which it will not quickly recover. Motives are various: danger if one stayed, exhaustion, hope of economic betterment, inability to prac- tise one's vocation or practise it properly, wish to get far away from Russia (to Australia's advantage), and many others. The consequences are the same. Many of the most talented and outspoken Poles have been lost to Poland. Among those who stay, many of the best educated do not enter, or leave, state employment, but drive taxis, become tradesmen, go into private business. Again the reasons are various, sometimes political, sometimes moral, sometimes financial. Among academics I met several who specialise in arcane theoretical areas because it is impossible to publish truthfully anything related to poli- tics or current affairs. An important question which Poles generally, and the *inteligencja* especially, ask is what will be the result for Poland of all this highly talented opting out. And of course, it is not just the problem of what Poland loses by many of its best people opting out; there is the question of who takes their place: careerists, dopes and thugs. Thus the notorious Polish 'negative selection' continues and now it need not even be deliberate. The jobs remain and *someone* will be found to fill them.

Given the all-pervasive hatred and distrust of 'them', 'the reds', 'the communists', it is inconceivable that the Party will find people of moral and intellectual stature to replace those whom it has driven out. For there is one thing on which 'society' is now agreed: its misfortunes derive from the system of power, not from a Bierut, Gomulka, Gierek or Kania whose replacement might do things differently. (When asked why my parents had not visited Poland after the war, I explained in terms of my father's anti-communist activity. Several people who scarcely knew me and had never met him asked me to pass on their congratulations.) In August the *New York Times* ran a moving account by Michael T. Kaufman, its Warsaw bureau chief, of the visit to Poland of his father, an 82-year old ex-member of the pre-war Polish Communist Party. He had sat in Polish prisons for nine-and-a-half years with, among others, Adam Michnik's father, Ozjasz Schechter. Among the many intelligent comparisons which the old man makes between pre- and post-war Poland, one seemed to me particularly striking:

> He said that when he was a young communist organiser in the 1920s, people in Poland had many ways to explain and account for their unhappiness and dissatisfaction. 'There was a pluralism of blame,' he said. 'A worker might blame the factory owner, some anti-semites blamed wealthy Jews, Jews said the problem lay with anti-semites, and the peasants resented wholesale merchants. Others pointed to Germans or Ukrainians as the source of the trouble. Meanwhile, we Communists, a small group, ran around saying, no, it's not a question of individual grievances, it is the system that is to blame. Now, after fifty years, I come back and what do I see? The whole nation knows perfectly well that the problem lies with the system and only the leaders are saying, no, the difficulties are the fault of individuals, former leaders, mistaken politicians, or, as during the anti-semitic purges of 1968, Jews.

So, unless there is some breakthrough, the nature of which I cannot imagine and some forms of which I fear to, the impasse between state and society will continue. Each side is strong enough to thwart the other's deepest ambitions, but not to realise its own. So for the immediate future, it seems to me that Adam Michnik's prognosis, smuggled out of gaol as he awaited his recent trial, will prove accurate:

> Yes, it is possible to govern in this way. So long as geopolitics is favourable, this system may last for quite some time. But it cannot rid itself of the stigma of an alien, imposed garrison. Repression has lost its effectiveness. Our imprisonment does not frighten anyone, nor will anyone be enslaved by it. This has been the case for the past five years.

Michnik goes on to give grounds for his heroic and profound optimism:

> They [the rulers] are much too confident. They forget that the sociology of surprise is hidden in the nature of the Leading System [Communism]. Here, on a spring morning, one may wake up in a totally changed county. Here, and not once, Party buildings burned while the commissars escaped clad only in their underwear. Edward Gierek, so beloved by Brezhnev and Helmut Schmidt, so respected by Giscard d'Estaing and Carter, within a week travelled from the heights of power into oblivion. *Sic transit gloria mundi.*

Poland's post-war history, and in particular Solidarity and its extraordinary and continuing aftermath, are striking testimonies to the 'sociology of surprise'. And it can be witnessed elsewhere in the bloc. One of the characteristics of political development in the satellite countries of Central Eastern Europe has been that 'the whole vast apparatus of domination which seemed omnipotent and omnipresent the day before, disintegrates the next day'. And it may be that Poland, unlike its neighbours, will avoid what has traditionally followed that collapse, in Poland itself, Hungary, East Germany and Czechoslovakia, as observed by three distinguished Hungarians, Ferenc Feher, Agnes Heller and György Markus:

> Once popular resistance is broken by external force (or even by no more than a threat of external force) the whole apparatus of domination (with a few changes at the very top) is reconstituted with remarkable ease. In an essentially unchanged form, it again attains that character of practical immovability and solidity which can even result in the memory of its collapse fading from the consciousness of its subjects – at least until the time when its next crisis approaches.

Poland is already an astounding exception in that the apparatus has only been able to reconstitute itself, not the cowed or hopeless population which has been the other pillar of 'really existing socialism'. I have no doubt that this Polish exceptionality will continue. Sadly, I also have no doubt that its bearers will continue to pay dearly for a system they neither want nor deserve. I hope Michnik's optimism will ultimately be vindicated, though I am not confident that it will. I also hope that nothing worse will befall Poland, though I am not confident that it will not.

*1986*

# Life in an Abnormal Country

Poland, as any Pole will tell you, is not a normal country. The Polish economy is a surreal shambles; everyday life is hard, drab and exhausting; queues are everywhere for everything; wages are low, prices high and inflation galloping. Not only is life nasty, horrible and brutish, but everything takes such a long time. And the whole country needs a coat of paint.

In outline these facts are well known. Countless newspaper articles inform Westerners that Polish shelves are usually empty, that what little is on them is rarely attractive or appetising, and that nevertheless people queue for it. Even a brief visit is enough to expose one to the shabby peeling monochrome of Polish cities; the huge and dilapidated housing estates at the edges of town; the random operations of hot water and phones; the absurd joke in the title of Warsaw's Hotel Grand; the tiredness, and at times hopelessness, of the best and – perhaps more surprising – the worst of the people one meets. And these obvious facts have contexts, consequences and social meanings which are less familiar – indeed astonishingly hard to imagine – outside Poland; in normal countries. All Poles, on the other hand, are experts on them. Yet their expertise is rarely articulated, and Poles find it frustrating to try and explain to foreigners. Where to start?

Let us try to imagine how and how long the inhabitant of a normal country, deposited in Poland with just the local median salary to live on, might survive. Let him be an academic, since I am one and know them best, and let us be generous and not schedule his visit for winter. How, in other words, would a *normal* person negotiate Polish reality on a Polish

salary? First he would find that salary pitifully small. An American colleague, for example, is shortly going to lecture in Poland for three
months. He is to be paid fifteen dollars a day, the equivalent of a full professor's monthly salary. While dollar equivalents are not the whole story,
they are not irrelevant to our visitor's problems. If he wanted virtually
anything foreign or anything good – salami, coffee, chocolate, electrical
goods, often even vodka – he would need dollars to pay at hard currency
shops *(pewex)*, for he would get these goods nowhere else. If he needed
foreign books: dollars again. If he stayed in a hotel, he would have to pay
in dollars or pay at the official rate of exchange, which is vastly (in mid-
1989 some seven times) more than the state-acknowledged and
exchanged free-market rate. If he needed and knew how to bribe, he
would need dollars. If he had anything left to save, it would be pointless
to leave it in złotys with inflation running at several hundred per cent.
He should do as countless Poles do and change it whenever possible into
green gold, even at a bad rate, because the currency will catch up. If he
enjoyed the life so much that he wanted to stay and buy an apartment, he
would have to become a złoty multi-millionaire – and pay in dollars.

If, for a treat, he were allowed to revert to his Western salary,
without any additional income or capital, he would immediately
become a local millionaire. That would make life easier, of course, but
he might find his newfound wealth frustrating and not always pleasant.
Frustrating, for if awesome wealth was a new experience for him, the
difficulty of finding something to spend it on might dull some of its
lustre. Worse still, he might become afflicted by the feeling that he had
done *nothing* to deserve his instant wealth. Spending time with people
he admired, perhaps some whom he loved, he might feel the awful
injustice of his easy profligacy and their practised care. Seeking to be
generous, he might just demonstrate himself as vulgar.

But let us return our visitor to Polish conditions. If he has found
somewhere to stay, for he cannot now afford a hotel, and if he has
bought what he can, he will have little to show for it, no money left, and
not much time to spare. Let us hope that he has the patience of
Methuselah or 38 million Poles, for otherwise he will not eat meat for
a long time. If he wants to make a local call, he will find the experience
excruciating; an international one, unbearable.

For the latter, one can wait days. Most Westerners in Poland find routine queuing intolerable after the first hour's novelty wears off. Poles too find the endlessness of everyday waiting infuriating and enervating, but it must be endured – particularly if they have children.

What if something breaks in our visitor's apartment – his washing machine, stove or toilet? Our visitor is unlikely to be the Renaissance figure found in every Polish academic family: the scholarly repairer of stoves, the beautiful and sophisticated expert on toilets. Naively he might think of going to a nearby shop and buying a replacement part; or calling – perhaps even complaining to – the manufacturer's representative. He should not voice those thoughts, lest his friends find him uproariously comical.

Imagine his surprise, then, when eventually he visits friends, academics earning the same salary as he, for a party. He may well be bewildered to find delicacies, even kinds of meat, which he has never seen in any shop. His hosts might have second jobs, relatives in the West, or have recently been on a fellowship not a cent of which would have been squandered. Or they may have had something that they were able to sell abroad, like the streams of Poles who never visit West Germany empty-handed and hope either not to return or at least to return with hard currency. (One sage drunk stopped me in the street a few months ago thinking I was a Pole who, because of my camera, must have been in Germany. 'Earn there, spend here,' he advised repeatedly. 'But, whatever you do, don't get it mixed up!') Whether they have any of these necessary luxuries, they will all know a great deal that he doesn't: the Byzantine operations, known affectionately as *załatwianie spraw.*\* Since the regular, public sources of supply are so impoverished, what Poles have that the outsider lacks is a vast array of talents and networks for finding things and fixing things. These skills can be impressive, but they are only developed because normality has broken down, and they don't come cheap, either in time or effort.

Think what *everyone* needs to know in Poland before he or she can deal with anything else. What pervasive training and experience in the

---

\* In Polish this phrase, translated literally, means 'arranging matters,' or 'settling things'. Neither of these, however, conveys anything of the layers of common social understanding contained in the Polish.

maintenance of skills that are useless in normal societies, indispensable there. And the time. The endless string of procedures necessary to prepare the ground, exploit opportunities, stock up reserves – toilet paper, matches, flour, sugar and other scarce luxuries – find replacements, think of alternatives, make do. The cultivation of contacts; the maintenance of reciprocities; the courting of useful beings. The searching and searching for sources of supply. And still the hours waiting for bread, meat, sugar, flour, petrol; the months for electric appliances or furniture; the years upon years for apartments. And then the many things which cannot be gotten, however long one waits.

A colleague has a child with asthma. The child was required to have twenty weekly injections. But medical supplies are catastrophic in Poland. Among countless other deficiencies it is very difficult to get single-use syringes, and impossible to rely on them being there twenty weeks in a row. The solution? Bribe a nurse (with a packet of coffee) and get the syringes in advance. My colleague had been in Britain on a fellowship for three months. He lived hard there, to be able to save the princely sum of £150. This treasure was laid aside for other necessities to do with his child.

So on special occasions, for special purposes, remarkable things can be done in Poland, in ordinary life as in politics. Our visitor will likely be struck by some qualities of character that the hardship often elicits.

On the one hand, one can see a sort of demeaning adjustment to the necessities of material success by those who aspire to be dollar, or at least złoty, rich. This has a hucksterish sleaziness to it, of which many Poles are ashamed. On the other hand, he will find among an extraordinary number of colleagues a level of serious, admirable *engagement* with matters of consequence which is hard to find in more pampered circumstances. Fewer top-of-the-line specialists, perhaps; many more truly engaged intellectuals who, unlike himself and most of his peers, have been genuinely tested.

In ways that no one is likely to have planned or wanted, Poland has come to instantiate some of Marx's better known prophecies. This is not a common view in the West. Often it is argued that contemporary communist states are travesties of Marxism, or at least that – whatever the consequences of his thought – Marx never envisaged or advocated anything like them. Yet credit where credit is due.

Marx loathed the alienating power of money over human lives. If one restricts oneself to Polish money, that problem has been solved: the currency is worthless. In *The Critique of the Gotha Program,* he looked forward to a time when 'the narrow horizon of bourgeois right' would be 'left behind', and so it has been. Far behind. He prophesied what Engels called the 'withering away' of state and law, and notwithstanding the best efforts of the Polish United Workers' party, that almost occurred before their resignation from (some of) the commanding political heights.

Above all, recall Marx on the division of labour. As he and Engels famously explained in *The German Ideology:*

> as soon as the distribution of labour comes into being, each man has a particular, exclusive sphere of activity, which is forced upon him and from which he cannot escape. He is a hunter, a fisherman, a shepherd, or a critical critic, and must remain so if he does not want to lose his means livelihood; while in communist society, where nobody has one exclusive sphere of activity but each can become accomplished in any branch he wishes, society regulates the general production and thus makes it possible for me to do one thing today and another tomorrow, to hunt in the morning, fish in the afternoon, rear cattle in the evening, criticise after dinner, just as I have in mind, without ever becoming hunter, fisherman, shepherd or critic.

Polish communism not only makes it possible to do 'one thing today and another tomorrow', it makes it necessary. Poles are hunting for something or other much of every day; they fish rarely, it is true – for the major rivers are dead (and their water, and thus tap water, undrinkable), poisoned by industrial waste – but they criticise all the time. And they exercise a variety of other finely honed talents – their genius for repair, for example – which Marx doesn't mention.

In sum, this is an industrial society which, perhaps for the first time in modem history, has managed to transcend the division of labour. It has produced a nation of Renaissance men, and especially women, who can make something out of nothing and commonly have to. It has achieved what Marx predicted would occur 'in a higher phase of communist society, after the enslaving subordination of individuals under division of labour, and therewith also the antithesis between mental and physical labour, has vanished'. These are achievements too rarely noticed or applauded by Marxists. The one small thing remaining is for society to 'inscribe on its banners: from each according to his ability, to each according to his needs!' But where to buy banners?

**The Depth of the Crisis**

In the first years of martial law in Poland, the following joke was popular. It was also plausible. A man is running through the street distributing leaflets. He is chased and eventually caught by the *milicja,* the much-reviled police. A *milicja*man notices that the leaflets are quite blank, and demands to know why nothing is written on them. The offender replies, 'Writing? Who needs writing? Everything's obvious.'

And so it often appeared. It was obvious who the bad guys were, obvious who were the good guys, obvious whom to oppose, whom to support. Of course it was never quite that simple. Difficult moral and prudential choices abounded, and some people handled them better, more admirably or sensitively, than others. Still it was obvious who had responsibility for what was going on and going wrong in Poland, and obvious that whatever the good guys did or didn't do, they were spared that responsibility. It is different today.

The new leaders of Poland have been handed a poisoned chalice. Both its donors and its recipients are well aware of that. That knowledge presumably consoled the former in their defeat and disgrace. And the latter accepted, knowing well the conditions under which they had gained power – or at least responsibility, because the military, police, transport and communications (no small combination) are still kept from them. How will it turn out?

The short answer is that nobody knows. That may always have been so in fact, since there is much in Poland's recent past that no one predicted – from the birth of Solidarity to the imposition of martial law to the holding of semi-democratic elections. Few Poles now venture confident predictions. How could anyone be confident, given not merely the scale of Poland's problems but also the extent to which any paths could be redirected and any particular solutions scuttled by decisive factors beyond the control of all the relevant Polish players?

For assorted reasons – genealogical, political, personal – Poland has come to mean more to me than any other foreign country. But my interest is purely that of an *amateur,* though in the full meaning of that word. So I shall merely try to suggest some elements of the mosaic which is forming but which might at any moment be shattered.

First and most obvious is the simple depth of the Polish economic crisis. Where are the experts who can confidently say how to climb out of it? Obviously freeing-up markets is necessary, and apart from the hardest *beton* (concrete) in the Party, who lack any social influence, everyone agrees. But while everyone favours a free market, different people understand the concept in different ways. The last ruling communist prime minister, Mieczysław Rakowski, favoured 'enfranchisement of the *nomenklatura*', that is, allowing the Party-appointed and anointed managers of state enterprises the legal right to operate privately on the side in various ways, often using state assets. Such stratagems reek of corruption, *nomenklatura* nepotism and a rigged playing field, but perhaps they might get *someone* interested in the success of the enterprise. The present government is unlikely to manifest much enthusiasm for such cosy communist devices, however.

Free-market liberals, recently enthused by the Harvard economist Jeffrey Sachs, favour radical freeing-up of the market. But in an economy driven into the ground by state monopolies, some Polish sceptics ask, 'What market?' Fast and massive deregulation will certainly cause a lot of social distress; more limited measures already have. Who will keep the lid on and how tight? Social democrats want social guarantees. But to whom and with what? Whatever distress is caused and whatever mistakes are made there are populists on the left of Solidarity and pseudo-populists in the Party, including the Party unions, ready to exploit them.

Poland's problems are political as well as economic. An obvious one is that Solidarity must rely for its survival as a government on two parties which until this year have been independent of the Communist Party only in name – the United Peasants' Party and the Democratic Party, both of which prostituted themselves for many years.

The Communist Party itself is more adept in taking power than in sharing it, but at the moment it has to settle reluctantly for the latter. There will be many Party members keen to make this unnatural situation short-lived. Shortly before the resignation of the communist prime minister, General Kiszczak, I asked a distinguished and experienced sociologist whether he thought a Pinochet-style coup – which some people were predicting – was likely. He replied that the possibility could not be excluded: 'There is only one decisive argument against it, and that is a bad one. It is that with our experience no one could be fool enough to think that a coup would solve anything. Of course that's true, but it's a bad argument.'

Still my own guess is that the Party is not at the moment a direct and positive threat. It has, after all, lost – lost even the power to intimidate – as a result of every repressive move (such as the murder of the Solidarity martyr, Father Popiełuszko) since the imposition of martial law. It will spoil, it will thwart, and it will oppose, but I doubt that it will seek or be able to topple the existing regime – at least for a while.

The Party is now a completely demoralised ragtag collection of factions, often covering – indeed mimicking – much of the natural political spectrum. It has even become fashionable for some Party members to call themselves social democrats, and the Party includes some leading Hayekians. General Jaruzelski has said – and I suspect that he might mean it – that a one-party state is a thing of the past. Since the Party is composed largely of careerists, many of these are likely to see some advantage in appearing decent since indecency hasn't worked. It might become habit-forming. Even if it doesn't, that is less relevant now. The Party is a sinking ship and the rats are leaving.

But other political problems remain and they lie deep. Paradoxically, in this most highly politicised of countries, there are few people with any experience of normal politics. As one political scientist stressed to me, Poland lacks Western-style political elites sustained by well-established political traditions, practices and procedures of parliamentary politics. One might add that what traditions existed – anti-semitism apart – have been deliberately extirpated over the last forty years. The Party has sought – fruitlessly as it turned out – to suppress all possibility of politics. It had short-term successes in maintaining what the sociologist Jadwiga Staniszkis has called a 'state without politics', at ruinous cost to the country. The Party has no skill in running a government, that is plain; and in its only real political contest it was not merely comprehensively trounced but appeared unable even to play the game. The Party's 'corridor skills' have failed. To what extent they will be enlisted to spoil the chances or exploit the weaknesses of the new government remains to be seen.

Solidarity, on the other hand, is extraordinary. Larger-than-life people involved in larger-than-life events, and remaining clean in the process. Heroic is not too strong a word for their achievements, for their leaders, and for many of their rank-and-file members. Courage was a major currency of the movement and it has paid off spectacularly. One of the brilliant election posters, conceived almost overnight, was not really exaggerating when it had a very large and familiar film shot of Gary Cooper in mid-purposeful stride. Above his head and in smaller format on his badge was *Solidarnosc.* In his gun hand, *Wybory* (elections). At the base of the poster: High Noon 4 June 1989.

What might have helped, however, as things have turned out, is some experience of normal, pragmatic, unheroic politics. But there has not been much room for that and not much of it around. Everything about Solidarity is abnormal, unpredicted. It sprang up, not exactly out of nowhere but where such a growth had never before occurred. It animated a nation to an extent no one imagined and its opponents clearly did not understand. It was beheaded in the one move – auto-invasion – that no one but its perpetrators predicted; beheaded, it seemed, cleanly and comprehensively. But the head re-grew, others were added, and, after a hard and testing period, their jailers and would-be executioners were forced to talk to them, campaign against them, and, at least provisionally, concede defeat to them. And what a defeat! The size of Solidarity's election victory shocked everyone, not least the leaders of Solidarity themselves. They agreed to contest merely 35 per cent of seats in the Polish lower house, the *Sejm,* and all the upper house seats, with four years – presumably learning years – before a decisive contest for power. As David Warszawski, a leading Solidarity journalist, put it:

> In a normal country, people go into politics to win power. We went into politics with the goal of becoming only an opposition, legalised and recognised as able to influence and criticise. Perhaps our grandchildren might take over, but nobody among us thought that we ourselves would do it.

Solidarity's victory was so crushing, however, and the Party's humiliation and subsequent disarray so complete that they have now been propelled to run the first free post-communist government.

Amazing and grand as this triumphal progress has been, it has not been a lesson in normal politics. It has all happened very, very fast and it has not come without price. It is not just that Solidarity has not tasted government before; after all, that is true of many political oppositions. It has had scarcely *any* experience of pragmatic, day-to-day politics, or large-scale administration; it has had no time to learn, and there is no institutional and cultural infrastructure of normal politics around to rely on or learn from. It will have to be a case of learning on the job.

And who will learn? The top leadership of Solidarity – like Wałęsa, Prime Minister Tadeusz Mazowiecki, and other leading figures such as Jacek Kuroń, Adam Michnik, and Bronisław Geremek – are men of outstanding calibre, morally, intellectually, politically. But my friends from Solidarity worry about the unpreparedness of many in what now is the governing party.

First, they say, since no one expected the sort of election victory that ensued, and since Solidarity was so much a moral movement anyway, meritocratic criteria were rarely uppermost in deciding who would stand and, as it turned out, win. Mietek was strong in the underground, Waldek didn't break under questioning, Piotr doesn't lie (I use fictional names). My friends, of course, admire each of these qualities and know how much it has often cost to display them. They fear, however, that such traits will not readily equip their possessors for what lies ahead.

And precisely what sort of movement is Solidarity? It began as a trade union, and speaking for the workers remains an important part of its present role. Quickly it came to voice increasingly political and universal demands. Clearly it was not merely a union, but at the height of its popularity (in 1981) representative of the nation, a nation which – like Isaiah Berlin's hedgehog – knew one big thing: it hated communists. It was a movement of opposition. Whatever else divided its members, opposition to the government united them. But that, as it were, is no longer interesting. It is now the government.

As that moment approached it became clear that Solidarity had no clear programme of reform, and that what programmes it did have did not all point in the same direction. I was in Poland until the day the former Minister of the Interior gave up trying to form a government. It was already clear that he would ultimately fail, but it was not clear when or with what consequences. At that stage it was also clear that there was no clear conception within Solidarity of what its role should be. Many people predicted that it would, or argued that it should, split into several normal programme- and orientation-based parties, reflecting political differences that hitherto had been sheltered under the great opposition umbrella but were real and marked: populists, social democrats, free-market liberals, Christian democrats. Such parties might have been ready to contest the first truly free elections, scheduled for 1993. But again Poland has been deprived of the time to develop normally. More subtle fears were expressed: that, after all, Solidarity too was a child of the communist system, and what it had not learned from that system it learned from the imperatives of conspiratorial opposition. People complain of 'Bolshevik methods', no compliment in People's Poland. The leaders nominated candidates, perhaps inevitable given the short time before the election. But there were also complaints that the leadership had moved with unseemly haste to cut off rivals. It did everything to make the election a choice between its candidates and the Party, and in the campaign advocated that voters for Solidarity cancel not only Party candidates but also independent non-Solidarity candidates. When it became clear that the newly created Citizens' Committees had done an extraordinary job in the election campaign by tapping roots with which Solidarity had lost touch, the National Executive Committee of the union resolved that the regional committees be disbanded. This demand was much resented and is unlikely to be followed.

Wałęsa also has caused resentment by his unilateral decision to demand government for Solidarity now. One senses that the leaders of Solidarity have little time for and no experience of the procedural pre-conditions of normal and civilised politics. As a friend close to the Solidarity leadership put it: 'I'd be less worried if someone around here was concerned to have a House Ethics Committee; but no one is.'

I don't want to exaggerate these purported deficiencies. Compared to its communist opponents, Solidarity has been a model of democracy, liberality and intelligence in conditions which have put each of these qualities to stern tests. Indeed, I don't know, and can hardly conceive, of another movement that could come from where Solidarity has come, survive the conditions it has survived, surmount the obstacles that have been continually and deliberately put in its way, and yet show the restraint and grace in dealing with its erstwhile tormentors and the courage in assuming its terrifying responsibilities that Solidarity has shown.

Prime Minister Mazowiecki is a man of honesty, depth, and courage. He also has powerful support from the church, which would have been uncomfortable with some of the other prominent figures from the lay left in Solidarity. Though the attentions of a friend like Cardinal Glemp are a mixed blessing – both morally and intellectually – the support of the church is crucial. Moreover the new government also has the support of Wałęsa and the Solidarity unions, and that will be important in the hard times to come. It also has two other key advantages. First, it can draw on an immeasurably larger and better pool of talent than its predecessors. For a very long time the *nomenklatura* has been filled by 'negative selection': bad people were chosen and good ones refused to serve. That is likely to change dramatically. Second, this government is truly committed to the transformation of a failed system. Its predecessors were committed to its maintenance, and they even failed in doing that.

These advantages are of incalculable importance. And all of them, and more, will be necessary to cope successfully with the problems Poland faces. One Solidarity activist explained a key problem to me this way, with rather effective oversimplification: 'Everyone knows *what* needs to be done. There is a little disagreement over *how* to do it. But there is no agreement at all about *who* should be asked to bear the pain and dislocation that will necessarily be involved. Once we get down to that, agreement falls apart and contingent factors will decide.' 'Contingent factors' is a euphemism for the balance of forces.

Poland is an ethnically homogeneous society since the Holocaust. But it is not socially homogeneous. Workers' interests are not the same as those of peasants nor of those whose jobs are threatened by reforms; there are millionaires who are expert in milking the existing system, parasites who live off it, paupers who do not, and many who might join or replace the millionaires and parasites if the system allowed them to. There are those in failing industries and those who could prosper if the vast, ramshackle state apparatus could somehow be made to let them breathe. And there are huge *organisations* – the Party, the administration, Solidarity itself, and the extraordinarily influential, if ineptly led, Polish Catholic church – which will demand a slice of the action, and seek to protect their own.

And responsible for carrying out whatever is decided, of course, are the *nomenklatura*, the million or so government servants who owe their jobs to Party approval. The government not only has to look to the future, it also has constantly to watch its back and check the till. If its policies are likely to benefit the health of the nation, they are unlikely to do wonders for the people charged with carrying them out. And these are people not notorious for altruism.

And what of the patient? Ultimately, whatever happens in government, it is Polish society which will register the results, as the Poles say, on their skins. Their skins are tired, stretched, bruised and sore. And the soreness is not merely physical, it is spiritual. Slovenliness, apathy, and amorality have come to characterise so many areas of productive and distributive work. A Polish shop display – at least in state shops – is close to being an oxymoron. The stuff is usually of low quality, and while many need to buy, no one has much interest in selling. Or look at any public building under construction: the gaping holes between brick and wood, the rubbish or bits of brick stuffed carelessly to plug gaps, the mortar which oozes messily like some sort of congealed pus in every direction but vertical or horizontal. Pilfering is standard practice in dairies, bakeries, building sites, perhaps everywhere but shipyards.

While one cannot be other than impressionistic about such things, there are worrying signs of civilisational decay, rot. There is hope in the simple fact that private shops and privately funded buildings (or church buildings) look different. But not all habits will disappear at once.

Finally, many Poles are very demoralised and depressed. I left, as I have mentioned, before the appointment of the new Solidarity-led government, and it may be – must be – that that, and recent changes elsewhere in the bloc, gave an important lift to morale. But so did the election victory, the round-table discussions between the government and Solidarity before that, and the remarkable televised debate between Wałęsa and the leader of the Party unions, which Wałęsa won in dazzling fashion. But given the underlying economic and social conditions, such lifts are a wasting asset. Their consequences had largely evaporated by July, notwithstanding what momentous political events were still occurring daily and that people knew that they were.

What is true and unique about the present moment is that, for the first time in forty years, the Poles have a leadership whose intentions they have reason to trust. That must count for a great deal. Moreover the events of the last ten years have shown that the Poles have the capacity to rally to causes in which they have faith. Nevertheless, euphoria is harder than most things to sustain in Polish conditions. It should be remembered that, notwithstanding the epochal significance of the June elections, a significant 38 per cent of potential voters voted for no one. Unless the new government has some quick and evident successes which people can feel, morale will dissipate quickly.

Of course people differ in their reaction to hard times. Some are optimists by character or vocation; some maintain ironic detachment from the realities of everyday life; some are absorbed in politics, and in Poland that is quite something to be absorbed in. But many talented people have left the country, most of those who remain are drained and some are defeated. I have known plenty of sad people in normal countries; but before I visited Poland I had never known a society that was sad.

### Whither Poland?
Poland's problems, then, are awesome. The new government has inherited a system which has destroyed the Polish economy and deeply

wounded the society. There is no doubt that this government, unlike all its predecessors, is determined to transform that system. There is equally no doubt that will be extremely difficult to do successfully. And ultimately two key ingredients are simply out of the Poles' control. They cannot decide what the Russians will do, and they cannot decide what we will do.

Everyone in Poland is aware that the breathing space which they have received since 1985 is due to Gorbachev. Everyone knows too that if Gorbachev fails, their future is endangered. Finally everyone knows that there is a good chance that he will fail (and, though few people worry about this, were he *really* to succeed, that might also be uncomfortable in the long term). But there is nothing much – beyond tactful diplomacy – that they or we can do about that.

On the other hand, we can do something about our own response. In the West – though the full extent of Poland's problems is only dimly grasped by Western onlookers – there is general sympathy for the Poles, mixed with admiration for their courage. Both sentiments are justified but neither instructs us on what is to be done. For too long the Bush administration seemed tentative, cautious and undecided about what and how much to commit to Poland's experiment with democratic reconstruction. It cannot be accused of over-generosity to date. There is concern in some government circles about the new government's capacity to survive. Well of course there is. Yet if this government fails, there won't be a better one.

Poland needs money, skills, infrastructure, which only the West can provide. It needs, to give an obvious but important example, a telephone system which allows international calls to be made without one having to give up a few days to do so: that is not merely a matter of convenience, but a precondition for substantial international connection and foreign investment. The country needs training in the development and maintenance of all sorts of microstructures – in civil society, in economic life and practice, in politics. The government also needs help in mitigating the social pain of necessary reforms. Otherwise this first attempt to build democracy from the ruins of communism will fail. And that would not be Poland's failure alone. It would be ours too.

Should Poland falter, the many and powerful forces – within Poland and nearby – who have been convinced all along that democracy and liberalisation are only for fools, will be given heart – and perhaps their heads. If the Poles succeed, that will be a triumph. If they fail, that will be a tragedy. Of course they cannot rely on the West to succeed for them. But they will not succeed unaided. We can either determine to help them meaningfully now when they need help – and in the process do ourselves a favour – or we can temporise, wait for sure bets, and fail. That choice is ours.

In an earlier essay, I quoted Joseph de Maistre on the French Revolution: 'For a long time we did not fully understand the revolution of which we were witnesses; for a long time we treated it as an *event*. We were mistaken; it is an *epoch*.' The same is true of the Russian Revolution. It has dominated this century. It has bequeathed a technology for seizing and maintaining power which has cost millions of lives and enslaved millions of people. It has reduced once-civilised countries to dilapidated ruins and has threatened still civilised ones with the same. It may be that this epoch is coming to a close. It is in everyone's interest that it does.

*1989*

# Gypsies, the Law and Me

I t is easy to be robbed in a big city, or a poor country, particularly a big city in a poor country. Pickpockets, muggers, false crowds, currency changers, short changers. Every tourist knows about them and many have met them. It's a common story, almost an expected incident of travel. People prepare for it as best they can. That may turn out not to be well enough and one is usually shocked to be robbed. Still it is the particular theft which is shocking, not the fact that theft of this sort has occurred. One is surprised in fact, as it were, not in principle.

I was robbed in a different way: by gypsies whose major weapons were simply words. Not particularly interesting words, and certainly not well-spoken. Just words. They used them, I became enmeshed by them – made vulnerable by and to them. Words – in particular, talk – had no power over my opponents. On the other hand, I turned out to be – as they knew I would be – powerless against the nets of civility which conversation throws over its well-behaved participants.

I was not merely surprised to lose my money but astounded to lose it thus. Ultimately I regained it – even made a small profit – but in the normal way of things I would not have, and it was the last thing I really wished to do.

This, then, is a tale of psychological, not physical, assault. The assault was preposterous from the start but it would have ended successfully – as it has countless times before and since – had not its almost willing victim reluctantly felt impelled to pursue the rule of law in a cause which scarcely warranted it, a country which hardly knew it, against a group of people who had never heard of it, with the aid of a police force which had for a very long time subverted it.

In 1988 I was invited to participate in a conference of scholars of Polish origin, to be held in Warsaw and Cracow in July 1989. This turned out to be shortly before the end of communism in Eastern Europe, but I did not know that; nor did my hosts.

I had considerable reservations about accepting the invitation, but I was finally persuaded by a Polish friend that I should attend, so long as I delivered a paper with some political and moral bite. So I wrote a piece on the rule of law, arguing that there was an enormous difference between societies in which law counted – such as the one from which I had come – and those where it simply didn't count – such as the one to which I had come. The paper was not an unqualified popular success in this officially sponsored function, but I was pleased to have given it. During several weeks in Poland I returned to the theme when I could, gave a press interview re-emphasising the point, and on the day I am about to describe offered my essay to a prominent independent journal.

I was approaching the end of my stay in Poland and wanted to buy presents for friends. Communist Poland had only one category of store in which one could anticipate finding much of any quality at all: hard currency (*pewex*) stores which sold to anyone, but only for Western cash. Such stores could be found in many places, but the best – still not much good – were in the best hotels – also not much good. So I walked to the Hotel Europejski, carrying two wallets – my normal złoty wallet in my jacket and a second, containing priceless dollars, secreted in the back pocket of my trousers.

Outside the hotel was a group of some eight or ten gypsy women, one of whom approached me and asked for 20 złotys. This is some fraction of a halfpenny, so without second thought I gave it to her. In gratitude for my 'generosity' she offered to tell my fortune without charge. This all seemed a pleasingly exotic diversion to me, and I figured – for at this stage I was still figuring – that I could handle myself in the middle of the day outside a well-populated open air coffee shop, against – if it turned out to be against – a woman half my size.

My interlocutor – for there was a lot of locution – talked to me ceaselessly and at great speed, explaining what she was doing and telling me about myself. Her hands kept moving in a rather mes-merising fashion as well. She asked for a cheap coin which I gave her. She made what I took to be some sort of blessing (more likely a hex) over it, stuffed it in my shirt pocket and told me it must stay there for three days. Why, I never knew; nor did it occur to me to ask what to do if, in sweltering mid-summer, I should choose to change my shirt.

She then asked to see the money of most value to me. Sensing my hesitation she loudly assured me that she had no designs on my money, and several of the other gypsies immediately drew closer and chorused endorsement. I had not yet surrendered my senses, but found myself impelled, by a combination of two rather different pressures, to sur-render my money. On the one hand the largest note in my złoty wallet was 10,000 zl – a sizeable amount in Poland, but equivalent then to under two dollars. So I reckoned I could survive its loss. On the other hand, to refuse the request would be to manifest distrust not only of the teller of my fortune, but of her companions, who by now had all engaged me in friendly conversation. That would be impolite.

I tendered my 10,000, she asked for my handkerchief, plucked from my head a hair which I could ill afford to lose, wrapped these together and mumbled something mysterious. This all happened very fast, accompanied by her reassuring and fortune-telling monologue.

She then asked me to show her my dollars. Again all in the interests of telling my fortune, not stealing it. I denied I had dollars. She rebuked me, saying her powers allowed her to see I had them. When again I denied, she said I mustn't lie with the blessed coin in my pocket. I still resisted, though somewhat shame-facedly for her friends again assured me that her intentions were wholly admirable. Again those professions were quite disarming.

She didn't stop her rapid talk, still simultaneously explaining her darting movements and exploring my soul; and then, out of the blue, she announced that I was particularly sad. I was recently distressed about someone important in my life. That happened to be true. She even had some characterisation of the distress, which seemed apt. It was all happening very fast, so I guess she only needed to throw out something that caught a psychological peg. But she certainly did that. I don't believe I was affected intellectually by this revelation – I didn't suddenly believe she had special powers – but I was psychologically disarmed by what appeared, in the heat, tension and disorientation of the moment, to be inexplicable insight. As if hypnotised I found myself reaching into various pockets trying to find where I had put the wallet in which my dollars were hidden.

When the wallet emerged the pace quickened. My fortune teller still kept talking, and her colleagues reassuring. Though for some time my apprehensions had been growing apace, they were still kept in check by the rudeness it would have demanded to show or act on them. Eventually her hand dashed at my wallet grabbing all but twenty dollars that I managed to retrieve. I grabbed her hand – though I was still reluctant to exert real force. There was an awful din and she vanished. The leader of the chorus – eager as ever to help me – pointed to a taxi and said she was in it. I rushed over to find an inoffensive gentleman somewhat bemused at the large, sweaty, looming Westerner peering into the window of his cab.

By now what has long been obvious to you had dawned on me. I had been conned and robbed. I was dazed but also angry. I returned to the remaining gypsies and accused them. They coolly replied that it wasn't them but her, and she was gone. I told them that I was going to the police. My erstwhile support group started to scream, loudly and odiously – there in the open air outside the coffee shop which I had imagined might protect me: 'You wanted to screw a gypsy girl; you son of a whore, you rapist.' 'Ten of us saw you trying to screw a gypsy girl. You Arab [Warsaw folklore has it that Arabs come to Poland for girls who are beautiful and cheap] trying to drag a gypsy girl into the hotel.' 'Anyway she's not here. Do you see her?'

I stumbled away, disgusted with myself for being so bewilderingly stupid, disgusted with the crescendo of horrible abuse that I was hearing, disgusted to be part of it – indeed the object of it, disgusted to be powerless in the face of it.

I entered the hotel, thinking at least to use my remaining $20 to buy something for my friends and also to put some distance between me and the scene outside. I felt desperate to get away from the squalor into which I had fallen. I certainly did not want to pursue the matter. I assumed the money had gone for good, since I would never see the fortune teller again. And I must also admit that I didn't want to hear the accusations against me repeated to someone who might believe them. After all, why not believe them? It was only my word against theirs, and I still had no idea that no one in Poland believes gypsies.

Just as I was almost convinced that I should do what I wanted to do – flee – I recalled that I had been preaching all around Poland about the importance of the rule of law. Yet the first time something illegal happened to me my almost overpowering instinct was to run for cover. I decided, with not a little reluctance, that I would have to pursue this. I went back to the gypsies who, with one exception, were still standing outside the hotel. Somewhat unbelievably, I lectured them on the immorality of their enterprise. I received the predictable, though this time even more vehement, response. I then went to the doorman of the hotel, and demanded to see the manager: 'You know what is going on here and you have a responsibility to warn or protect those who don't. Why don't you?' He sent me to a more senior doorman, whom I approached followed by my mocking chorus. He replied loudly to my rebuke: 'We all know what's going on. So does the *milicja*. But there's nothing anyone can do about it.' The gypsies laughed triumphantly, I called them a band of thieves, they called me a rapist, and I skulked into the hotel.

In truth I was partly relieved that it appeared I could do nothing, because there was nothing I actually wanted to do but escape. I was also struck – indeed increasingly amazed – by the psychological cleverness of what had just been done to me. My brief and speedy encounter had induced and had depended upon a quite remarkable degree of psychological disorientation. Later I heard of some Warsaw actresses who, fascinated by the process, used to take small amounts of money and allow themselves to be robbed in this way.

Friends in Solidarity had told me that soon after martial law had been imposed, underground Solidarity had issued instructions to people who were to be interrogated, to say nothing. Not just little; nothing. I had imagined I understood why: interrogators know the business better than those they interrogate and anyway they can put apparently innocent pieces of information together to confound a later victim, who imagines they know more than they do. What I never understood till that day, however, and have since confirmed, is that once talk has begun, it is almost impossible for a civil person not to be at a disadvantage with people who have no use for civility. Or rather, who have very good use for it, but in whose own moral economy it has no weight at all.

Perhaps this is all the more the case if – as here – the stakes are insignificant, real danger non-existent and the interlocutors women. One has less reason to be on guard and less psychological ability to be. Had I been accosted by men, I imagine I would have been at the same time more cautious and less concerned to be polite. This too is presumably ideologically unsound, but I guess my gypsies took it to be a safe bet.

Finally, not only had I been robbed cleverly but I was being kept at bay, again by nothing more than the psychological discomfort on which my tormentors were confident that they could rely. Primitive strangers knew all they needed to about me, exploited that understanding and had been justly rewarded for their skill. Nevertheless my admiration – though real – was not unalloyed.

At that juncture the senior doorman entered the hotel. I decided to tackle him again. 'Is it really true that no one can do anything about this?' He replied, 'Once I used to chase them away, but I was warned that one night I would find a knife in my back. So I don't interfere. I've got to live and it's not my affair. If anyone's stupid enough to talk to gypsies, that's their problem.' 'But, I'm not Polish,' I protested. 'I don't know anything about gypsies.' 'Everyone in Europe knows about them.' 'But I'm from Australia.' At this he softened.

He explained that he had spoken as he had outside, in part to reassure my entourage. But all was not necessarily lost. 'It all depends on the policeman. If he's dumb you're gone. If he's smart he can fix you up. You say you've still got twenty dollars. Slip it to him and he'll find your gypsy. There was an Austrian here recently. He lost two thousand dollars, but he told the policeman there'd be something in it for him and got his money back in no time.' Since my only reason for pursuing the matter was my damned rule of law, I decided I couldn't slip any policeman anything but that I would call the police. The doorman offered to call them for me. 'I will call them from inside the hotel. But after that I can't be involved. It's your affair.'

I waited tensely for a good while, still apprehensive about the coming encounter between the alleged thief and the alleged rapist. In the meantime, an expatriate Polish couple from France stumbled through the hotel door. They had lost one million złotys in the same way as I had lost my dollars. I suggested they stay with me and wait for the police.

In due course our *milicjant* arrived. I should explain that another reason for my ambivalences was that the *milicja* in communist Poland were universally loathed as the dumb thugs of the communist regime. (Among other things, they assume the place of 'Polaks' in Polish jokes.) Since all my friends were in the opposition, I felt soiled, disloyal, going to the *milicja* for aid. All the more so when our *milicjant* appeared, looking and behaving like a poor extra in a B-grade cop show. He strutted, barked monosyllabically and wore small reflective sunglasses which made him seem somewhere between ominous and ridiculous. My heart sank as he bundled – actually squeezed – the three of us into the back of his small Polish Fiat.

Our gypsies were nowhere to be seen, which he said was unsurprising given their two good hauls. Still they would re-assemble outside the Hotel Forum, and he would pick them up there. So it was. The fortune teller was not there, but all her accomplices, including the one most vociferous about my sexual ambitions, were. We told him that the major player was not about, but that did not bother him. He went to the leader of the group – my former ally – and told her he was taking her to jail. At that her resistance melted away, as – it turned out – he knew it would. He explained that gypsies fear nothing more than imprisonment. She reassured us that she would return our money, left a hostage with us and disappeared. I had to give an estimate of what my wallet had contained, because I wasn't at all sure. I stressed that it was an estimate and she wagged her finger sternly at me, saying: 'Don't add on, sir. Whatever you do, don't add anything on.' Suitably chastened I did the best I could to remember the exact amount. She was away for some good time, time enough indeed for our hostage to start cursing quietly. Eventually, however, she returned, giving me my money and calling me away from the people I was with. She said that I no longer had any business to be there and should go home. The *milicjant* had already told me, however, that I should return to his base for paper-work. Since he had the address of the friends with whom I was staying, and I had no wish to cause them any trouble, I said I would not leave. In any case I was meant to be doing this for the rule of law. I couldn't just pocket my money and run. The gypsy started to swear at me again, but with little conviction. She was in rather a weak position.

This was all the more the case when it was discovered that she had only come up with 900,000 złotys, instead of the million that the other couple had claimed to lose. The cop arrested her and said that we all would have to go to his base, but then since she was rather large and there were three of us victims and he only had a Fiat, I was asked to walk. I did so, but not knowing the *milicja* bases of Warsaw and being reluctant to ask, I got lost. Eventually I asked a pretty couple of girls if they knew where the *milicja* headquarters were. They looked at me with haughty disdain and said that they knew nothing of such places. I con-gratulated them, diffidently explained that I had been robbed and wan-dered aimlessly about.

Eventually I found the base and entered it to discover my *milicjant* hot and bothered about what he should do next. He couldn't hold the gypsy long, because none of us had actually been robbed by her. On the other hand, he was not prepared to release her, unless these Westerners, who could make life difficult for him these days, were satisfied. Eventually someone brighter than he suggested that we make and sign statements that we had been fully recompensed. The couple had been short-changed and I simply didn't know if I had, but we decided to cut our losses and sign. That evening I discovered I had overestimated, by twenty dollars, the amount I had been carrying. Though my gypsies had reassembled at the Europejski next day when I returned to make my purchases, I didn't return the money.

*1990*

# Traps for Young Players in
# Times of Transition

The first of the leading peculiarities of the present age is, that it is
an age of transition. Mankind have outgrown old institutions and
old doctrines, and have not yet acquired new ones.... In all other
conditions of mankind, the uninstructed have faith in the
instructed. In an age of transition, the divisions among the
instructed nullify their authority, and the uninstructed lose their
faith in them.

– John Stuart Mill, 'The Spirit of the Age' (1831)

When introducing neophyte enthusiasts to a complicated game,
it is common to warn of 'traps for young players'. It may be
worthwhile to explain such traps to those for whom the post-communist 'twisted path to democracy' is a game that they would like to watch
from the sidelines or perhaps even play but that seems confusing and
hard. I will not address all such pitfalls, merely ten of them – one for
each year since the collapse of communism. Awed by the scale and pace
of changes in the region, beginners often have to rely on what is written
by specialists, by those who in more-established and successful fields of
research might be called experts. They are right to consult such writings, but in doing so they should be aware of some of the things that
commonly influence what they read, other than the facts of the matter.
Their reading will otherwise be fraught with risk.

In this area, first of all, the distinction between scholarship and daily journalism is thinner than among commentators on, say, the Peloponnesian War. In post-communism studies, nothing dates as fast as yesterday's journal article. Writings from 1993, which took the victory of ex-communists in Poland, Lithuania and Hungary as convincing evidence that post-communist Europe was moving backward into the future, seem quaint, now that these parties have all, for the time being, been defeated. Similarly, articles which explained in 1996 that no one could defeat Mečiar in a Slovakian election and that if they did he would not leave (and similarly for ex-communists in Bulgaria and Romania) today seem more than just three years old. All the more so, when such inaccurate predictions were buttressed with erudite references to the peculiarly non-Western cultural baggage which guaranteed that these states would never become democratic. (Orthodoxy has been routinely invoked to explain failed or half-way reforms in Bulgaria, Romania and, of course, Serbia. With Slovakia, absent middle classes were the usual suspects.)

The 'yesterday's scholarship, today's fish wrapper' quality of much post-communist research is not surprising, nor is it necessarily a reflection on the IQ of the researchers. Instead, it is an intrinsic feature of this new game, which was once known as the 'transition from dictatorship to democracy' but is now more coyly called a 'transformation', destinations unspecified. The game is, after all, only ten years old, and there is therefore no one in the world who has been playing at it, or even aware of it, for very long. That we are not always successful at this game should not surprise us. Virtually none of the so-called experts on the region's previous political game, the one known as communism, had a clue that it was about to end and be replaced by something else. Their expertise has not become irrelevant, but it is somewhat devalued by predictive failure, and much of it has in any case been superseded by the fast and furious movements of the past ten years. The new game is as complex and unpredictable as the old one seemed (wrongly, as it turned out) predictable. As a consequence, the distinction between the deadline-driven journalist and the contemplative scholar is often obscure.

Second, neophytes should keep in mind, for they will not always be told, the great diversity of and within the countries that constitute the various world of post-communist Europe. Twenty-seven countries with four hundred million inhabitants, and I do not know how many time zones, constitute 'a region' in name only. These countries have very different pasts, and they will have increasingly diverse and probably divergent futures. They had one enormously important factor in common: they were ruled by communist parties almost all of which were backed by Moscow. But though that rather large fact about their past contributes to their present and gives them many common problems, it does not determine what they do about those problems or what new things happen to them. So if anyone delivers breezy assessments of the future of democracy or capitalism or whatever else in 'post-communist Europe' you have reason to be on your guard, or at least to ask for what lawyers call 'further and better particulars'.

Moreover, diversity is found not merely among states but also within them. Diversity of regions, classes, ethnic groups, age cohorts, social and political processes, of winners and losers, winners who will be losers, and losers who will be winners. Although the paths to democracy and capitalism are entwined, they are not the same path despite their occasional overlap. And some people and countries walk better, farther, faster, more safely on one than another. And there are many other paths as well, and they often confusingly cross and branch. No wonder people lose their way.

Third, because there is a lot written about the 'region', it always helps to know something about a specialist's biography in order to grasp where he or she is coming from, in both the literal and the Californian sense. That is because in the present state of transitology, where someone is coming from often has as much to do with what they say as does what, ostensibly, they are talking about.

Begin with the literal sense: it helps to know what country a commentator is from or writing about. I am struck by how much better post-communism looks to Poles or Polologists than it does to Romanians or Romanologists, which is understandable enough if you compare the present situations of Poland and Romania. Harder to understand is why it looks so much better to Poles than to Hungarians, given that Hungary has also fared relatively well. Until you know that a Hungarian optimist is a contradiction in terms, you will not understand why so much more miasmal gloom emanates from the pretty Danube than from the ugly Vistula. (I once asked a particularly clever and particularly pessimistic Hungarian colleague whether his pessimism was a way of guarding against disappointed hopes if things were to turn bad. 'No,' he responded, 'nothing works in Hungary, not even pessimism.') And quite apart from optimism and pessimism, commentators commonly identify as central to the whole region problems that figure only locally. A young player should check to see if what seems all-important to Polish discussion is considered equally vital in Budapest or Bucharest. Frequently it is not, yet local specialists or specialists on particular parts of the 'region' write, all too often, as though their own experience were of region-wide significance.

Fourth, provenance other than merely geographical is also important. All too often, questions posed and answers given tell us more about a particular scholar's intellectual biography than they do about the matter under discussion. Historians, for example, are prone to recall past legacies, many long past, when thinking about present problems. Sociologists also talk of legacies, but usually they are relatively recent. And political scientists and economists! They have no memory at all. They are far more impressed with what lies ahead than with what lay behind. Indeed, it is not always clear that they think anything important ever happened before they arrived on the scene.

It is rare to find economists invoking Mongol or Byzantine footprints of the past to explain what they find distressing in the Russian present; less so to find historians who do. Ex-Sovietologists are likelier to go back a bit further than economists but not so far as historians – to Gorbachev, say, or, if they are of an antiquarian turn of mind, to Lenin. Locals and area specialists tend to insist on the ineffable peculiarities of the regions they hail from or study. Westerners, particularly Americans, often combine a lack of local knowledge with the conviction that it is not necessary to have much. We are all human, after all. It is hard not to sympathise. Many leading transitologists – particularly those interested in the fate of democracy – were already experts on other subjects and other places, particularly Latin America, when communism suddenly became 'post'. New fields of interesting and important endeavour opened up, and, understandably, scholars packed their bags and moved in. Equally understandably, having already mastered Spanish or Portuguese, some of them have been reluctant to learn Hungarian or Romanian. Easier to seek universal patterns that link what they know with what they want to talk about. And so we witness wars between the transitologists who do precisely that and the scholars who have given their lives to Russia or Romania and do not like to be lectured about what is going on there by someone just off the plane from Bolivia.

At issue are not just differences in attitudes toward the past. Economics, law and even political science seem to breed 'can-do' optimists, happy to be brought in to explain to benighted locals what they must do to get from where they are – say, Bucharest – to where they should be – Boston, for example. History, and to some extent sociology, breeds pessimists who are inclined to believe that locals need not make a great effort to move on because they will not get far, starting where they are and carrying the overwhelmingly heavy baggage that they do. The technical term for this baggage and its consequences is 'path dependence'. It need not translate, though it often does, as the Slavic or Magyar equivalents of the Irish peasant's response to a request for directions to Dublin: 'I wouldn't start from here.'

This autobiographical element in what passes for science may be inevitable, given the novelty and difficulty of the problems now being addressed by those whom my friend Claude Karnoouh calls '*specialistes du post*.' It is at any rate almost universal. And there is nothing especially wrong with it, apart from the fact that young players are often unaware of it and do not realise that many authors who ostensibly write about the region are actually talking about themselves. (And – after the initial excitement of 1989 had waned and before Kosovo exploded – largely to themselves as well.)

Fifth, young players should treat single-factor explanations of the present with care. Commentators frequently select one particular factor – such as the burdens of history, hostile cultural legacies, peasant fatalism, 'learned helplessness', 'civilisational incompetence', webs of 'dirty togetherness', the presence (or absence) of shock therapy, and so on – from among the many potentially relevant ones. And this single, overprivileged factor may be invoked to explain manifold contemporary developments – for example, the weaknesses of the rule of law, democracy, market economies, civil society, etc. A young player should always ask if the writer has fairly considered competing explanations. For a general methodological difficulty afflicts every attempt to explain the sources of disappointment in post-communist societies: there are so many potential explanatory candidates, and so many of them point in similar directions. Thus, is it hostile political culture, state weakness, Orthodoxy, poverty, the 'poisoned gift' of vast mineral wealth, or bad weather that explains the weakness of the rule of law in, for example, Russia? Sad to say, Russia has them all, and not much in the way of the rule of law. How to choose? Even if we eliminate the weather, since Norway and Iceland appear to have overcome it, the answer to our question still seems overdetermined. Worse still, it is not clear that these potential explanatory factors are unrelated or exclusive alternatives. In the conditions of post-communism, they seem so entangled and mutually reinforcing that it is extremely hard to pry them apart.

The sixth trap concerns that common pastime, calculating the costs of transformation. As the Polish sociologist Andrzej Rychard points out, such costs are often spoken about:

> without any reference to the conceivable costs of no transformation at all. One may say that the fall of communism was an indirect proof that the functioning costs of the previous system were too high. What is more, from the very beginning of the changes, one of the ways to mobilise political capital preferred by politicians of certain orientations was to treat the costs which persisted beyond the life of the former system and were connected with its 'fall' as transformation costs. After all, it was also a matter of argument whether those were costs of the changes or, perhaps, costs inherited from communism. And the argument could never be unequivocally brought to a conclusion since, inter alia, the functioning costs of the former system are difficult to calculate. Undoubtedly, it is one of the paradoxical gains of the transformation that the market order which is being introduced allows for the calculation of costs and generally presents the problem of costs

much more clearly. If, therefore, the chance to assess the costs of the transformation is a good, the impression that the costs are high is partly a consequence of the fact that they were never calculated before.

Seventh, so much is made of the parlous state of democracy, of the market, civil society and so on, in the region that one should always ask, though transitologists do not always ask, the deepest question of social research: compared to what? Specifying the comparisons one has in mind – in particular, what we are comparing with what and why – will not in itself solve anyone's problems, but it might clarify what the problems really are.

Eighth, let me suggest another point of comparison helpful for weighing what has been achieved in particular countries in the region: non-events. I have in mind coups that never occurred, violent conflict that did not erupt, the happy avoidance of certain dreaded election results, and so on. Once these non-events turn out to be non-events there is a tendency to ignore their significance. But the ease with which they have become non-events in several countries in the region is worth serious contemplation. And from my own observation, it took some nervous moments in several countries for even relatively experienced players to conclude, with relief and then confidence, that they really were non-events.

The ninth trap is spelled out in an observation of Joel Hellman's, regarding that excellent book *Rebuilding the Ship at Sea*, by Jon Elster, Claus Offe and Ulrich Preuss: that it 'presents a more complete and more compelling explanation of the obstacles to institutional consolidation than of the conditions for success. This creates a certain bias toward failure in the analysis, which may not be warranted given the experience of transition to date'. Whether or not this is true of the book Hellman is reviewing, it is very common. It stems from cultural pessimism, the difficulties of the present, the loss of faith in grand narratives, and many other things. But you do not have to scratch hard or often to find it. The conclusions of writers exhibiting this bias are not always pessimistic, but when the final analyses are not gloomy, they often seem at least surprising and under-explained.

And this brings me to my final trap: the seductive, often apparently irresistible, charms of pessimism. Pessimists, of course, often have good reasons. To the extent that pessimism flows from insightful understanding of states of affairs and possibilities, it might well be what it used to be called under communism: well-informed optimism. But deep insight is not always its source. Sometimes it is just a cast of mind, and at other moments just a failure of imagination, however understandable when times are hard. The same, of course, can be, and has been said of certain kinds of optimism. Someone – perhaps it was Henry James – observed that those who lack the imagination of disaster are doomed to be surprised by the world. In 1914, and not only then, many were. The same mistake is often at work: direct extrapolation from one's estimation of the present (and past) to pessimism if the present seems harsh, optimism if the reverse.

In hard times and places, pessimism often seems warranted by the abundance of what, in his sparkling book *To Craft Democracies*, Giuseppe di Palma calls 'hard facts' – cultural, political, social, and economic legacies that may plausibly be taken to render happy outcomes difficult and are taken by many to rule them out. As he points out, however, difficulty does not mean necessity: 'whatever the historical trends, whatever the hard facts, the importance of human action in a difficult transition should not be underestimated.' Di Palma is making a theoretical point about the unwarrantedness of pessimistic – sometimes structural, sometimes cultural – determinism: not only has it often led to predictive failures but it is based on theoretical error. The error also has a moral dimension, since it can turn out to be self-fulfilling. Observers who find such determinism appealing might keep in mind that actors in difficult circumstances are not always helped by it. In the absence of overwhelming evidence that the future is closed (and one rarely has such evidence), there are good reasons to look for ways in which it might turn out to be open. Or, at a minimum, kept open.

Having observed Poland, and then some other parts of the region, since 1985, I offer this last point as the self-criticism of a somewhat bruised pessimist – bruised, because my pessimism so often seemed warranted by the evidence and yet was so often proved wrong, while the buoyant optimism of recidivist gaolbirds like Adam Michnik seemed heroically irrational and yet often proved prophetic. I have learned from this not only to admire Michnik's judgment, among other things, more than my own but also to be suspicious of the ease with which pessimism seems sensible, even required, in hard circumstances. I am also pleased it never occurred to him to listen to people like me.

*1999*

# Parables of Hope and Disappointment

What follows are ten parables.* The number is, of course, arbitrary. There could be more or less, and no one remembers how many parables there are in the Bible. Still, once I had passed three, it seemed inappropriate to stop at nine or go on to eleven. Like three, after all, ten has a biblical resonance.

My parables begin with hopes rather than promises, because my memories of 1989 are more of the former than the latter. One quickly forgets the nervousness (and widespread pessimism) of 1989, too easily imagining retrospectively that everyone thought the future would be rosy or easy. That is not what I recall. Still, hopes were high.

It is common to think of disappointment as a natural and direct response to distressing developments, and then go on to ask what was it about these developments that led to the disappointment. To seek the sources of disappointment in later results, in other words, rather than in earlier anticipations. And of course, a lot has happened in the region, especially in its southern and eastern parts, that must disappoint anyone, whatever their hopes. However, I am intrigued with the other end: the hopes themselves. Some disappointments follow from, indeed sometimes flow inevitably from, the nature of the originating hope. Some hopes are inherently unrealisable, and my first parable has to do

---

* In July 2001, the World Congress of the International Institute of Sociology was held in Cracow. The theme of the congress was 'The Moral Fabric of Contemporary Societies'. It included a plenary session on 'Eastern Europe after Communism: Promises and Disappointments'. What follows are my remarks at that session, updated in minor ways.

with them. However, there are other sorts of hopes that spawn disappointment precisely when they are realised, and the rest of my discussion will be concerned with hopes of that sort.

This is not the whole of the story, and in some countries it is only a small part of it. By emphasising this aspect I do not mean to diminish or trivialise the more profound problems – of which there have been plenty that would distress anyone who had to endure them. Yet, since memories are short and local pastures so easily can seem brown, it is perhaps worth recalling that not everything that disappoints us flows from what it has strangely brought us to. Some comes from what we ourselves bring to it.

The significance of disappointment-spawning hopes varies, as does the increasingly diverse range of post-communist experiences. I know Poland best, and there I think the character of originating hopes plays an important part in subsequent disappointments, a part that is often overlooked. It is not insignificant in quite a few other countries as well.

Parables are usually identified by name, the parable of the Good Samaritan or the parable of the Prodigal Son, for example, and are often recalled by those names, when people have forgotten all else. In keeping with that tradition I will name each parable and then explain it.

## 1. Impossible Dreams

Adam Michnik once distinguished two sorts of former dissidents: those who hated communism because they didn't like dictatorship, and those who hated it because it failed to recognise they were greater than Homer. Some of the former, like Michnik himself, are pleased with post-communism since they are now free. The latter generally are not, since they are still ranked behind Homer. There are parallels to this sort of frustration in many domains of post-communist life. Some people hoped that once communism was removed, their own or their country's rise would be simply unstoppable. Disappointment followed, in direct proportion to the magniloquence of the ambition, like night after day. And this might have been predicted. If fervent hopes cannot be realised, they are likely to lead to disappointment, and if the hopes are sufficiently grandiose, disappointment will not only be inevitable but great. Any attempt to satisfy such hopes is bound to disappoint.

## 2. The Irish Question

In *1066 and All That*, that wonderful introduction to the whole of English history from its beginning as 'top nation' until its Fukuyamaesque end (when America became 'clearly top nation, and History came to a .'), it was explained that nineteenth-century British prime minister Gladstone 'spent his declining years trying to guess the answer to the Irish Question; unfortunately, whenever he was getting warm, the Irish secretly changed the Question.' Questions in this region, too, have changed over time. In the first years after the collapse, many novelties – the end of communist despotism, the first free elections, politicians who were voted out of office, and then left, court decisions that were obediently followed by those in power – were seen as remarkable achievements in those countries where they occurred. As indeed they were. Now, these things are taken for granted in countries like Hungary and Poland and some other countries, too. Sights have been set higher. Different questions are being put, and many people will not be satisfied until they receive satisfactory answers. When they do, they will ask further questions.

## 3. The Wisdom of Chou En-lai

Those who imagined that, after the collapse of communism, it could be easy and quick to establish democracy, rule of law, prosperity, and equality – together and at once – were doomed to disappointment. But twelve years is a short time in the development of the institutions of any social order, unless they collapse quickly. Recall Chou En-lai's response, when asked to assess the results of the French Revolution: it is too soon to tell.

## 4. Silly Questions, Silly Answers

Many post-communist initiatives are rightly regarded with disappointment and not only because they fail to satisfy bizarre or shifting or premature expectations. For some answers (good or bad doesn't really matter) are bound to frustrate, since they respond to bad questions or questions that are badly posed. Here the problem is not that the expectations are unfulfillable or that they change. Rather it is that fulfilling them – however successfully – is often the wrong thing to try to do.

That problem will occur whenever the question is foolish in principle, or, as a poor translation of a sensible question, it becomes foolish in context. Certain questions of this second sort have been common among legal missionaries from self-confident metropoles and their eager converts.

The sensible, but difficult, question often asked is: What can be done about what works badly here? That is often translated, particularly by western missionaries and advisers in the region, as: What works well at home, or in 'normal' countries, or in the West? When the first question becomes the second without further thought, or indeed whenever it is answered without first finding answers to deeper questions about the conditions and possibilities of institutional transplantation – about what is left behind in transportation and what is likely to be met on arrival, about how to mesh with (and yet transform) local institutions, expectations, social interests, history – such questions will often lead to answers that look foolish, and might well be. But a deeper truth is that any answer will be foolish, however clever it is, so long as it is the answer to a silly question.

## 5. The Seven-Year Itch

Some people get exactly what they want when they marry, but they find, after some time, that it does not satisfy them. This phenomenon is known in English as the seven-year itch. Similarly, some hopes have issued in disappointment in the region, even though they were fully realised. Communism collapsed, freedom of speech ensued, capital flowed in (to some countries), queues disappeared, a variety of goods appeared on shelves. And still they are disappointed. You find such disappointment expressed, for example, in aphorisms like, 'We wanted justice, we got the rule of law,' or, 'We wanted civil society, we got NGOs' (even though the rule of law and NGOs once seemed the unattainable jewels of the supposedly normal West to many in the abnormal East). People who had to bribe shop assistants to set aside toilet paper, or who, plastic bag in hand, had to engage in hunting expeditions for the same precious commodity, or had to latch onto queues for who knows what, just in case there was something worth getting at the other end, now are unsatisfied by the arid impersonality, predictability and speed of their visits to the supermarket.

## 6. The Aria Competition

There is a story about an aria competition, in which the second con-
testant was awarded the prize as soon as the first stopped singing. The
judges presumed that whoever followed the first competitor could not
be worse. People often thought that way about communism. Thus it
was common (and right) to attribute many of the worst problems of
communism to its monopolistic and inescapable state. Many drew
from this accurate diagnosis the prescription that the state's power
should be drastically diminished. The more the better. Unfortunately,
in some of the most miserable post-communist societies, that is precisely what happened. Soon, fear of the state was succeeded by fear of
real and imagined criminality. People on fixed incomes or state subsi-
dies and salaries had to face the decline, sometimes collapse, of state
budgets. Then there was the price to everyone of a state that cannot pay
its officials, enforce its judgments, collect taxes, and so on. Not to mention the gobbling up of state assets, on the cheap, by oligarchs, tycoons,
*biznesmeni*, and so on. Here the failure of social and political theory
was a failure to realise that the opposite of a bad thing is not necessarily
a good thing. One might rather hope for an altogether different thing,
such as a state that is strong in a way different from that which is
familiar – not despotically, for example, but infrastructurally.

Again, an example particularly evident in Poland is the reaction to
the now-fulfilled hope that politicians or the group they belong to or
the 'political class', as it is called there, would be different from what
went before. The ideal type of the former was a disciplined single party,
committed to Marxist ideology, and devoted to the achievement of
communism, or, more prosaically by the end, to the maintenance
of pervasive party control. The government in power when these
remarks were first made (July 2001) faithfully fulfilled the dream of a
change to all that by being chaotic, undisciplined, publicly committed
to no ideology or too many, and devoted to capitalism, indeed, so
keen to promote it by personal example, such as corrupt openness to
bribes and lobbying, that it was hard to find word of anything else in
Polish newspapers, apart from advertisements. And still some ingrates
were unsatisfied, so unsatisfied, in fact, that they recently and not
for the first time voted in the successor party to that of the former

communists, filled though it is with faces familiar to anyone with a long memory.

A contrasting dream fulfilled in Poland and several other countries, was for a 'rule of law revolution' that eschewed the brutality of communist and other revolutions. One of the emblems of this new alternative was the lack of vengefulness against former agents of the communist state. That has been so well achieved that a major disappointment, expressed publicly, today flows from the successful enrichment of former apparatchiks, managers, secret police, and *nomenklatura* generally, who trade off little-disturbed networks of connection, information, and thus power.

The most tragic examples of prizes awarded too soon are connected with one of the great and realised hopes of late communism: national independence. In Poland, Hungary and other countries with few or small national minorities, it was a hope not merely realised but largely salutary in its consequences. In several other countries, it was a source of overwhelming calamity. In Yugoslavia, it was such a calamity that it appears in some circumstances that the second competitor (or successor social system) might even be worse than the first, to which it was not unrelated.

### 7. No Such Thing as a Free Lunch

Some people believed that everything they hoped for could be cost-free, yet many costs of transformation were inevitable. If not taken into account, disappointment was bound to follow. And, indeed, many costs occurred which surprised everyone, and some of these have been very painful. Partly this was a failure of the social theory behind the original hopes, so the realisation of the prices to be paid is more painful than anyone expected.

Some of these costs were inevitable aspects of transformation, such as the inequalities attendant on capitalism; social, psychic and economic dislocation; political, legal and other inexperience; and many of the other things that make life hard in the new post-communist world. Some were not inevitable, but predictable, such as the time it all takes. Some of the worst, such as the efflorescence of predatory nationalism in some but by no means all parts of the region, were predicted by no one. Many of these costs are very hard to bear.

### 8. But Send the Bill to the Right Address

Some hoped that when communism collapsed, it would be replaced as night by day. Instead, much of it has stayed around, including many structures and processes that pollute the atmosphere literally and metaphorically, with many costs still being paid. These are arguably better attributed to what went before than to what is done now, but commonly are not.

### 9. The Aesthetics of Hope, or the McDonald's Problem

Isaiah Berlin liked to quote an American philosopher's aphorism that 'we have no reason for supposing that the truth, when it is discovered, will necessarily prove interesting.' Analogously, we had no reason for supposing that post-communist democracy, rule of law and market economy, if attained, would prove enchanting – particularly once memories of the alternative had worn away. But many people imagined otherwise and are, therefore, distressed to find even the most successful post-communist orders so tacky. They bemoan the booming of McDonald's just as they do supermarkets, sometimes nostalgically recalling, sometimes frivolously forgetting, that communism was rich in neither.

### 10. The Monism of Hope; the Plurality of Disappointments

Another insight of Berlin's, on which he insisted with greater frequency than he quoted the above aphorism, was that not everything we want is going to be compatible with everything else we want. The post-communist experience, even in its most successful versions, confirms that in spades. Many initial hopes were monistic, in Berlin's sense: the end of communism would deliver what we want, and not what we did not want. Instead it has, at times, delivered both. It is a pity, perhaps, but if Berlin is right it cannot be escaped. For it is a truth, not just of post-communism, but of the human condition, and that, the Bible tells us, is hard to avoid in this life.

*2002*

# Publication Details

Many of these essays had footnotes or lists of sources when they were first published; they can be found there.

'Richard Krygier', excerpt from 'The Sources of Civil Society I', *Quadrant*, October 1996, 12–22.

'Roma Krygier', excerpt from my eulogy at her funeral in August 1999, later published as 'Roma Krygier, 1918-1999' in *Quadrant*, November 1999, 60–63.

'Hybrids and Comparisons', Chapter 1 of Martin Krygier, *Between Fear and Hope: hybrid thoughts on public values*, ABC Books, Sydney, 1997.

'Worse Than Provincial – Parochial', published as 'The Many-Faceted McAuley', *Eureka Street*, December 1999, 32–37.

'The Curate's Egg', excerpt from Chapter 4 of Martin Krygier, *Between Fear and Hope: hybrid thoughts on public values*, ABC Books, Sydney, 1997.

'Subjects, Objects and the Colonial Rule of Law', published as 'The Grammar of Colonial Legality: Subjects, Objects, and the Australian Rule of Law,' Geoffrey Brennan and Francis G. Castles, eds, *Australia Reshaped: 200 Years of Institutional Transformation*, Cambridge University Press, Cambridge, 2002, 220–60.

'The Character of the Nation' (with Robert van Krieken), Robert Manne, ed., *Whitewash: On Keith Windschuttle's Fabrication of Aboriginal History*, Black Inc., Melbourne, 2003, 81–108.

'Neighbours: Poles, Jews and the Aboriginal Question', La Trobe University Essay, *Australian Book Review*, April 2002, 37–43.
A longer version with Australian and Polish citations appeared in *East Central Europe/L'Europe du Centre Est: Eine wissenschaftliche Zeitschrift*, 2002, 29, 1–2, 297–309.

'The Rhetoric of Reaction', *Griffith Review*, May 2005, 79–91.

'Between Fear and Hope', Chapter 2 of Martin Krygier, *Between Fear and Hope: hybrid thoughts on public values*, ABC Books, Sydney, 1997.

'The Uses of Civility', Chapter 3 of Martin Krygier, *Between Fear and Hope: hybrid thoughts on public values*, ABC Books, Sydney, 1997.

'The Good That Governments Do', Chapter 5 of Martin Krygier, *Between Fear and Hope: hybrid thoughts on public values*, ABC Books, Sydney, 1997.

'In Praise of Prejudice', *Best Australian Essays 2003*, Black Inc., Melbourne, 2003, 121–31.

'The Price of Purity', excerpt from Chapter 6 of Martin Krygier, *Between Fear and Hope: hybrid thoughts on public values*, ABC Books, Sydney, 1997.

'Conservative liberal socialism revisited', *The Good Society*, 2002, 11, 1, 6–15; an earlier version appeared as 'In Praise of Conservative-Liberal-Social Democracy', *Quadrant*, May 1992, 12–23.

'Stalemated in Poland', *Commentary*, 1986, 81, 3, 15–23. Also in *Quadrant*, March 1986, 19–26.

'Life in an Abnormal Country' *The National Interest*, Winter 1989/90, 18, 55–64. Also in *Quadrant*, Jan–Feb 1990, 10–16.

'Gypsies, The Law and Me,' *Quadrant*, November 1990, 28–31.

'Traps for Young Players in Times of Transition', *East European Constitutional Review*, Fall 1999, 63–67.

'Parables of Hope and Disappointment', *East European Constitutional Review*, Summer 2002, 11, 3, 62–65.

**Books by Martin Krygier**

Robert Kagan, Martin Krygier and Kenneth Winston, eds, *Legality and Community: on the intellectual legacy of Philip Selznick*, Rowman and Littlefield, New York, 2002.

Martin Krygier and Adam Czarnota, eds, *The Rule of Law after Communism*, Dartmouth, Aldershot, 1999.

Martin Krygier, *Between Fear and Hope: hybrid thoughts on public values*, ABC Books, Sydney, 1997 (the text of the radio lectures on which this book expands can be found at www.abc.net.au/rn/boyers/97boyer1.htm).

Martin Krygier, ed., *Marxism and Communism: posthumous reflections on politics, society, and law*, Poznań Studies in the Philosophy of Sciences and the Humanities, Rodopi, Amsterdam – Atlanta, GA., 1994.

Eugene Kamenka and Martin Krygier, eds, *Bureaucracy: the career of a concept*, Edward Arnold, London; St. Martin's Press, New York, 1979.

*In press:*

Adam Czarnota, Martin Krygier and Wojciech Sadurski, eds, *Rethinking the Rule of Law after Communism: constitutionalism, dealing with the past, and the rule of law*, Central European University Press, Budapest, 2005.

Wojciech Sadurski, Adam Czarnota and Martin Krygier, eds, *Spreading Democracy and the Rule of Law?: implications of EU enlargement for the rule of law, democracy and constitutionalism in post-communist legal orders*, Springer Verlag, Berlin, 2005.